Governance, Conflict, and Natural Resources in Africa

Governance, Conflict, and Natural Resources in Africa

Understanding the Role of Foreign Investment Actors

HANY GAMIL BESADA

McGill-Queen's University Press
Montreal & Kingston • London • Chicago

© McGill-Queen's University Press 2021

ISBN 978-0-2280-0543-8 (cloth)
ISBN 978-0-2280-0544-5 (paper)
ISBN 978-0-2280-0707-4 (ePDF)
ISBN 978-0-2280-0708-1 (ePUB)

Legal deposit second quarter 2021
Bibliothèque nationale du Québec

Printed in Canada on acid-free paper that is 100% ancient forest free (100% post-consumer recycled), processed chlorine free

We acknowledge the support of the Canada Council for the Arts.

Nous remercions le Conseil des arts du Canada de son soutien.

Library and Archives Canada Cataloguing in Publication

Title: Governance, conflict, and natural resources in Africa : understanding the role of foreign investment actors / Hany Gamil Besada.
Names: Besada, Hany, author.
Description: Includes bibliographical references and index.
Identifiers: Canadiana (print) 20210108800 | Canadiana (ebook) 20210108819 | ISBN 9780228005438 (cloth) | ISBN 9780228005445 (paper) | ISBN 9780228007074 (ePDF) | ISBN 9780228007081 (ePUB)
Subjects: LCSH: Natural resources—Africa. | LCSH: Investments, Foreign—Africa. | LCSH: Conflict management—Africa.
Classification: LCC HC800.Z65 B47 2021 | DDC 333.7096—dc23

This book was designed and typeset by studio oneonone in 11/14 Minion

This book is dedicated to my late father, Gamil Fawzy Besada (1945–1995), who always guided me and remains the source of my inspiration.

Contents

Figures and Table   ix

Foreword   *Franklyn Lisk*   xi

Preface   xv

Abbreviations   xix

Introduction   3

1   Understanding Conflict and Resource Management   29

2   Studying Resource Management and the Role of Foreign Actors   58

3   Ghana: The Transformative Potential of Hydrocarbon Resources   78

4   Sierra Leone: From Blood Minerals to Development Minerals?   123

5   Ethiopia: Land Distribution as Developmental Tool   168

Conclusion   201

Notes   221

References   227

Index   277

Figures and Table

Figures

1.1 Political Economy of Natural Resource Governance (PENRG) framework 55
5.1 Land leased to investors in Ethiopia by village 179
5.2 Composition of merchandise exports for 2014–15 195

Table

1.1 Governance structures at the private, public, and regional/global levels 41–2

Foreword

In this intellectually inspiring book, Dr Hany Besada, who has written extensively and advised on the management and governance of natural resources in Africa, offers an innovative political economy analysis of the role of foreign economic actors involved in natural resource exploitation in the development process in three different types of African nation states – politically stable, post-conflict, and conflict-challenged. He introduces a pioneering concept, the Political Economy of Natural Resource Governance (PENRG), as the theoretical framework for analyzing a key issue in academic and policy circles: the complex relationship between governments and foreign investors, and its impact on development as represented by three interlinked "pillars" of progress: growth, peace, and stability. The approach adopted allows for a "bi-directional" analysis of this relationship: assessing the impact of the behaviour of foreign economic actors on the goals associated with these three pillars of development, and how conditions associated with these pillars affect the contribution of foreign investors to development. This summary underlines the complexity of the analysis involved in bringing out this book. Dr Besada's critical analysis, based on the enormous research he has undertaken and his deep expertise on the subject, including his involvement in the drafting of the AU/UNECA Africa Mining Vision (AMV), provides a new and stimulating way of thinking about natural resource governance architecture, the actors involved, and their responses to inherent challenges.

I am pleased to be associated in a mutually respectful, collegial manner with this illuminating study. This book grew out of the author's PhD thesis, submitted to the University of Warwick, which I co-supervised with

Professor Stuart Croft (currently vice-chancellor and president of the university). I have known the author for well over a decade since his days as young researcher at the Centre for International Governance Innovation (CIGI) in Waterloo, Canada, where we interacted professionally on my numerous visits. I take some credit for attracting Hany to Warwick to undertake a research project on natural resource governance that focuses mainly on national and subnational governance systems illustrated by country-specific case studies, rather than only on international governance systems, thereby providing an opportunity to sketch out the analytical parameters for a multilevel governance approach.

Another quality of the book that adds to its richness concerns the empirical research undertaken by Dr Besada to test the central premise concerning the nature of natural resource governance in relation to three different state types. As an "insider," I know that the findings of the study are derived from evidence meticulously gathered by the author through "on-the-ground" field research undertaken in three African countries: Ghana, Sierra Leone, and Ethiopia. This involved desk research, information and data collection, personal observation, and structured interviews of actors at various levels of decision making, from the local community to the central state, and within both the public and private spheres of operation.

The incisive nature of the analysis and the quality of the empirical research on which the book is based make it a compelling and readable contribution to a better understanding of the international political economy of development on natural resource governance. The integrative-oriented PENRG theory advanced by the book goes beyond economic gains to assess additional development impacts of foreign investment, including peace dividend and social stability. Those committed to the promotion of sustainable development will welcome the approach of Dr Besada in presenting natural resource governance not as a goal in and of itself, but as an important part of achieving larger societal goals of poverty reduction, inclusive growth, and sustainable development. Hence, one of the conclusions of the book implies the need for a wider governance architecture based on strategic alliances or convergence between actors in a national context – i.e., foreign investors, state/government representatives, and civil society organizations – and international financial and standards governance institutions.

I hope, first, that this book reaches and informs thinking people (researchers and policy analysts in universities, supranational institutes and think tanks in both the North and the South), and practitioners (policy decision makers in government and the private sector and operational staff of civil society organizations) in Africa and beyond; and, second, that as many of them as possible become not merely observers of the development process and its consequences, but advocates of and even participants in the new political economy of natural resource governance that this book espouses.

Professor Franklyn Lisk
Politics and International Studies Department, University of Warwick
December 2020

Preface

The potential of Africa's abundant natural resources is enormous. Yet, for decades, many countries on the continent have dramatically failed to transform that immense economic potential and wealth into tangible benefits in terms of sustainable socioeconomic development, enhanced state and human security, and inclusive, broad-based economic development. Thus, the governance of African natural resources will have a profound impact on the future prospects of the continent, because, more than ever before, extractive industries are creating new processes of state making and state building while also reshaping political, social, and economic roles throughout the continent. Moreover, effective natural resource management in Africa will be critical to achieving the Sustainable Development Goals (SDGs) adopted by the United Nations as well as to realizing the African Union's Agenda for 2063.

Written with these pressing issues in mind, this book touches upon several subthemes to provide a better understanding of the role of foreign-owned enterprises in the management and governance of natural resources in Africa. These include: the roles played by foreign state-owned and private-sector actors (collectively referred to as foreign economic actors in extractive industries); the efforts made by foreign actors to implement policies and practices that demonstrate corporate social responsibility (CSR) and promote inclusive natural resource management and economic development at the national and community levels; and the role of natural resource extraction for Africa's peace and security.

My motivation and inspiration to write this book is to appreciate, understand, and provide informed policy analysis and options to governments, the private sector, and civil society in resource-rich African countries. This motivation reflects the need for economic planning and governance restructuring on the continent, beginning at its very foundations, to ensure that natural resources are used effectively to achieve a degree of economic transformation required to alleviate poverty and allow countries to maximize the true and full potential of their resources in a sustainable and inclusive manner.

From 2015 to 2016, I served as senior regional advisor at the African Minerals Development Centre of the United Nations Economic Commission for Africa (UNECA). While there, I established and helped build the Centre's mineral linkage division aimed at promoting local content, procurement, mineral beneficiation, and value addition, and supporting chain analysis in Africa's mineral sector. This work afforded me a unique opportunity to deepen my understanding of the issues covered in the book.

Furthermore, having lived, worked, and travelled in more than forty-five countries on the African continent and seen abject poverty, economic dislocation, joblessness, civil strife and violence, environmental degradation, deepening inequality, and growing youth frustration, I was profoundly interested in finding solutions to the paradox of Africa's natural resources. In other words, given the continent's incredible natural resource wealth, it is vital that prudent management and governance is critically examined, evaluated, and supported to ensure that governments, mining communities, and the larger population reap the benefits that have eluded most resource-rich countries thus far. My thinking has always been that new and comprehensive knowledge on these burning issues may be useful for practitioners to effectively reverse Africa's misfortunes on natural resource wealth and help ensure that the expectations of the African people are met when it comes to utilizing natural resources for sustainable economic development and inclusive prosperity.

Therefore, I have chosen to write this book on the role of foreign-owned enterprises in the management and governance of natural resources in Africa because it goes to the heart of the continent's development programs and ambitions, as well as some of the leading development theories and practices. In an effort to develop a theorization of the impact of foreign direct investment (FDI) through foreign-owned private actors, I developed a new theoretical framework, the Political

PREFACE xvii

Economy of Natural Resource Governance (PENRG). The intent is to create an improved analytical tool for conceptualizing the impact of natural resource governance on peace, stability, and economic development in Africa.

On the empirical front, my study draws its data from the extensive fieldwork I conducted in the three case study countries – Ghana, Sierra Leone, and Ethiopia – over an extended period of time. These data are complemented by comprehensive desk research. I chose the three countries for two main reasons. While the first of these has to do with my ability to conduct research fieldwork while working for the UNECA as its senior regional advisor, the second underpins my theoretical framework. For the particular purpose of this study, Ethiopia neatly fits into the category of a conflict-threatened country; Sierra Leone is a classic example of a post-conflict, resource-rich country; and Ghana is an excellent example of a stable, resource-rich country. Much of the existing scholarly literature on natural resource management and governance focuses on foreign investors in particular and conflict risks in general. Less is known, however, about the role of economic actors in the extractive sectors of countries with differentiated political stability, as the case selection above illustrates.

This book fills that gap by addressing the lingering puzzle of how foreign-owned enterprises, operating in Africa's extractive sectors, affect peace, security, and economic development in specific political contexts, especially in countries with differential primary resource commodities. A core argument of the book is that the role of foreign state-owned and private-sector actors in natural resource governance and management in Africa depends mainly on the various strengths, weaknesses, and levels of governance structures in stable, post-conflict, and conflict-threatened states. Moreover, the case studies (Ghana, Ethiopia, and Sierra Leone) show the extent to which a lack of alignment between bureaucratic, administrative, and political structures on the governance and management of a country's natural resources can negatively affect its stability, peace, and development. From tax evasion to a lack of local beneficiation and capacity building, the destructive nature of the extractive industry's practices and structures can be devastating. This is important, as it contributes to knowledge about the impact of foreign-owned enterprises on governance and management of Africa's natural resources. This, in turn, could lead to policy recommendations for promoting positive developmental outcomes in Africa, especially in the context of the growing presence of actors from China and other emerging powers, the pending launch of the African Continental Free Trade Area (AfCFTA), and other factors.

This book is based on my PhD thesis and so I am profoundly and deeply appreciative to a remarkably long list of people who helped paved the way for this research. Specifically, I wish to thank my two program supervisors: Professor Stuart Croft, who has since become vice-chancellor and president of the University of Warwick, for his unwavering support and guidance over the past years; and Professor Franklyn Lisk, for his endless guidance, unparalleled dedication, and invaluable commitment toward this book. This research project has also benefitted greatly from the professional experience and knowledge that I gained while working in a number of institutions and organizations, including the South African Institute of International Affairs, the Africa Business Group, the Centre for International Governance Innovation, the North-South Institute, the UN Secretary-General's High Level Panel on the Post-2015 Development Agenda, the University of Ottawa, Carleton University, the United Nations Economic Commission for Africa, and the United Nations University Institute for Natural Resources in Africa. At these organizations and institutions, I met some amazing people with whom I had the great fortune to work; in particular: Dr Cristina D'Alessandro, Dr Fatima Denton, Professor Timothy Shaw, Dr John English, the Honourable Alvin Curling, Ambassador Mokhtar Lamani, Ms Neuma Grobbelaar, Ms Elizabeth Sidiropoulos, Mr Michael Sudarkasa, Professor Caroline Andrew, Dr Dennis Willms, Professor Nelson Sewankambo, Mr Joseph Ingram, Dr Andrew Cooper, Dr Kojo Busia, Dr Homi Kharas, Professor Fantu Cheru, Dr Manmohan Agarwal, Mr Daniel Schwanen, Professor Blair Rutherford, Dr Pius Adesanmi, and Dr Elias T. Ayuk. This research project has benefitted greatly from my interactions with all of them.

Abbreviations

ACEP	African Centre for Energy Policy
ACET	African Center for Economic Transformation
ADLI	Agricultural Development Led Industrialization
AfCFTA	African Continental Free Trade Area
AfCOP	African Community of Practice on Managing for Development Results
AfDB	African Development Bank
AGC	Ashanti Goldfields Corporation
AGRA	Alliance for a Green Revolution in Africa
AMDC	African Minerals Development Centre
AMV	Africa Mining Vision
APC	All People's Congress (Sierra Leone)
ASM	artisanal and small-scale mining
AU	African Union
BDUS	Biofuel Development and Utilization Strategy
CAADP	Comprehensive Africa Agriculture Development Programme
CBNRM	community-based natural resource management
CDAS	community development agreements
CDFS	community development funds
CDSA	Centre for Development and Security Analysis
CIA	Central Intelligence Agency
CIFR	Center for International Forestry Research
CNRMCS	Community Natural Resources Management Committees
CSOS	civil society organizations

CSR	corporate social responsibility
DACDFS	diamond area community development funds
DAG	Development Assistance Group (Ethiopia)
DFID	Department for International Development (UK)
DNRMCS	District Natural Resources Management Committees
DRC	Democratic Republic of the Congo
ECOWAS	Economic Community of West African States
EIA	environmental impact assessment
EIA	Ethiopian Investment Agency
EIF	Enhanced Integrated Framework
EITI	Extractive Industries Transparency Initiative
EPRDF	Ethiopian People's Revolutionary Democratic Front
FAO	Food and Agriculture Organization
FDI	foreign direct investment
FPIC	free, prior, and informed consent
FSS	Forum for Social Studies
GBL	Georgette Barnes Ltd
GCDD	Ghana Center for Democratic Development
GIPC	Ghana Investment Promotion Centre
GIZ	Deutsche Gesellschaft für Internationale Zusammenarbeit (German Agency for International Cooperation)
GNPC	Ghana National Petroleum Corporation
GRI	Global Reporting Initiative
GTP	Growth and Transformation Plan (Ethiopia)
HDI	human development index
HRW	Human Rights Watch
ICMM	International Council on Mining and Metals
IEA	International Energy Agency
IFAD	International Fund for Agricultural Development
IFC	International Finance Corporation
IFFS	illicit financial flows
IFPRI	International Food Policy Research Institute
IFS	Institute for Fiscal Studies
IGF	Intergovernmental Forum on Mining, Minerals, Metals and Sustainable Development
IIED	International Institute for Environment and

	Development
IMF	International Monetary Fund
IPE	international political economy
ISO	International Organization for Standardization
ISS	Institute for Security Studies
ISSER	Institute of Statistical, Social and Economic Research, University of Ghana
ITA	International Tin Association (formerly ITRI)
ITSCI	ITRI Tin Supply Chain Initiative
JTTC	Jubilee Technical Training Centre, Takoradi Technical University (Ghana)
KAFSP	King Abdullah Food Security Program
KAIPTC	Kofi Annan International Peacekeeping Training Centre
KITE	Kumasi Institute of Technology, Energy and Environment
KPCS	Kimberley Process Certification Scheme
LCC	Local Content Committee
LICUS	Low-Income Countries Under Stress List
LPI	Land Policy Initiative (Ethiopia)
LSM	large-scale mining
MAB	Minerals Advisory Board (Sierra Leone)
MC	Minerals Commission (Ghana)
MCO	Mining Cadastre Office (Sierra Leone)
MDGS	Millennium Development Goals
MEP	Ministry of Energy and Petroleum (Ghana)
MFED	Ministry of Finance and Economic Development (Ethiopia)
MLG	Ministry of Local Government (Sierra Leone)
MMMR	Ministry of Mines and Mineral Resources (Sierra Leone)
MMRPA	Ministry of Mineral Resources and Political Affairs (Sierra Leone)
MPF	mining policy framework
NACE	National Advocacy Coalition on Extractives
NGO	non-governmental organization
NIU	National Implementation Unit (Sierra Leone)

NMA	National Mineral Agency (Sierra Leone)
NMJD	Network Movement for Justice and Development
NNRMC	National Natural Resources Management Committee
NRGI	Natural Resource Governance Institute
OECD	Organisation for Economic Co-operation and Development
OPEC	Organization of the Petroleum Exporting Countries
PASDEP	Plan for Accelerated and Sustained Development to End Poverty
PENRG	Political Economy of Natural Resource Governance
PRI	Principles for Responsible Investment
PRMA	Petroleum Revenue Management Act (Ghana)
PSNP	Productive Safety Net Programme (Ethiopia)
RUF	Revolutionary United Front (Sierra Leone)
RWI	Revenue Watch Institute
SDGS	Sustainable Development Goals
SLEITI	Sierra Leone Extractive Industries Transparency Initiative
SLPP	Sierra Leone People's Party
SMB	Société Minière de Bisunzu
SMBC	Sumitomo Mitsui Banking Corporation
SMES	small and medium-sized enterprises
SNNPR	Southern Nations, Nationalities, and Peoples' Region (Ethiopia)
TGE	Transitional Government of Ethiopia
TPLF	Tigray People's Liberation Front
TRC	Truth and Reconciliation Commission
TWN	Third World Network
UCDP/PRIO	Uppsala Conflict Data Program at the Department of Peace and Conflict Research, Uppsala University, and the Centre for the Study of Civil War, Peace Research Institute Oslo
UN	United Nations
UNAMSIL	United Nations Mission in Sierra Leone
UNCSD	United Nations Commission on Sustainable Development

ABBREVIATIONS

UNCTAD	United Nations Conference on Trade and Development
UNDP	United Nations Development Programme
UNECA	United Nations Economic Commission for Africa
UNEP	United Nations Environment Programme
UNGC	United Nations Global Compact
UNICEF	United Nations Children's Fund
UNIPSIL	United Nations Integrated Peacebuilding Office in Sierra Leone
UNU-INRA	United Nations University, Institute for Natural Resources in Africa
UNU-WIDER	United Nations University, World Institute for Development Economics Research
UPEACE	University for Peace
USAID	United States Agency for International Development
VGGT	Voluntary Guidelines on the Responsible Governance of Tenure of Land, Fisheries and Forests
WB	World Bank
WFP	World Food Programme

Governance, Conflict,
and Natural Resources
in Africa

Introduction

Background and Context

In recent years, there has been a great deal of evidence to suggest that for resource-rich countries, an abundance of natural resources could either be a curse or a blessing depending on the governance structures in place. From the African countries' overreliance on a few natural resources and the economic insecurity spurring from their inability to diversify production (Wohlmuth et al. 2007) to the critical role that energy production, mining extraction, and land deals have played in the destabilization of political, economic, and social structures (Ross 2013; Demissie 2017; Bracco 2018; Matondi, Havnevik, and Beyene 2011; Anne 2012), the governance of African natural resources will shape the future of the continent.

Whether an abundance of natural resources proves to be a curse or blessing depends on the nature, extent, and outcome of an individual country's effort and experience in governing and managing such assets. How individual countries manage and exploit Africa's resources is fundamental to their ability to enhance both state and human security while fostering inclusive, broad-based economic development. Extractive industries are creating new processes of state making and state building, and reshaping political, social, and economic roles and relationships (Schubert, Engel, and Macamo 2018). Analyzing and understanding these evolutions will be critical in bridging the divide between the natural and social sciences (Ali, Sturman, and Collins, forthcoming). Effective natural resource management is also critical to achieving the Sustainable Development Goals (SDGs) recently adopted by the United Nations.[1] Ghana, Namibia, and Botswana are examples of countries where natural resources have been used for the betterment of the populace by contributing to sustained socioeconomic development over the past decade, with varying degrees of success and under different conditions and challenges (Grant, Compaore, and Mitchell 2015).

Africa is fortunate to have some of the most sought-after natural resources in the world. These resources comprise large deposits of a variety of minerals including 60 per cent of the world's diamonds, 40 per cent of the world's phosphate, 30 per cent of the world's cobalt reserves (SMBC 2011), proven oil reserves of 130 billion barrels, $1.5 trillion in projected gold reserves, 18 per cent of the world's uranium, and other strategic rare minerals, along with an estimated 300 million hectares of potential land for rain-fed agriculture (Ahlenius 2006; Al Jazeera 2016; Dasnois 2012). The continent also boasts eighty transboundary rivers and lake basins, and seventeen large catchment areas, each exceeding 100,000 square kilometres.

Despite these natural resource advantages, many African countries have failed to transform their enormous economic potential and wealth into tangible benefits in terms of sustainable socioeconomic development, human security, and peace. Encouragingly, however, there is evidence to suggest that the continent is home to a small but growing number of countries that have begun to harness energy, mineral, and land resources to promote sustainable economic growth and broad-based inclusive development. Concerns around governance, leadership, and structural transformation of the extractive nexus, combined with new challenges such as the green economy and technological advances, have been explored by researchers and support the conclusions of this book (Hanson, D'Alessandro, and Owusu 2014).

This volume introduces the Political Economy of Natural Resource Governance (PENRG) framework. With this framework, and via the use of three variables – growth, peace, and stability – I intend to develop a theorization of the impact of foreign direct investment (FDI) through foreign-owned private actors. As a political economic study at the national level, I have purposely excluded considerations at the local and global levels in the aim of focusing on this particular level of analysis. While recognizing the potential limitations of such an approach, including the disconnect between local and national implementation of global corporate policies, I would also underline that this manuscript is aimed at providing

Introduction

lesson-learning experiences for decision makers, primarily at the national level. Moreover, while focused chiefly at the country level, and on the policies, decisions, and behaviour of foreign-owned corporations when dealing with national politics, this book is also inspired by on-the-ground research in local communities.

Nevertheless, it is critical that the reader complement this read with local case studies to assess the impacts of foreign investments on specific communities' land uses, profit repatriation, and other conservation struggles, while also assessing the behaviour of foreign-owned capital in terms of tax avoidance in the natural resources extraction sector, among other issues. These considerations should be inscribed in an analysis of corporate behaviour not only in the countries of the Global South but also at the global level to assess alignment, or potential lack of alignment, with national-level practices (Geppert and Williams 2007).

As described above, the PENRG framework, as a national-level analytical tool, does not preclude attention to local struggles. The debate around the applicability of policies across multiple scales, including the national and the local levels, is marked by what Cash and Moser describe in the environmental sphere as a "lack of systematic way of thinking about and addressing the challenges involved in integrating science and policy across multiple scales" (2000). A similar conclusion can be drawn from the political approach to developmental issues, for which the links between national decision-making processes and local consequences are often misunderstood. Recognizing this trend, the PENRG framework fully embraces a multiscale analysis and provides the necessary flexibility to integrate local impacts of foreign-owned extractive investments. It also appears clear that, of the PENRG framework's three constituent pillars – growth, peace, and stability – at least two are profoundly impacted by local-level contexts. The propensity for spillover of local conflicts impacting regional, national, and continental levels underlines the importance of feeding PENRG from local experiences (Rustad et al. 2011).

In turn, the stability of political systems, social organizations, and economic structures at the national level are profoundly impacted by local-level impacts of foreign-owned corporations. This has been exemplified in numerous cases throughout the continent, including Nigeria (Frynas 2000; Ikelegbe 2005; Omeje 2013), South Sudan and Sudan (Patey 2007 and 2012), and Equatorial Guinea (McSherry 2006; McFerson 2009; Appel

2012). Recent developments in the Democratic Republic of Congo and the militarization of copper and cobalt industrial mines at the request of foreign mining companies also show the risks for localized issues to spread quickly across regions and impact national politics, economic systems, and social stability (Sanderson 2019).

As described above, the PENRG framework rests on a triptych constituted of three pillars: growth, peace, and stability. Throughout this manuscript, we can see that by assessing these three pillars, we can determine the impact of foreign-owned investments. To take another approach, I will argue that the situation resulting from the entry of foreign-owned corporate capital into the extractive sector of one of the countries in this study is defined by the levels of stability, growth, and conflict in that country. At the same time, these three characteristics will be profoundly impacted by the manner in which these investments are conducted at the national level – and, as noted above, by local realities. By selecting these three broad pillars, I intend to provide a framework encompassing the developmental discourse's ideal conditions, namely a politically and socially stable, conflict-free country with strong economic growth. As such, I hope to provide a framework that is sufficiently broad to cover most situations, while allowing for refinement of the analysis specific to each case study. Consequently, my goal here is not to exclude additional variables – such as strong political discourse in opposition to national government policies in Ghana, regionalization of extractive conflicts in Ethiopia, or health catastrophes in Sierra Leone – but to provide the reader with a framework that articulates these factors to support an integrated analysis.

Research Objectives

In line with this objective, the book will touch upon several sub-themes to provide a better understanding of the role of foreign-owned enterprise in governing and managing natural resources in Africa:

- The roles played by foreign state-owned and private-sector actors, collectively referred to as foreign economic actors in extractive industries;

Introduction 7

- The efforts made by foreign actors to implement policies and practices that demonstrate CSR and foster inclusive mineral development agreements promoting relevant economic development at the community level;
- The role of natural resource extraction in peace and security contexts, as evidenced by comparison of stable, post-conflict, and conflict-threatened resource-rich African states; and
- The evaluation of instances in which intervention by foreign actors did not result in an improvement in capacity building and natural resources governance, and instead hampered development and contributed to financial mismanagement, environmental degradation, poor labour standards, loss of livelihoods, and increased conflict with local communities.

In each of the selected country case studies, three core research questions will form the basis of investigation and argument, and define what answers are sought through interviews, desk research, and the like:

1 How does the evolving role of foreign-owned enterprises, including state-owned and private (close or listed) companies, affect peace, stability, and economic development in the African context?
2 What determines whether these actors play a positive or negative role in achieving peace, stability, and economic development?
3 In what areas of policy changes and reform could recommendations be made so as to promote positive, impactful, and sustainable development outcomes?

Responses to these questions will contribute to existing knowledge about the role of foreign-owned enterprises in fostering stability or instability, and prosperity or poverty, in natural-resource-rich African countries with different political situations: Ghana (politically stable), Sierra Leone (post-conflict), and Ethiopia (conflict-threatened).

Three Political States

The states considered in this study fall into three categories:

A *politically stable country* is understood as holding the characteristics of good governance and strong institutions, regular economic growth, and robust development prospects (Cubitt 2014).

A *post-conflict country* is perceived as having divided societies in the process of economic reconstruction and peacebuilding, but not (yet) having strong governance or institutional legitimacy (Wolff 2011; Roberts 2008).

A *conflict-threatened country* displays good economic performance and has strong state institutions based on the developmental state model, but nevertheless has existing undercurrents of ethnic or social tension, linked largely to resource-sharing, which threaten peace, and political and social stability. Deficiencies in governance, economy, and nationhood constitute the key defining characteristics of a conflict-threatened country (Brock et al. 2012).

These classifications stem from existing research and policy definitions on each country in this study. In 2017, the Fund for Peace classified Ethiopia as a country that has experienced a significant decline in stability, due primarily to ongoing anti-government protests (Fund for Peace 2017). For Sierra Leone, most scholars agree that the country remains in a post-conflict situation, conducting peacebuilding for purposes of reconstruction and development (Neethling 2007; Quinn 2016; Bertone 2014; Jinguishi 2015). Ghana, despite surface-level turbulence, is regarded as a stable country (Knoope and Chauzal 2016; Cooke 2016).

The study results will contribute to knowledge about the impact of foreign enterprises on development (experiences, lessons learned) and, ultimately, lead to policy recommendations for promoting positive developmental outcomes. In addition, key variables will be isolated to help create a unique, broader framework for analysis. In using the PENRG framework to assess the outcomes and influences of foreign-owned enterprises on governance structures in the three case countries, the intent is to create an improved analytical tool for conceptualizing the impact of natural resource governance on peace, stability, and economic development in Africa.

Introduction 9

Based on gaps in the literature on political economy and the impact of foreign-owned enterprise on development, and information gathered during fieldwork in Ghana, Ethiopia, and Sierra Leone, I argue that, in consideration of governance design, foreign-owned private-sector activities vis-à-vis natural resources have ushered in unprecedented economic growth in stable Ghana. Those areas where foreign investments failed to bring about improvements are also evaluated, shedding light on instances where such investments may have hampered development and fuelled conflict – as in the case of post-conflict Sierra Leone – and raising the question as to why private-sector natural resource investment has served as a source of continued instability and low-level conflict in Ethiopia. Ultimately, the different outcomes of these investments hinge on the relative robustness of the case countries' governance structures, as per the tenets of the PENRG framework.

Existing literature on natural resource governance identifies certain continuing knowledge gaps: whether private actors involved in the natural resource sector contribute to peace, stability, and prosperity (particularly in terms of governance quality and development outcomes) and the role of foreign-owned enterprises in post-conflict recovery contexts. Based on the case studies, the argument is made that the role that foreign-owned enterprises should play in stable countries is to promote and nurture sustainable development; in post-conflict countries, they should support economic reconstruction as well as state building and peacebuilding; and in conflict-threatened states, they should enhance state building and broad-based economic development. To put it bluntly, the private sector's overarching consideration is economic – the raison d'étre of their existence. The UN recently estimated that its Sustainable Development Goals (SDGs) constitute a \$12 trillion economic opportunity for the private sector, as their achievement will require a massive global undertaking that includes that sector's participation (Vali 2017). Similarly, much has been written on the economic costs of conflict, a motivating factor in the private sector's involvement in building and maintaining peace and stability. While the private sector is only one of many actors, its influence over public policy is central to favouring peace and stabilization (Khan and Ahmed 2014).

That said, the private sector has thus far been readily sidelined in these conversations, with governments and the non-profit sector viewing these actors as part of the problem rather than a vehicle for solutions – although this viewpoint has begun to shift since the early 2000s and the publication of several volumes on the untapped potential of business in peacebuilding (Sandole and Staroste 2014, 25). More recently, corporations are being viewed as a magic bullet for the issues and challenges faced by the non-profit sector, which has thus far been unable to act as an effective and permanent antidote to endemic development challenges; for its part, the private sector seemingly faces the same intractable issues as other actors who have come before it, but without a structural mandate to "do good" (McEwan 2017, 48).

This is in contrast to research suggesting that private-sector actors may have a highly political role in conflict and post-conflict settings, despite little interest, capacity, or legitimacy regarding their ability to participate in these conversations (Ford 2015, 151). Of course, the necessity for them to engage voluntarily in CSR practices continues to be debated in policy and academia, for there is no clause that mandates companies to act in ways that benefit anyone except their shareholders. This integrative-oriented theory, based on a holistic and collaborative approach that associates the economic, political, social, and environmental needs of communities with corporate business practices, appears promote peace and stability (Issifu 2016). But, putting aside for one moment the over-whelming agreement at the international level and among development practitioners that CSR is quintessential to conducting business in the modern era, foreign-owned enterprises create environments conducive to their long-term enrichment by investing in peace, stability, and econ-omic growth. Brauer and Tepper Marlin (2009) calculated that the cessa-tion of violence would generate a "peace dividend of approximately 13.1% of the 2007 gross world product." This analysis has since been taken up by an increasing number of studies and illustrates the macroeconomic benefit of peace and stabilization for profit-driven organizations (Prandi and Lozano 2010).

Indeed, these objectives are summarized throughout this work as the dependent variables of peace, stability, and economic development. In pursuing them, foreign-owned enterprises create the environment for re-liable and skilled workforces and predictable political institutions while

Introduction

minimizing risk. Therefore, while not mandated to perform these functions in each of the three different political contexts examined in this study, given the benefits and dividends described above, it is in the private-sector actors' best interest to adopt practices and policies that promote a stable, peaceful environment. The success of foreign-owned enterprises in doing so hinges on strong governance at both the local and national levels. This involves putting in place structures that hold foreign actors accountable and help realize the outcomes of their investments and activities. In the chapters that follow, each of these roles and impacts by foreign-owned enterprises will be discussed and examined in turn.

To explore the impact of foreign-owned corporate investments in Africa, the concepts of peace, stability, and economic development should be clearly defined. While peace may seem to be simply the absence of war, in this book it is defined as freedom from disturbances at the social, economic, political, and environmental levels. As Royce (2009) states, peace is a "two-dimensional construct with both objective and subjective measures that must be studied within specific micro to macro contexts." In this context, the present research tackles this multidimensionality of the concept of peace as we analyze local, national, and global objective and subjective measures to integrate peace in the governance of natural resources.

In terms of stability in a political context, Ake (1975) reminds us that political stability is profoundly linked to the concept of obedience to the law and depends on the capacity of individuals to obey the social, political, and economic regulations in place to support or undermine the system's stratification. In the realm of natural resource governance, stability is defined as the ability of foreign-owned enterprises to adhere to domestic laws and regulations but also to be cognisant of the economic and social institutions in the countries where they operate.

Finally, a key concept – and probably the most controversial – is economic development. While economists in the past have defined economic development in parallel to materiality and material progress, current approaches use more indicators and place the notion of poverty, and poverty reduction, as a top indicator. While economic development is still measured by macroeconomic indicators, such as GDP per capita growth, trade levels, and level of FDI, the addition of socioeconomic aspects is crucial. With respect to the governance of African natural resources, economic development is tightly linked both to macroeconomic indicators of exports and production, and to population well-being.

While typologies other than politically stable, post-conflict, and conflict-threatened are described in the case studies that form this book – particularly the multiplicity of post-conflict environments – a broad approach was adopted to produce context-adaptable solutions (Brown et al. 2011). Well-structured empirical research was undertaken to test the central premise concerning the nature of resource governance with respect to each type. The findings from my analysis will help to inform the literature on the governance of natural resources, political economy, and investigations of the impact of foreign enterprise on development, as well as policy recommendations regarding the role of foreign investors and foreign-owned companies in the enhancement, or otherwise, of natural resource governance and the contribution of such entities to the overall development process.

Due to the malleable definitions surrounding foreign-owned companies, this research is characterized by its consideration of a multiplicity of actors. The increasing interconnectedness of economies and economic actors blurs the lines around the origin of capital flows and investments, and makes the distinction between local and foreign-owned companies somewhat complex. As investments are made in critical strategic areas, during periods of unstable global markets, state-owned enterprises emerge as significant players in land deals and in projects involving the extraction of mineral-rich deposits and energy development. Among others, China's Exim Bank, Qatar's Zad Holding Company, and the United Arab Emirates' World Islands, in Dubai, are strong examples of major public investors in Africa's natural resources portfolio.

Surprisingly, sovereign wealth fund (SWF) investments in energy, mining, and land projects remain sporadic (Cotula et al. 2009). An acknowledgment of the role of public-owned entities in direct investments should not override the overwhelming participation of privately owned or listed companies in such investments. Though supported by state/country initiatives, including government-to-government investment treaties, loans, and guarantees, private companies conduct the bulk of investments in

Introduction 13

these types of projects on the African continent (Cotula et al. 2009; Herring 2015).

This research presents an opportunity to advance new knowledge on the diversity of roles attributed to foreign-owned enterprises operating in resource-rich countries with different political contexts via a new theoretical framework: the Political Economy of Natural Resource Governance (PENRG). But it also constitutes an innovative contribution to investigating the impacts of foreign-owned enterprises on peace, stability, and economic development and thereby providing a basis for generating new policy recommendations for the private sector and state governance in resource-rich African countries. Similar to an international political economy (IPE) framework as it relates to national development and transformation policies and outcomes, the natural resource governance framework will be interpreted and incorporated into an analysis of governance-related factors that impact development and transformation (e.g., policy choices and decision-making processes, institutional mechanisms for transparency and accountability, public financial management, opportunities for inclusive growth and equality). Through PENRG, the role of foreign-owned private-sector companies is analyzed in terms of their contribution to economic growth, peace, and stability at both the national and local levels.

At the national level, the analysis will conceptualize the key actors' roles in a number of specific conditions and environments, all of which, the current literature tells us, can impact the effectiveness of natural resource governance, overall stability, and prosperity and development – including taxes, government revenues, employment creation, and the implementation of laws. At the local level, where extractive and productive activities take place, the analysis will conceptualize actors' roles in terms of employment generation, revenues shared with local communities via renegotiation of contracts, and community development agreements that ensure CSR activities produce more tangible results. By considering how these actors can help to strengthen industries linked to the natural resource sector via value addition, beneficiation, and local content, the hope is that new insights will be formed and guidelines for policy recommendations developed based on these insights.

Over the last ten years, policies and practices adopted by foreign-owned enterprises that have invested in resource-rich African states have been insufficiently reviewed and evaluated – especially in environments characterized by weak governance. In his 1995 article, Rosenau adopts a very broad definition of global governance. Despite being a somewhat different concept, his approach is of particular interest in defining governance. He states that governance encompasses "systems of rule at all levels of human activity from the family to the international organization in which the pursuit of goals through the exercise of control has transnational repercussion" (Rosenau 1995). Applied to natural resources, this definition appears attractive due to its broad approach. Extractive activities should be understood to affect the whole community and every sector. In this sense, governance of natural recourses is constituted by a system of rule through which, at every level, the exercise of control has repercussions. There is a lack of literature chronicling the progression of these foreign actors' contributions to natural resource management and sustainable broad-based economic development in resource-rich African countries. Scant attention has been given to problems that have emerged as a result of poor corporate practices and their impacts on sustainable peace in post-conflict and conflict-threatened states specifically. The need for an increased awareness of these trends is critical in light of activities by foreign-owned companies: for example, 230 Australian mining companies are involved in over 600 projects in forty-two African countries, representing more than $45 billion in investments (Edwards et al. 2014).

While we have defined here the concept of global governance, it is critical also to understand the different levels and types in which such governance may take form. The present book focuses on national and subnational governance systems and explores only slightly the impact of international governance systems. As we examine our three case study countries and the impact of foreign investments by global corporations on their governance systems, it appears clear that the focus should remain on national governance and how it cascades down to the local level to support broad-based development. As such, we aim to adopt a governance definition fed by a multilevel governance approach, which is defined as follows by Ian Bache and Matthew Flinders: "First, that decision-making at various territorial levels is characterized by the increased participation of non-state actors. Second, that the identification of discrete or nested territorial levels of decision-making is becoming more difficult in the context of complex overlapping networks. Third, that in this changing context, the role of the state is being transformed as state actors develop new strategies of coordination, steering and networking that may protect and, in some cases, enhance state autonomy" (Bache and Flinders 2004).

This typology of multilevel governance is further explored by Hooghe and Marks, who address the dual, but non-exclusive, processes of dispersion of multitasking authority and the creation of specialized, geographically overlapping systems (Hooghe and Marks 2002). This approach lays emphasis on the role of non-state actors, including non-profits and, of interest for this study, foreign corporate entities. In terms of governance type, while we acknowledge the differentiation between voluntary and mandatory systems, the goal of this book is to assess the impact of policy requirements on foreign corporate behaviour and the influence that these actors have on national regulatory frameworks. Consequently, the origin of the corporate governance system has only a limited impact on our study. Finally, in an effort to define governance processes and their impact on local communities and the developmental state of a country, it is important to deconstruct what we mean by a *governance system.*

For the future of Africa and its countries' natural resource governance, it is crucial to have in-depth knowledge of the impact of such massive investments on economic, social, and political structures. As such, each case study is organized according to three research questions: what are the impacts of foreign-owned companies on natural resource governance? What are the causes of these impacts? Which regulatory and policy sectors should be explored to provide positive outcomes?

Extensive field research in the three case study countries, complemented by desk research, was undertaken in order to obtain and understand the perspectives of local stakeholders and thus better address perceived deficiencies in the literature on African natural resource governance. A particular goal of this research was to obtain a more balanced perspective on foreign-owned enterprises currently operating in Africa's natural resource sector and the role that they are, can, and should be playing in supporting stability and prosperity in conflict-threatened, post-conflict, and stable countries. In so doing, the historical contributions of foreign actors to improving political governance, economic stewardship, and capacity building in African natural resources management are examined in each chapter.

Africa's Energy, Mineral, and Land Resources: Envisioning the Future

Hydrocarbon Resources: From Destabilization to Development?

On the African continent, energy use has risen by 45 per cent since 2000. Despite this increase, sub-Saharan Africa in particular remains badly affected by a very weak supply of energy, including a severe shortage of electrical infrastructure. The electrical grid remains unreliable throughout much of the sub-Saharan region, with mini- and off-grid systems accounting for 70 per cent of the electricity provided in rural areas. With more than 500 million people in the region expected to lack connection to an electrical grid by 2040, costly back-up generators fuelled by diesel or gasoline will be needed for the foreseeable future (IEA 2014).

Although such challenges are significant, Africa is poised to improve on both its conventional and renewable energy deficits thanks to continued development of hydroelectric power, which is steadily gaining capacity in the Democratic Republic of the Congo (DRC), Ethiopia, Mozambique, Guinea, and other sub-Saharan countries – although only approximately 5 per cent of Africa's hydroelectric power potential has been exploited (Ben Aïssa, Ben Jebli, and Ben Youssef 2014, 12). While the potential of renewable energy is high – and forms part of the sustainable development agenda – its uptake across the continent is currently low (Karekezi and Kithyoma 2002; Deichmann et al. 2011; Tenenbaum et al. 2014; Ben Aïssa, Ben Jebli, and Ben Youssef 2014). Yet, geothermal energy is expected to become the second-largest energy source in Ethiopia and Kenya by 2040, and two-thirds of mini- and off-grid electrical systems in

Introduction 17

rural sub-Saharan Africa are expected to derive their energy from solar photovoltaics, small-scale hydroelectric power, and wind turbines over the same period. Moreover, the use of bioenergy, derived from wood and charcoal, is also expected to remain a critical domestic energy source for the continent well into the future.

Despite significant technical potential for offsetting the use of non-renewable energy sources in sub-Saharan Africa, renewables remain a considerably slim component of electricity production (Deichmann et al. 2011, 215–16). This is a bit disheartening, considering that a multitude of studies indicate that "renewable energy consumption plays a vital role for increasing economic growth and an energy policy planned to increase the share of renewable energy in total energy consumption is very effective in reducing greenhouse gas emissions" (Ben Aïssa, Ben Jebli, and Ben Youssef 2014, 12; Bhattacharya 2016). Mini-grids have been proposed as a means for bringing renewable energy to rural Africa, where only small segments of the population across most countries on the continent enjoy access to stable and affordable electricity (Eder 2015). And yet, four out of five Africans use fuelwood and other biomass for cooking, and it is anticipated that a 40 per cent rise in the demand for bioenergy over the course of the next twenty-five years – not unlikely given the continent's anticipated population growth – would impose a significant strain on Africa's forestry stock. Despite the potential energy contributions to be made by these sources, Africa currently constitutes one of the world's most promising regions in terms of hydrocarbon resources (IEA 2014).

Nearly 30 per cent of the global oil and gas discoveries of the last five years were made in Africa (IEA 2014). Though Nigeria remains the hub of the continent's hydrocarbon sector, ongoing theft and militant activities in the Niger Delta are deterring investment and impacting production in the sector negatively, thereby reducing the competitiveness of the country's output in the face of emerging producers (PwC 2016; Muvunyi 2016; Ukiwo 2009; Ikelegbe 2013). Though it is believed that African crude oil production will decline from more than six million barrels per day (mb/d) in 2020 to 5.3 mb/d by 2040, continental demand for oil products is expected to double and reach 4 mb/d over the same period (OPEC 2017). This suggests that the continent's net contribution to the global oil balance could be curtailed in the coming years. Meanwhile, natural gas reserves have the potential to serve as an engine of domestic economic development, provided the correct regulation, prices, and infrastructure are put in place. Despite the resource's promising outlook, as much natural gas is flared as is consumed in Africa, with an estimated one trillion cubic metres having been flared to date. Based on current consumption levels, such volumes would be enough to power the whole of sub-Saharan Africa for more than a decade (IEA 2014).

According to PwC, Africa has proven natural gas reserves of approximately 502 trillion cubic feet, located primarily in Nigeria, Libya, Algeria, Egypt, and parts of East Africa including Mozambique and Tanzania (Temkin 2017). In 2013, six of the top ten oil and gas discoveries were made in Africa, while the continent maintains about 7.5 per cent of the world's proven oil reserves (PwC 2017, 3). Indeed, PricewaterhouseCoopers concludes that Algeria's 121.9 billion barrels of shale gas potential places it third globally. This increase, combined with an improved regulatory environment, would bolster government revenues and economic expansion. Bazilian et al. (2013) have illustrated the critical link between hydrocarbon resource–rich countries and increased access to electricity in a context of effective governance. Notably, a poor and inadequate supply of domestic electricity is regarded as one of the most pressing obstacles to the growth of African enterprises – especially pertinent if the continent as a whole should seek to drive an economic boom with sustainable energy projects, including nuclear power (IEA 2014; Kessides 2014).

Indeed, Andersen and Dalgaard suggest that since 1995, significant economic impact has been lost due to a lack of reliable electrical infrastructure, including physical infrastructure, which economic analysis by Deloitte argues will inhibit projected annual economic growth across the continent over the next decade (Pottas 2014; Andersen and Dalgaard 2013). In addition, global markets for hydrocarbons have been increasingly volatile over the last decade, dropping below US$30 per barrel in 2016 from US$125 in 2008, before averaging at US$70 per barrel the following year (Krauss 2017). If this trend continues, coupled with more fervent international trends toward economic "greenification," African countries may not be able to depend uniformly on the hydrocarbon sector for major contributions to their domestic economies (Nkomo 2017).

Introduction

For a long time, the oil-and-gas sector was considered one of the main destabilizing factors in African resource-rich countries like Nigeria, Equatorial Guinea, or Gabon, as it had favoured the rise of anti-democratic regimes. Nonetheless, foreign-owned actors working within a strong and appropriate governance framework can be, and should be, considered as partners in a country's socioeconomic long-term development.

African Mineral Wealth as a Stabilizing Resource

Mining has been a critical economic activity for the continent, especially sub-Saharan Africa, since the colonial era, when large volumes of minerals began to be mined and processed for international markets (Dumett 1999; Cleveland 2015; Mark-Thiesen 2018). Africa's mineral economy has grown significantly since the first South African diamond rush in 1869, and is widely regarded as a strategic producer of precious raw materials. Today, mining is responsible for the largest contribution to GDP in many African countries, and the continent as a whole produces more than sixty mineral products including several of the world's most lucrative and strategic minerals, such as gold, platinum, and diamonds (Besada 2006; AfDB 2012). Underexplored and underexploited, the continent is estimated to hold 30 per cent of the world's total mineral reserves, including 40 per cent of its gold deposits (Besada 2006).

More recently, the continent experienced a dramatic transformation of its mining sector. Many African governments have established investor-friendly policies and relaxed their control over the sector. As early as 1986, Ghana became one of the first countries in sub-Saharan Africa to reform its mining regulations and provide a regulatory system that, through the passage of the Minerals and Mining Law, allowed foreign ownership within its gold mining sector (Berry 1994). Today, despite the development of stricter mining codes (for example, the DRC's 2018 mining code significantly increased taxes on strategic minerals), more than forty African states have amended their mining legislation to attract greater foreign direct investment (FDI) as a means of developing their mineral resources (Besada 2013; Harvey 2014). The current trend of "resource nationalism" – defined by Jeffrey Wilson as not merely economic bargaining but a process with profound repercussions on "political institutions and their influence on governmental objectives and policy strategies" (2015) – does not always reflect stricter governance.

However, it does translate into an increased awareness of the criticality of resource supply to the global economy, and of constituents' expectations as to the role of their political system regarding resource extraction. These new national-level statutes have facilitated the privatization and deregulation of the sector, enhanced the incentive framework in which mining companies operate, and redefined the obligations and rights of foreign and local investors. These statutes also provided incentives, such as more liberal immigration laws for expatriates and reduced taxation levels, while introducing import tax exemptions for equipment to be used by mining companies in their operations. Together, these changes resulted in a boom in mining exploration across the continent (Besada 2013; Campbell 2003).

In addition, there is a growing acknowledgment that mining companies can bring economic benefit to Africa through skills and technology transfer, greater innovation, more affordable financing, and higher-quality products and services (George 2015; Heymann 2014). Against this backdrop, there has been increased attention in public policy debates on the value of investment from foreign public and private actors in the African mining sector, which has led to the development of new forms of governance, including Pan-Africanist mining regulatory proposals (Nhemachena and Warikandwa 2017). There has also been a concomitant growth in awareness regarding the role played by foreign investment actors in commodity-driven economic planning. The view, however, that foreign majority-owned mining corporations have generally benefitted host countries and local mining communities in Africa in terms of revenue and infrastructure development is not shared by all (Chuhan-Pole, Dabalen, and Land 2017).

Critics contend that foreign mining interests exert a direct influence on political stability and social cohesion, which is due, they argue, to the socioeconomic and environmental disruptions caused by mining operations, especially in countries like Nigeria (Smith 2011; Amunwa and Minio 2011, 8; Courson 2009; Vidal 2015) and the DRC (Nest 2011). Under pressure from advocacy groups, protest movements, and international organizations, some multinational companies operating in the extractive sector

Introduction 21

have become more aware of the need for positive community relations as well as a social licence to operate among local stakeholders. Discussions on corporate social responsibility (CSR) have emphasized that mining industries abroad should adopt ethical business practices, while many Western countries have implemented legislation or created forums to ensure that businesses incorporated within their jurisdiction adhere to acceptable standards of labour rights, environmental protection, and expectations regarding their contribution to socioeconomic development in host countries (Yakovleva 2017; Essah and Andrews 2016; Viveros 2014; Besada 2013). Whether such injunctions by corporate actors have been an effective medium for driving peace, stability, and economic development will be investigated further as part of this book's case study chapters.

Over the past decade, various global and regional initiatives have emerged, including the UN Global Compact, the Global Reporting Initiative, the OECD's Guidelines for Multinational Enterprises and Due Diligence Guidance for Responsible Supply Chains of Minerals from Conflict-Affected and High-Risk Areas, the Principles for Responsible Investment, the Natural Resources Charter, and the Africa Mining Vision (AMV). These voluntary regulations focus to varying degrees on ensuring good corporate behaviour and accountability (Gugerty and Prakash 2010). There is general consensus among civil society organizations (CSOs) and governments that CSR, broadly defined, needs to be about more than merely complying with government regulations and laws.

The African mining sector has been plagued by irregularities and endemic corruption, leading many experts to support the resource curse theory. This book, however, supports an innovative approach that considers foreign-owned mining actors as important partners to sustain broad-based economic development, particularly in post-conflict states such as Sierra Leone.

Land Resources: From Land Grabbing to Sustainable Use

The publication of an alarming report by the international social movement GRAIN (2008a) brought international attention to a new topic: international investments in and acquisitions of land by foreign investors, primarily but not exclusively in Africa. It is important to point out from the outset that both negative consequences and tangible benefits may result from increased investment in land resources in Africa by international investors (Lisk 2013).

These developments in foreign land acquisition underline the significance of land as a critical natural resource in most sub-Saharan African countries. They arise at a time when some of these countries are still trying to come to terms with a land crisis linked to their colonial legacy and characterized by structural inequality, land tenure insecurity, communal impoverishment, and environmental stress. Makki and Geisler even referred, controversially, to land investments by outside interests, mainly foreign ones, as "recurring ways in which states use cosmographies of power and *terra nullius* narratives to remake places identified as empty, underutilized or underproductive" (2011).

Since the end of colonialism in much of Africa and the demise of apartheid in South Africa in 1994, land reforms have been at the core of southern African societies' aspirations toward democratization and socioeconomic reconfiguration. While the International Food Policy Research Institute (IFPRI) claims that land acquisitions may have the potential "to inject much needed investment into agriculture and rural areas in poor developing countries" (von Braun and Meinzen-Dick 2009, 1), it also warns about the potential negative repercussions for the rural poor in recipient countries. This phenomenon is termed *developmental stimulus from land grabbing*, whereby researchers have been striving to understand the developmental impact of large-scale land acquisitions in African states, particularly by foreign private-sector actors. An extensive academic literature has focused on the negative consequences of large-scale land acquisitions (LSLAS), ranging from land grab–induced displacement (Thomson 2014) to an increased gender-based imbalance in household activities (Fonjong and Fokum 2015).

However, other studies have explored the potential beneficial impact that such transnational investments might have on human rights and economic development through agro-industrialization (Wisborg 2013; Lisk 2013). Ethiopia is at the centre of this land-grab or land-sale development trend/stimulus (depending on one's perspective). According to figures from the Ethiopian government, close to forty foreign countries have bought or leased prime agricultural land in the country (Vidal 2011).

Introduction 23

The Ethiopian government argues that it needs multinational investment in its agricultural sector to spur development and industrialization, especially as more than 80 per cent of the country relies on agriculture for subsistence (Schiffman 2013). India has acquired 600,000 hectares of agricultural land in Ethiopia, followed closely by firms from Saudi Arabia (Anwar 2016). Ethiopia has earmarked some 11.5 million hectares of agricultural land for lease or sale to foreign multinationals (Chandran and Gardner 2017). Land acquisitions in Africa, especially in Ethiopia, have been driven by the increasing scarcity of land and water resources, as well as export restrictions (e.g., export taxes and export bans) imposed by major global food producers during times of high food prices, which has resulted in a "growing distrust in the functioning of regional and global markets" (IFPRI 2009).

Land deals have become a national security strategy for countries facing forms of environmental scarcity or preparing for future energy shortages. At the same time, in 2007–08, burgeoning agricultural commodity prices increasingly attracted private companies (agri-food businesses, bio-energy corporations, investment funds, and so on) and public-private partnerships to invest in land acquisitions as the world headed into financial crisis. The impact of sharp increases in international prices pushed major exporting countries to introduce tariffs or even bans, destabilizing the global markets. To insulate themselves from the elevated prices of an unstable market, wealthy food-importing countries began to invest heavily in overseas lands (Cotula 2013).

This massive scale of investment and land acquisition during a triple global crisis (in terms of food, energy, and financial uncertainty), together with the prevailing problem of land tenure insecurity in most "recipient" countries, calls for greater scrutiny as to how and why these investments and land deals are occurring. It is also important to examine their local, regional, and global repercussions on social, economic, and political structures. In the southern African region alone, deals have proliferated at an unprecedented rate. Assessments of the potential impacts of these investments differ greatly, but experiences in case study countries, including Ethiopia, illustrate the destabilizing effects of land deals on national political structures and the need for robust, stable governance systems (Matondi, Havnevik, and Beyene 2011).

As illustrated earlier, land deals provide a strong example of interference by foreign-owned companies in national natural resource governance systems. Indeed, this book supports a new research paradigm to understand how land-related investments by foreign actors can and should support long-term development and stability in African countries.

While appearing subjective, exploration of the positive and negative roles played by foreign-owned enterprises focuses on issues pertinent to creating a sustainable environment in terms of social, economic, political, and environmental concerns. Positive impacts of foreign-owned economic actors centre on but are not limited to: inclusion of local communities in the investment project, implementation of appropriate efforts toward redistribution of created wealth at the state and local levels, and integration of CSR practices together with on-the-ground translation of these internal policies. On the negative side, the destabilization of socioeconomic systems and the creation of enclave economies, wherein financial and political benefits from extractive activities in resource-rich countries filter toward political and economic elites at the expense of larger segments of the population, constitute negative corporate impacts that affect long-term peace, stability, and economic development.

Three Countries: A New Framework

Prior to examining the three case studies, this research begins with two framework chapters that present, explore, and clarify key *concepts* and *methods* pertinent to the research as well as literature topics covering the resource curse, the evolving role of foreign investors, and the role of the private sector in sustainable growth paradigms. In addition, there will be a robust acknowledgment of the project's proposed PENRG framework, a further expansion of the book's three primary research questions, and an outline of how the investigation was designed to obtain relevant empirical evidence and advance the analysis.

In each of the three case studies, the challenges and opportunities created by the expanding role of foreign-owned enterprises are viewed through a new theoretical framework. In particular, the growing presence of traditional and emerging state-owned and private-sector actors in natural re-

Introduction 25

source management in Ghana, Sierra Leone, and Ethiopia as they relate to stability, peace, security, and broad-based economic development (prosperity) is analyzed. Thematically guided histories for each case country and current knowledge on natural resource governance provide context.

Ghana and Its Hydrocarbon Resources: A Case Study

Since the 1980s, Ghana's economic growth has been increasingly tied to the mining sector, which is largely dominated by gold. Ghana's lucrative natural resources, stable political landscape, and increasingly diverse economy have seen it emerge as the second-largest economy in West Africa (after Nigeria). With its established democratic system, prudent natural resource management, steadily declining national poverty rates, and consistent economic growth – culminating in middle-income status in 2011 – Ghana has traditionally been regarded as a model for development in sub-Saharan Africa (Chamlee-Wright 1997; Killick 2010). Despite various efforts and improvements, the country has nevertheless confronted several challenges in recent years that have prevented its mining fiscal system from functioning more effectively (Amponsah-Tawiah and Dartey-Baah 2011; Standing and Hilson 2013, Ayee et al. 2011). These challenges include gaps in the monitoring and verification of capital expenditures, loss of carryover provisions, and transfer pricing mechanisms. Consequently, Ghana's extractive sector is highly susceptible to illicit financial flows (IFFS) (ACEP 2015).

The extractive sector has the potential to play a significant role in Ghana's future economic development and transformation, social progress, and poverty reduction, as well as greater environmental protection. For this to occur, the country's forthcoming forty-year National Development Plan must give the sector the attention it deserves, placing it at the core of Ghana's future, long-term development strategy and establishing the infrastructure needed for its responsible development. This includes a well-planned and -financed industrialization process for the transformation of mining and mineral resources, which cannot happen if this process and these resources are not considered tightly linked to and necessary for agricultural development, given that agriculture is a key economic sector (Owusu-Ansah and Smardon 2015). This case study also underlines the connections between gold and cocoa (Snapir, Simms, and Waine 2017) as well as downstream linkages between oil and construction, and between gold mining and other sectors of the economy (Tenkorang and Osei-Kufuor 2013). The intention is to demonstrate that specific natural resources, and the progress toward improving their governance, do not exist in isolation from the rest of a country's economic system. Along this interconnected chain, foreign-owned investment actors, together with the Ghanaian government, may be key drivers of transformational change.

The Mineral Wealth of Sierra Leone: A Case Study

Sierra Leone is undergoing post-conflict reconstruction and state building following brutal civil wars fuelled by resource predation. Reconstruction efforts, particularly in the extractive sector, have focused heavily on private-sector growth (Del Castillo 2008; Andersen 2011). In Sierra Leone, diamond extraction by a variety of foreign-owned enterprises, via legal and illegal means, played a crucial role in the country's destabilization and provided a primary means of finance to armed rebel groups leading up to and during the civil conflict (Jakobi and Wolf 2013). Recent efforts to resuscitate the economic livelihoods of communities devastated by conflict have placed great emphasis on "good governance" in small-scale diamond-mining communities. Nevertheless, resurrecting viable and transparent diamond- and gold-mining industries in the country has been problematic, as the "peace dividend" continues to elude many communities due to a lack of foreign investment and persistent corruption within political institutions that hamper reconstruction and peacebuilding efforts (Beevers 2015).

But despite considerable achievements in recent years, Sierra Leone's post-conflict environment continues to impact investment and the degree to which it can diversify its economy (Marda and Bangura 2010). Indeed, the country's long-term stability and the consolidation of its democracy require that it move away from resource extraction as the dominant source of revenue. The aftereffects of the conflict include a severe shortage of skilled workers and managers, rampant corruption, a lack of infrastructure (roads, telecommunications, and supplies of water and energy), cumbersome customs procedures, a weak judiciary, the absence of an effective

Introduction 27

land-titling system outside the western area around the capital, Freetown, and a limited banking system (Le Billon 2008; US Embassy, Freetown 2011). These drawbacks in terms of development and ease of doing business deter much-needed foreign investment in the extractive and other key sectors.

Ethiopia's Vast Land Resources: A Case Study

For Ethiopia, natural resource governance with respect to land constitutes a particularly crucial dimension of its development. Agriculture has long been the central axis of its economy, and commercial agriculture and large-scale investments have been considered critical to the development of this sector. One of the main challenges presented by commercialized agriculture is that instead of creating employment, it replaces labour-intensive farming techniques with machinery and other technology that can degrade the surrounding environment (Khairo, Battese, and Mullen 2005).

Although foreign investments in Ethiopia's agricultural sector have culminated in improved infrastructure, large-scale agricultural investments are particularly problematic when one considers that Ethiopia, and East Africa more broadly, are disproportionately affected by hunger and other food security concerns. Though such investments have the potential to offer much in the way of knowledge and technology transfer, there is also evidence to suggest that land acquisitions in Ethiopia have displaced smallholder agriculturalists and pastoralists from their ancestral lands without providing them with compensatory employment opportunities (Moreda 2015).

On the other hand, the book seeks to investigate whether the adoption of alternative governance models may constitute a workable solution. This case study demonstrates that governance models that prioritize, via foreign-owned enterprises, the production of labour-intensive crops, meaningful consultations with local communities, and due respect for local knowledge of agricultural production processes may spur possible administrative changes that could facilitate inclusive and sustainable growth (Adenew 2004). In addition, fostering participatory industrial crop production allocation frameworks and lending greater support to domestic firms producing agricultural inputs are other means of empowering growth and mitigating instability in Ethiopia. A re-evaluation of legislation that has recentralized land administration functions, as well as a reconsideration of the Ethiopian government's general approach to pastoral and shifting cultivator groups, could also benefit the citizens (Little et al. 2010). Ethiopia's agricultural sector nevertheless offers development opportunities for well-regulated foreign actors and constitutes a complex linkage between foreign investment and Ethiopia's interethnic fragility.

This research should shed light on the role that foreign state-owned and private-sector actors have historically played in the governance and management of natural resources in these three distinct countries. It also addresses the political conditions that are unique to each, and how they shape the environment for foreign-owned enterprises operating in the natural resource sector. By addressing the role of foreign actors and the local political conditions that affect them, this research endeavours to identify patterns and relationships evolving in the face of new investment flows from traditional and emerging investors, and how African governments and communities have responded to the social impacts of such investment.

By focusing on the factors that influence whether foreign actors contribute to or alleviate instability, conflict, and prosperity, this research aims to contribute to broader debates and academic discourses on the role of foreign actors within the natural resource sector by providing guidelines for an improved analytical framework that can be used to interpret and clarify concepts about natural resource governance, sustainable development, and violent conflict in Africa. A second goal is to help enhance discussion surrounding on-the-ground experiences and lessons learned – those of host governments, foreign actors, local communities, and international organizations – that could be relevant to developing policy that promotes development outcomes in the natural resource sector.

CHAPTER 1

Understanding Conflict and Resource Management

Conceptual Overview

The management of natural resources is now an important debate in the political economy of national and international development, both in policy and academic circles. In particular, the discussions that characterize this debate have far-reaching strategy and policy implications for the ability to attain sustainable development in developing countries. Indeed, one area of emerging consensus is the critical importance of *governance* – defined here as "the deficiency or effectiveness of public and private sector institutions" – as the key to understanding the prevalence or absence of violent conflict (peace and security) as well as economic development pertaining to natural resources in Africa (Alao 2007; Collier 2007; Acemoglu, Robinson, and Johnson 2002). Weak, corrupt, or undemocratic governments may be unable or unwilling to invest resource revenues in sustainable economic development, or to provide the necessary regulatory environments for responsible and accountable business practices (Ballentine 2006). Host governments of resource-rich countries, local communities in extractive areas, and foreign-owned enterprises can all play a crucial part in influencing and determining strategies, policies, and the nature of the institutions that govern how resources are managed, as well as whether resource wealth contributes to sustainable economic development in the Global South.

In Africa, effective management of the continent's abundant natural resources could be the key to poverty alleviation and lasting prosperity. However, recent history suggests that poor resource management often results in the chaotic and wasteful deployment of human capital, the depletion of the resources on which societies' economic livelihoods are based and, in extreme cases, violence and political instability at both the national and regional levels (Ross 2012; Buckles 1999; USAID 2006; UNDP 2011). Indeed, natural resource wealth alone is not sufficient to contribute to the peace, security, and economic development of resource-rich countries (Torvik 2009). The generation of positive development outcomes, including the reduction of poverty, is grounded in effective governance, which encompasses both the government's ability to utilize resource revenues effectively and the policies and practices of other actors such as businesses and NGOs. In this sense, questions surrounding the governance of natural resources become critical to ensuring that resource wealth contributes to the development of resource-rich countries, rather than precipitating cycles of violence and sustaining widespread poverty.

The increasing frequency of dialogue and roundtable discussions between various stakeholders in the extractive industries – revealed in part and reflected by this research – illustrates the growing concern in the global community, including even among international business organizations and multilateral institutions, that a reconciliation between sustainable economic development and business objectives must occur by encouraging a more responsible exploitation of natural resources (UNECA 2016). Key concerns from a governance perspective include: the absence of clear regulations and mining codes; insufficient adherence to the rule of law; an absence of fiscal, monetary, and budgetary discipline; the presence of few public-private partnerships that are pro-poor in their orientation and design; poor skills and limited resources in government departments; muted encouragement of open dialogue between government and civil society; and little, if any, transparency and accountability. These deficiencies demand an improved and visible governance system in Africa's natural resources sector so as ultimately to promote peace, security, and economic development.

From the perspective of African stakeholders – including the national leaders, domestic investors, and development practitioners interviewed during the fieldwork for this research project – effective natural resource governance is increasingly regarded as the key determinant of the continent's economic growth and investment opportunities, especially if official

Understanding Conflict and Resource Management

aid levels continue to decline (IDEA 2018; Rodríguez-Pose and Cols 2017, 67; Ovadia 2017). African leaders have come to recognize that the manner in which the continent's resources are managed and developed is integral to their ability to mobilize more resources domestically, contribute to sustainable economic and social development, and enhance peace and security (Fabricius et al. 2013). This is evidenced by the outspoken support by African leaders for the Africa Mining Vision, including the African Union's Addis Ababa Declaration. Given the changing global order brought about by the rise of emerging economies such as China and India, and their increased trade with and investment in Africa, an improved understanding of natural resource governance on the continent – its direct impact on peace, security, and economic development, and how its governance is likely to evolve – is of greater importance than ever.

The literature to date denotes a range of perspectives on the impact of natural resource governance on peace, security, and economic development. It has been argued that foreign investors are to some extent contributing to the transfer of skills, knowledge, and technology to host countries through their operations (York 2012; Evans 2015; Zhou 2017, 328; *World Finance* 2015; Turok 2013), although the literature is also filled with examples of these so-called beneficiation outputs failing to appear in any meaningful, tangible, or sustainable way. Foreign investment in extractives can also facilitate innovation, more affordable financing, and higher-quality products and services. In contrast, research findings indicate that resource-rich economies in Africa have suffered lower economic growth due to the phenomenon known as "Dutch disease," which refers to the economic challenges associated with rapid growth in exports of raw commodities. This lower growth may give rise to an increase in the value of a country's currency and exert an impact on the decline of other sectors of its economy (Van Der Ploeg and Poelhekke 2017, 206).

This is in contrast to the resource curse, a paradox in which countries endowed with abundant natural resources tend to achieve, at a statistically significant level, fewer development metrics than other countries. For example, based on evidence from forty-one countries between 1970 and 2006, Frynas, Wood, and Hinks argue that non-resource exports are seen to decrease by an average of 75 per cent while imports rise an additional 25 per cent (2017, 235). Others, including Behzadan et al. (2017), suggest that Dutch disease originates solely from the unequal distribution of re-source rents. The literature, however, is not uniformly supportive of the resource curse hypothesis, with some proposing that it is a "statistical ar-tefact created by either endogeneity or omitted variable bias"; that research tends to falsely equate a comparative advantage in resource products with abundance; or that many wholly fail to recognize the nature of develop-ment as inherently imperfect (Ross 2015; Wright and Czelusta 2004; Fran-kel 2010).

There is also undisputed evidence that corruption is endemic in many of Africa's resource-rich countries where there is already a high degree of income inequality (AfDB 2007) and low poverty reduction rates (Ite 2005). Indeed, research shows that corruption has particular and visible impacts on per capita GDP growth, while lowering efficiency in the allocation of public goods, discouraging foreign direct investment, and restricting general economic production (Baliamoune-Lutz and Ndikumana 2009; KPMG 2016; Lučić, Radišić, and Dobromirov 2016; Hodge, Prasada Rao, and Duhs 2011). Consequently, public policy debates on the governance of Africa's natural resources are now central to discourse and dialogue, at the continental and regional levels, on financing sustainable economic and social development, as well as promoting peace and security.

Much of the existing scholarly literature on natural resources manage-ment and governance focuses on foreign investors in particular and con-flict risks in general; less is known, however, about the role of economic actors in the extractive sector in post-conflict and conflict-threatened countries (Woodward 2010). This is a lingering puzzle: in specific political contexts, how do foreign-owned enterprises operating in these areas im-pact peace, security, and economic development, especially in countries with differential primary resource commodities? Bush and Opp (1999) underline the somewhat paradoxical fact that conflict can serve as a cata-lyst for positive economic and social development. The potential for con-flict to galvanize cooperation and peaceful development has been noted, particularly with respect to water resources (UN 2016). What has occurred in Sierra Leone since the end of the civil war in 2002 might also apply to economies reliant on minerals and hydrocarbons.

The experience of armed conflict may generate strong incentives for the political elite to secure the consent of the governed and create representative and effective governing institutions to extract resources more efficiently – although whether this has occurred and what role foreign-owned enterprises play in this regard have yet to be determined (Tilly 1975). Le Billon, for example, suggests that the abundance of natural resources may encourage parties in an armed conflict to sustain it rather than work toward peace, as the former is far more profitable that the latter. Peace, he argues, removes key sources of revenue for all parties, including international, intervening actors, who lose immediate access to natural resources when a functioning local government is created during post-conflict reconstruction (2001, 578). In Angola, for example, oil revenues made it possible for conflicting parties to build loyalty through rent dispersal and control, preventing meaningful governance reform while perpetuating economic inequality (Le Billon 2001). Indeed, political commentators such as Blattman and Miguel (2010) have observed that the connection between foreign investors, national and international private-sector organizations, and institutional transformation in the context of natural resource governance is not clear. In the chapters that follow, this research project hopes to shed light on the relationship between these variables through case studies on Sierra Leone, Ghana, and Ethiopia.

If foreign-owned enterprises – both state-owned and privately owned – are to support sustainable economic development, peace, and security in stable, post-conflict, and conflict-threatened countries, then an inclusive approach to the governance of natural resources is required. Ideally, in stable countries, foreign-owned enterprise revenues should help to bolster economic growth and sustainable human and physical development, CSR practices, and capacity building. In post-conflict countries, foreign-owned enterprises could contribute to post-conflict reconstruction, economic transformation and development, and governance enhancement. Finally, in conflict-threatened countries, foreign-owned enterprises could contribute to a conflict containment strategy through judicious involvement in land transactions and investments. Based on the existing literature, greater accountability and CSR, the reinvestment of resource revenues into social services and poverty reduction programs, and diversified economic development are ideal objectives for all stakeholders (Peschka and Emery 2011). However, given the wide range of challenges and the complexity of underlying issues in diverse political environments, an improved analytical framework is needed to better understand the changing interactions between foreign investment actors, natural resource governance, and political stability and instability in Africa. The PENRG framework could provide researchers with a new tool for analyzing how foreign-owned enterprises affect sustainable economic growth and poverty alleviation, peace, and stability in stable, post-conflict, and conflict-threatened countries in sub-Saharan Africa.

This line of enquiry is crucial to Africa's development considering the continent's ongoing need for foreign capital and technology transfer (Agola 2016), the increasing significance of FDI in the natural resources sector (Bokpin, Mensah, and Asamoah 2015), and the effects these could have on trade and fiscal policies designed to promote sustainable development.

Governance Structures

Governance structures in sub-Saharan African countries are institutions and policies – both national and local – that determine the interaction between companies, the country, and its citizens. Examples of elements of governance structures include the means to translate resources into tangible benefits for citizens, national ownership of resources, the enactment of fiscal rules on the use of revenues, and the existence of strong public institutions, including oversight bodies and the justice system.

For the purposes of this research study, companies are deemed to be foreign-owned enterprises – an aggregate grouping of foreign investment actors. Such enterprises may be wholly or partly state-owned, -controlled, or -sponsored companies or privately owned companies (listed or not) that operate in large-scale resource industries in the host countries. Whether a company is state-owned or a private, corporate actor is likely to have a critical impact on how investments are pursued. As Amighini, Rabellotti, and Sanfilippo (2013) argue in the Chinese case, while private companies are attracted by large markets and strategic assets in a risk-averse approach, state-sponsored or -controlled enterprises follow the strategic needs of their home country, with little concern over risk. While an analysis of the differences, in terms of processes and impacts, on the investment's host country between private and state-owned corporate actors would be an invaluable addition to the literature, this study does not undertake such an analysis.

In Ghana, the key industry is hydrocarbons; in Sierra Leone, mining; and in Ethiopia, agriculture (Kopf 2017; Commonwealth 2017). Ghana currently has four major hydrocarbon fields, with total proven reserves of 2,312.4 billion cubic feet of natural gas and 883.4 million barrels of oil, which, as of 2018, are being explored and exploited under seventeen petroleum agreements (Ghana Petroleum Register, n.d.). Diamonds are well known for their role in driving civil conflict, and Sierra Leone has some 7,700 square miles of active diamond fields covering nearly 25 per cent of the country's surface area, along with other mineral resources such as gold, bauxite, rutile, ilmenite, and iron ore (MMMR, n.d.[b]).

Foreign involvement in the natural resource sector in Africa is a direct consequence of the continent's lack of the capital and technology needed to develop such infrastructure projects, and of supportive government policies such as openness to trade and tax incentives. The need for accumulation of capital and technology in fast-growing emerging economies over the past three decades, taking into consideration strategic and national interests, explains the recent phenomenon of South-originating FDI in Africa's natural resource sector. China's massive investments in securing cobalt supplies from the Democratic Republic of the Congo (DRC) is only the latest example of South-South FDI in strategic acquisitions (Payne and Zhdannikov 2018).

How citizens, civil society groups, and the international community view foreign-owned enterprises depends largely on how local and national governments in resource-rich countries manage their relations with the private sector. For example, governance systems determine whether private-sector actors are viewed with praise (as in the case of Ghana), as pivotal players in peacebuilding and reconstruction efforts (Sierra Leone), or with general suspicion and as a destabilizing factor (Ethiopia). Corporations' reputations also depend on how integrated they are within the governance structures set up by these countries to manage resource rents and investments. These structures operate within the broader frameworks and commitments that governments agree to as part of their national visions and economic priorities – as well as in relation to the AMV, which was adopted by African leaders at the 2009 Addis Ababa Summit.[1] An additional factor that determines how foreign-owned enterprises are perceived by host populations is the structure of their own governance frameworks.

These national governance structures are integrated to global systems of governance of natural resources. While the EITI provides a transparency framework at the country level regarding the award, management, and monitoring of financial flows in the extractive industries, the OECD has focused on the supply-and-demand side of corruption at the national and international levels (OECD 2016). Exploring 131 real-life corruption cases in the extractive industries, the OECD report provides analysis of anti-corruption measures covering the whole value chain. Many examples of initiatives exist at the global level to tackle corruption issues in the extractive sector and ensure alleviation of socioeconomic inequalities at the local and national levels. From the Resource Governance Index of the Natural Resource Governance Institute (NRGI) to the Responsible Mining Foundation's Responsible Mining Index (RMI), a wide variety of tools are available. However, as Acosta argues, "understanding and measuring the impact and effectiveness of these initiatives is a matter of proposing and empirically validating a causal link between interventions and governance improvements" (Acosta 2013). In this sense, the role of non-state actors is critical for assessing and understanding the processes at play in natural resource governance at the international, national, and local levels (this book tackles the issue from the national level). As Young highlights in regard to environmental concerns, "although states remain central players in natural resources and environmental issues, nonstate actors have made particularly striking advances both in the creation of environmental regimes and in efforts to make these regimes function effectively once they are in place" (Young 1997). This trend of nonstate actors' involvement in global governance structures for extractive industries – as definers of standards and good practices, and implementers of legal systems – is critical to assess the ability of states like Ghana, Ethiopia, and Sierra Leone to create governance frameworks.

State actors remain, however, at the core of defining global governance frameworks for extractive industries, particularly through cooperation organizations – either the traditional North-South system or the increasingly important South-South and Triangular models (Besada, Tok, and Polonenko 2019). The most widely accepted frameworks for managing the social and environmental costs of investment projects in the Global South remain the International Finance Corporation (IFC) Performance Standards and the Equator Principles. As an assessment tool to review private-sector projects and investments in developing countries, the IFC Performance Standards converge with other international norms, such as the UN Global Compact, the UN Norms on Transnational Investments and Other Business Enterprises with regard to Human Rights, and the OECD Guidelines for Multinational Companies (Morgera 2007). Carbonnier's approach to natural resource governance systems at the international level exposes how the energy supply security concerns of rich countries have shaped the global governance framework. The inadequacy of this framework to the needs of resource-rich countries, usually in the Global South and transit countries, underlines the importance of a reconceptualization of extractive governance and the increased institutionalization of voluntary initiatives (Carbonnier 2011).

Similarly, the influence of rich importing states, mostly but not exclusively in the Global North, on the definition of social and environmental standards casts doubt upon the applicability of such instruments in low-income countries. This trend has been brilliantly described by Dreher, Lang, and Richert in their analysis of the political economy of the IFC lending system. They found that "IFC loans go to companies and countries whose interests are better represented." Linking these findings with the allocation of seats at the IFC's board, the researchers found that companies investing in countries with board seats have higher incomes than companies investing in countries without seats (Dreher, Lang, and Richert 2019). Such influence at the financial level translates all too easily into how the IFC Performance Standards are defined. In this sense, this book tackles the discrepancies between international norms on natural resource governance and their applicability at the national level through three case studies of resource-rich countries: Ghana, Ethiopia, and Sierra Leone.

Foreign actors have the potential to bring about transformational changes in the economies and social fabrics of conflict-affected and post-conflict states. They could also serve as engines for growth in stable, resource-rich democracies in Africa. However, this can only be achieved with strong, coherent, and strategic national and local governance structures that clearly define the role of the private sector. Such structures must not only take the companies' interests into account, but also spell out their responsibilities to all stakeholders, including mining communities.

International Political Economy and Natural Resources FDI

Much of the International Political Economy (IPE) research has focused on the relationship between democratic institutions and the flow of FDIS through the assessment of political risks, mostly in developing countries. Interestingly, democratic regimes are seen as the lower governance system risk for investments, as the multiplicity of actors able to block legislative changes provides a stabilizing factor in legal systems (Tsebelis 2002). Another critical factor is the transparency of the avenues available to corporations to influence the political sphere (Jensen 2008), a factor closely linked to the transparency of democratic political regimes that allow companies to observe and anticipate changes in the legal framework (Rosendorff and Vreeland 2006). While these concerns link the political system to the political risks, for foreign companies, of investing in a specific country, Jensen makes a compelling argument regarding the political risks for national leaders who renege on engagement with foreign-owned corporations (Jensen 2006).

These concerns are central to the research presented in this manuscript. The political regimes in Ethiopia, Sierra Leone, and Ghana have profound impacts on the investments made by foreign-owned corporations in the natural resources sector.

Theoretical Framework for Country Case Studies

According to Hout, traditional structural political economy "understands development as a permanent process of institutional restructuring, with the aim of achieving resource redistribution. This process, which requires particular elites to give up certain privileges in favour of the poor, involves conflict ... [and specifically] the political struggles that result from the expected opposition of (parts of) the elite that do not wish to give up their privileges" (Hout 2015, 88–9).

Understanding Conflict and Resource Management 39

The structural political economy approach to analyzing natural resource governance is narrow in focus and deals strictly with governance reform and the politics of structural reform, particularly the restructuring of existing institutions and governance arrangements (Hout 2015). In this light, each case study begins by outlining the country's political economy, with a historical overview of the relationships between governance structures and economic, social, and development outcomes. The case studies deal with laws, regulations, and policies – or, in the absence of such, with other governance structures that desire to transform resources into tangible benefits for citizens. National and local governments, political and economic elites, traditional authorities (chiefs and community elders), foreign state-owned and private-sector actors, and local communities are considered as key actors in governance and structural reform activities.

Governance structures are inherently linked to country type (i.e., stable, post-conflict, or conflict-threatened); they inform state capability and guidance for foreign investors/foreign state-owned and private-sector actors, and influence how such actors affect peace and stability, and economic development outcomes. My theoretical approach may be used to assess country narratives, conditions, and relevant outcomes in support of my core argument that the role of foreign state-owned and private-sector actors in natural resource management in sub-Saharan Africa depends on the various strengths, weaknesses, and levels of governance structures in stable, post-conflict, and conflict-threatened states.

In his highly influential paper "Concept Misformation in Comparative Politics," Sartori (1970) stresses that researchers must define concepts correctly in order to know exactly what their theory will test. Further, he argues that conceptual precision helps researchers choose the right methods for testing their theory (Collier and Gerring 2009). This research applies the theory of structural political economy to the analysis of foreign-owned enterprises' roles, state stability or instability, and country governance structures. Through a modified PENRG approach, the research investigates how the contribution of foreign-owned enterprises to state stability or instability, peace, and economic development is derived from the outcome of their investments. These investments are not only shaped by governance structures, but also interact with such structures to produce outcomes. Traditional thinking in existing literature suggests that in the absence of strong policies, institutions, and long-term vision, foreign investments in natural resources could lead to state instability (Cabrales and Hauk 2011). Alternatively, foreign investment could lead to increased state stability.

Two related notions or terms of importance to this research are *instability* and *conflict*, which require clarification: they refer to competition and rivalry over the control, distribution, and consumption of natural resources. Instability and conflict are therefore understood as existing within a spectrum: they can range from confusion and frustration among members of a community over specific development actions to violent clashes between armed groups over resource ownership. Instability and conflict also connote widespread social unrest that threatens the political stability and security conditions of entire countries. Foreign investments in natural resources could increase instability and conflict by contributing to corruption, creating socioeconomic inequalities, providing funding for arms, providing arms directly to warlords and militias, disrupting environmental and social systems, and contributing to Dutch disease. Instability and conflict can also refer to land grabs, poor labour standards, environmental degradation, the importation of foreign workers, and a lack of accountability in government budgets, resulting in tension between civil society groups, private actors, and governments.[2]

With regard to governance structures, Table 1.1 presents political and economic examples found in this research. This research also draws on Cox's critical approach to international political economy (1981). Cox strives for a holistic approach, questioning the nature of institutions, social relations, and power dynamics by examining their origins and anticipating future characteristics. In brief, he is concerned with broad, cross-cutting themes as opposed to more micro-level, specific details. As part of the PENRG framework, which I introduce below, my research employs Cox's critical approach to outline the relationship between foreign private-sector actors and their effects on stability and instability in the three case study countries. It also informs how this research project addresses the roles of foreign-owned enterprises, state stability or instability, and whether governance structures and the involvement of foreign actors contribute to stability or instability in resource-rich African countries.

Importantly, Cox distinguishes between problem-solving theory and critical theory. He states that problem-solving theory "takes the world as

Table 1.1

Governance structures at the private, public, and regional/global levels

LEVEL	STRUCTURE
Private	Revenue-sharing agreements; wealth-sharing agreements; production-sharing agreements; exploration and mining licences; oil-sharing agreements; policies on selective treatment, cost-recovery measures, and quality-control mechanisms; training programs; International Organization for Standardization (ISO) certification; joint ventures with government and other companies; mining community development agreements (CDAs); community development funds (CDFs); projects including community outreach; CSR practices reflecting an actor's role as a socioeconomic development and security partner (beyond merely complying with government laws and regulations); ethical business practices; initiatives to promote forward and backward linkages; economic diversification and beneficiation; community development funds.
Public (local)	Local governments, departments, and agencies; commissions; committees; institutional frameworks and mechanisms; incentives; policies; strategies; programs and plans; community development programs; projects; public relations; forums to ensure that companies uphold human rights standards, environmental protections, and broad-based socioeconomic development; principles of free, prior, and informed consent (FPIC); technical assistance arrangements; channels to engage with civil society and local communities; conflict resolution strategies that foster mutual trust among workers and develop social capital within communities; local-level funding for social projects and economic activities; community-based natural resource management (CBNRM) interventions.

Table 1.1 Continued

LEVEL	STRUCTURE
Public (national)	National and local governments, ministries, and departments; agencies and tax authorities; the judiciary; special courts; commissions; committees; legislation and laws; regulations and regulatory mechanisms; revenue- and production-sharing agreements; joint ventures and public-private partnerships; resource allocation mechanisms; monitoring and evaluation arrangements; institutional frameworks and mechanisms; transparency and accountability mechanisms; incentives; policies; strategies; programs and plans (including privatization programs, infrastructure development, and poverty alleviation); community development programs; projects; contracts; investments; standards; best practices; mining and CSR codes; public relations; forums to ensure that companies uphold human rights standards, environmental protections, and broad-based socioeconomic development; FPIC principles; technical assistance arrangements; peace agreements and ceasefires.
Regional/global	Extractive Industries Transparency Initiative (EITI); United Nations Global Compact (UNGC); Global Reporting Initiative (GRI); OECD Guidelines for Multinational Enterprises; commodity-specific OECD guidance; Principles for Responsible Investment (PRI); Natural Resource Charter; Africa Mining Vision (AMV); Publish What You Pay; certification schemes such as the Kimberley Process Certification Scheme (KPCS); regional and global benchmarks.

it finds it, with the prevailing social and power relationships and the institutions into which they are organized, as the given framework for action. The general aim of problem-solving is to make these relationships and institutions work smoothly by dealing effectively with particular sources of trouble" (1981, 128–9). While problem-solving theory is analytical, critical theory is holistic. Therefore, Cox contends that critical theory "does not take institutions and social and power relations for granted but calls them into question by concerning itself with their origins and how and whether they might be in the process of changing ... Critical theory is directed to the social and political complex as a whole rather than to the separate parts" (129).

Cox also suggests that where problem-solving theory might be seen as conservative, critical theory can be seen as utopian. However, he argues that this interpretation misunderstands the objective of critical theory, nothing that the "aims [of critical theory] are just as practical as those of problem-solving theory, but it approaches practice from a perspective which transcends that of the existing order, which problem-solving theory takes as its starting point. Critical theory allows for a normative choice in favour of a social and political order different from the prevailing order, but it limits the range of choice to alternative orders which are feasible transformations of the existing world" (130).

Employing Cox's critical theory, this research project aims to identify possible alternatives for state governance structures to guide potential impacts of foreign-owned enterprises on peace, stability, and economic development. Accordingly, the case studies explore the impact of foreign-owned companies on peace, stability, and economic growth in relevant sectors, the emergence of new sectors, and experiences and lessons learned that could be relevant to policies aimed at promoting positive developmental outcomes. Benefitting from the absence of restricting factors in the critical theory approach, the three cases also contribute to the development of an improved analytical framework, introduced at the end of this chapter, for conceptualizing natural resource governance and stability in Africa.

A critical remaining question is the impact of globalization processes and, more generally, the neoliberal economic system on the three countries at the centre of our study. While much research tends to highlight the negative trends that the global financial system has encouraged, and still does, on the African continent, it appears important to mention this debate. Indeed, the destructive structural adjustment programs of the 1980s and 1990s have tarnished subsequent interventions by global financial institutions in the countries of the Global South. Re-politicizing questions of financial flows and, generally speaking, the international political economy of foreign investments is important to assess the trends in regulation and incentivization of investments. Campbell's study of the complementarity between national regulations in the mining sector and international norms has been critical in this context. She supports that "no amount of local governance is sufficient if not accompanied by legal and fiscal frameworks designed to meet development objectives and which are implemented in the context of good international policies and rules" (Campbell 2003). In the land and agricultural sector, the work of Haroon Akram-Lodhi, Borras, and Kay (2009) is critical to approach the role of globalized policies and financial systems in processes such as land privatization and the ability of global corporations to establish themselves as developmental actors, as we will see throughout this book.

Literature Review

This section will survey relevant issues pertaining to the governance and management of natural resources, particularly in the African context, in the academic literature. Its aim is to highlight the key intellectual debates with which this research project engages. Through an examination of relevant issues pertaining to the governance and management of natural resources in the academic literature, specifically in the three case study countries, the literature review coalesces key debates within a single framework to allow for more effective policy analysis.

A True Resource Curse?

Conflict over the control, distribution, and consumption of natural resources is ubiquitous. However, the nature of that conflict is determined by the social, political, and economic contexts in which people interact

Understanding Conflict and Resource Management

(Ayling and Kelly 1999). These conflicts range from confusion and frustration among members of a community over specific development actions, to violent clashes between armed groups over resource ownership, to widespread social unrest that threatens the political stability and security environments of entire countries. Foreign investors and private-sector actors – including ranchers, large-scale landowners, and private corporations in industries such as forestry, mining, hydroelectric power, and agribusiness – are becoming increasingly influential in resource management decisions. Consequently, they are also important actors with regard to maintaining or encouraging peace and security in developing countries (Buckles 1999). This dynamic is being driven by the globalization of multinational enterprises, the fiscal policies of financial institutions, the actions of developing countries' governments, and the increased demand for resources among emerging economies (Cotula et al. 2009).

Burgeoning literature on the "resource curse" and the "paradox of plenty" has established strong linkages between resource abundance and corruption, authoritarianism, economic decline, inequality, and violent conflict (Karl 1997; Sachs and Warner 1997; Ross 2012). Resource abundance in particular provides both finances and motives for armed conflict, while rent-seeking and patronizing behaviour further erodes political institutions and economic well-being (De Soysa 2002; Collier and Hoeffler 2004; Ross 2004). Moreover, a wealth of resources may relieve governments of tax collection pressures, reduce fiscal discipline, and hinder the diversification of other sectors of the economy – in other words, engender the "Dutch disease" (Gupta, Bornhorst, and Thornton 2009). This said, not everyone agrees with the resource curse concept, and some claim that its existence is tied to other, unknown factors and statistical anomalies (Ross 2012; 2015).

As illustrations of how a wealth of natural resources can lead to protracted conflict, Sierra Leone and Liberia are good examples. Both conflicts were inextricably tied to the diamond trade in those countries, which enabled the growth of rent-seeking, one-party states that failed to promote economic development. Instead, the diamond trade presented incentives and opportunities for rebel movements to organize armed insurgencies (Keen 2005; Miguel and Bellows 2006). Nevertheless, the specific conditions under which the resource curse contributes to instability and conflict remain poorly understood, with countries such as Equatorial Guinea and Gabon maintaining a precarious stability despite enduring nepotistic and authoritarian governments (Humphreys 2005; Basedau and Lacher 2006).

It is widely believed that on average, the economies of resource-rich countries tend to grow less rapidly than those of resource-scarce countries, a phenomenon explained by the "resource curse" theory. Sachs and Warner (1995) were among the first scholars to examine the intricate relationship between economic growth and natural resource endowment. They concluded that when differences in macroeconomic policies and initial income levels were accounted and adjusted for, resource-rich developing countries were destined to experience slower growth on average. Theoretically, this should not be the case, as abundant natural resources could play a positive role in promoting economic development. A significant natural resource endowment has the potential to boost an economy via initial and continued investment, skills transfer, infrastructure development, employment creation, revenue for central and local governments, and social development through the implementation of CSR projects (Sachs and Warner 1999; Murphy, Shleifer, and Vishny 2000).

Various explanations have been put forth over the years as to why natural resources have not facilitated economic growth in many developing states over the past decades. One such explanation revolves around governance as central both for promoting sustainable and equitable growth, and reducing the likelihood of conflict and disagreement among relevant stakeholders, including mining community leaders, the general public, policy makers, foreign investors, and private-sector actors (Burnside and Dollar 2000; Easterly, Levine, and Roodman 2004; Glaeser et al. 2004). It is further argued that in the absence of governance structures, these stakeholders waste resource revenues while exhausting natural resource deposits to the detriment of future generations and potential economic development.

Scholars in the natural resource governance field have argued that increased and continued government control over the extractive industry, high and often skewed dependence on the extractives sector, and continued neglect of other primary sectors, such as agriculture, have all resulted in diminished revenue and increased unemployment. These reasons account for how natural resources may inhibit broad-based economic growth and poverty alleviation in poor, resource-rich countries, particularly those in Africa (Shahnawaz and Nugent 2004). Given these countries' inordinate dependence on natural resources for government revenue, there appears to be a diminished reliance on tax revenue, which has contributed to reduced accountability within the sector. This is particularly the case with regard to the distribution and expenditure of resource earnings.

In terms of fiscal management, resource revenue in poor, resource-rich countries that suffer from poor governance can negatively affect developmental goals. For instance, such situations are often evident where substantial aid flows are misused. Corrupt regimes, many of which are driven to remain in power by any means, typically resort to lowering taxes as a way to gain public support. Oil-producing countries, for example, often subsidize domestic gasoline prices, even though this is deemed to be economically unviable in the long term (Bacon 2001).

In situations characterized by poor governance – in the extractives sector in particular – resource revenues are generally found to be unevenly distributed. In many instances, these revenue streams are squandered while the economy continues to stagnate. In this context, the Dutch disease framework is central to the literature pertaining to economic stagnation in resource-rich developing states. Corden and Neary (1982) observe that manufacturing and other non-primary resource sectors in resource-rich countries endure tremendous difficulties due to domestic currency appreciation. That is, as excessive earnings from the extractives sector are captured by the domestic, non-tradable sector, the national currency appreciates in real terms, affecting the competitiveness of non-extractive sectors. Sachs and Warner (1997) contend that, particularly in the African context, Dutch disease has affected economic growth as part of the wider, negative consequence of an immoderate reliance on the extractive sector.

Karl (1997), Collier and Hoeffler (2004), and Omeje (2013), among other authors in the schools of neo-Marxist dependency modelling, environmental scarcity theory, and "greed versus grievance" theory, have argued that there is a positive and evident correlation between conflict and extractive economies. This is primarily due to the terminal nature of extractive economies, and the realization thereof by those in positions of power, resulting in corruption, graft, ecological conflict, and economic depression

(Omeje 2013). Others have coined the term "economic imperialism," a form of neo-colonialism designed to export wealth from resource-rich countries to the developed West (Veltmeyer 2013). This narrative is posited as well by Wengraf, who, through a Marxist lens, denotes how extractive economies in sub-Saharan Africa are once again faced with the pressures of militarism, resource wars, and development "aid" that is conditional on a perpetual licence to return wealth abroad (2018; Shaw et al. 2006).

That said, despite these relationships, which have been acknowledged by Auty (1993), Gelb (1988), Sachs and Warner (1995), Ross (2001, 2003), and UNCTAD (2011), studies have equally challenged the notion that extractive economies inevitably lead to economic stagnation, decline, and conflict (Davis 2009). Consideration of the above political theory approaches is given throughout the work, particularly in the discussions of the influence of foreign-owned private-sector actors on peace, whether their operations contribute to or mitigate conflict in the three case study countries, and how governance of natural resources structures and systems can curb detrimental relationships, activities, and interactions in the resource sector.

Another challenge related to overreliance on the natural resource sector for revenue lies in the specificity of assets and geography. Assets tend to be stationary and are closely tied to mining operations. Any investments in equipment, infrastructure, and facilities are generally linked to specific mines and geographic regions within resource-rich states (Joskow 1987). The sector, furthermore, tends to be capital-intensive, especially with regard to exploration and extraction activities. The most prominent assertion by scholars has been that natural resources development in many resource-rich countries has resulted in only a few forward and backward linkages, while negatively affecting local industries given that the latter tend to be divorced from the international economy (Sachs and Warner 1995).

The historically poor management of natural resource revenues by African governments raises questions regarding the opportunities and challenges that might stem from integrating new stakeholders into processes of natural resource governance. The extractives sector could serve as the basis for long-term economic development, provided that governments – supported by the involvement of foreign investors and the private sector

– implement a long-term vision regarding the management of these resources. Examining the types of policies and initiatives that could be adopted by stakeholders to support African governments and enhance development outcomes is a key concern. This research hopes to add to current knowledge by exploring the role of additional stakeholders, namely foreign-owned enterprises, on natural resource management in Africa.

The Evolving Role of Foreign Investors and the Private Sector in Encouraging Sustainable Development, Peace, and Stability in Africa

With increased investment in Africa's mining sector spurred by new and improved mining legislation and incentives, African governments and civil society have closely examined the socioeconomic contributions and the impact of these investments on both national economies and local communities. In recent years, a great deal of accumulated evidence has suggested than an abundance of natural resources may be more of a curse than a blessing (Auty 1993). For instance, Gelb (1988) found that resource-rich economies suffered from lower economic growth – a finding that has been confirmed by Sachs and Warner (1995).

Linkages between foreign investors, the private sector, and violent conflict have also been the topic of recent investigations (Besada, Ermakov, and Ternamian 2009; Hameed and Mixon 2013; Bannon and Collier 2003). Foreign investment and other private-sector involvement can increase conflict by contributing to corruption, creating socioeconomic inequality, providing funding for arms or providing arms directly to warlords and militias, disrupting environmental systems, and contributing to Dutch disease. For example, multinational firms operating in the DRC were directly implicated in violent massacres and fiscal improprieties with local authorities (Ballentine 2006). On the other hand, foreign investors and private-sector actors are central agents of global trade and investment, which are crucial to the sustainable growth of African economies (Collier 2007). They also play a critical role in post-conflict recovery (Woodward 2010), an area of research with the potential to shed greater light on the specific conditions under which private actors involved in the natural resource sector may contribute to peace, stability, and prosperity, and what form this might take.

While the literature has tended to highlight the potential outcomes arising from foreign investor engagement within the natural resource sector, less is known about the mechanisms that determine the specific effects that arise from such interactions. Indeed, the literature remains focused on a number of key areas and themes, exposing gaps in knowledge. Thus far, few efforts have been made to investigate thoroughly how governance structures operate in the contexts of natural resource management, the bolstering of extractive economies, and guiding private-sector actors so as to leverage them as assets for translating resource wealth into sustainable economic growth, peace, and stability. Research inevitably tends to focus on what governments should do as opposed to the causal relationship that exists between the structures of resource governance and the outcomes facilitated by private-sector actors. Providing policy recommendations as to what these actors ought to do to promote objectives such as peace, economic growth, and stability is, however, a fundamental starting point to the discussion of how governance structures should be developed so as to advance these goals.

Foreign investment in Africa's extractive industries has also been a hot topic in light of what some commentators characterize as "resource nationalism." Jesse Ovadia explores this trend extensively and discusses the impacts of local content policies on foreign investment. He asserts that "local content policies, which promote local and national participation in extractive industries, are essential for the sustainability of resource-led economic development" (Ovadia 2014). While this approach has been identified and supported by many international organizations, including the World Bank and various UN agencies, it is also important to emphasize the limits of such approaches as exemplified in the cases of the DRC and Tanzania. Both countries recently adopted stringent mining codes that increased tax levels on international miners, spurring contestation. While increasing tax levels remains a long step away from increased local content, the introduction of local content clauses, including a mandatory 10 per cent participation of Congolese nationals in all mining enterprises, as well as participation in infrastructure development, are interesting and compelling new requirements (DRC 2018). The case of the DRC is particularly interesting as the country controls vast amounts of critical minerals, including cobalt, which have been identified as strategic raw commodities with exports taxed at higher levels. In addition, in 2018, the government of Tanzania established a 51 per cent mandatory threshold for domestic ownership of national companies in every mining project. In the latter case, however, Dodoma quickly amended the law and decreased this level to 20 per cent for fear of limiting international investment in the country's mining industry. Ovadia's approach to local content, mostly related to oil extraction in the Gulf of Guinea, supports the creation of "state-led development" inscribed in a capitalistic approach (Ovadia 2017; Ovadia and Wolf 2018). The concept of state-led development is closely linked to the "developmental state." The latter is defined by Ovadia as a way of understanding the role of the state in economic and social development, and the possibilities for positive state intervention in the economy through a "set of processes and institutions that produce a set of developmental outcomes" (Ovadia 2018). While this analysis is based on the state's role in regulating extractive industries, we aim here to illustrate that the state is not the only player to provide a regulatory system for the industry, and that foreign investment may also drive change and support sustainable practices to advance broad-based development.

Another critical debate to consider in this literature review is the role of certification bodies and their credibility in light of global supply-chain complexity – such as the case of the International Tin Association's Tin Supply Chain Initiative (ITSCI). The debate over certification of tin exports from the DRC region is quite problematic and illustrates the limitations of foreign-owned companies in promoting sustainable, long-term, broad-based development. As Steven Young notes, "downstream manufacturing industries are 'governing at a distance' the management practices of upstream raw material producers" (2018). However, the risk of supply-chain contamination and the possibility for high levels of corruption that such frameworks allow threaten the whole sustainability approach as represented by regulations such as Section 1502 of the Dodd-Frank Act or EU Regulation 2017/821 (to be implemented in January 2021). This risk is critical and has been observed in the DRC's North Kivu province, where the Société Minière de Bisunzu (SMB) left the ITSCI certification scheme following allegations that the supply chain was contaminated with minerals tainted by human rights abuses (Mahamba and Lewis 2019; UN 2018).

It is also critical to emphasize the inherently capitalistic nature of these frameworks as competing entities to provide services to downstream brands. In the case of the DRC, the ITSCI scheme competes with the Better Sourcing Program implemented by the RCS Global Group, which questions the ability of these frameworks to provide long-lasting impacts for local Congolese communities. Similar analysis has been performed regarding the ability of the Kimberley Process Certification Scheme (KPCS) to adequately certify diamonds as "conflict-free" (Santiago 2014). Similarly, the definition of "conflict diamonds" adopted by the KPCS only accounts for minerals that fund rebel armies and excludes de facto illegal and immoral uses by governments and corporations (Rush and Rozell 2017; Smillie 2013).

Applicable Existing International Governance Frameworks

International governance frameworks are critical to this study, as they provide a link between foreign-owned corporations and the extraction of natural resources in a specific context. As such, the development, over the past twenty years, of standardized tools allows for better comparison and understanding of each country and its minerals, hydrocarbon, and land sectors. For this book, the focus will be on two frameworks that will help support our analysis of the governance of natural resources in the three countries explored, Ghana, Sierra Leone and Ethiopia.

The Extractive Industries Transparency Initiative (EITI), in place since 2003, aims at providing a comparative approach to governance issues in the extractive industries, including the mining and hydrocarbon industries. The framework is based on the "EITI Standard Requirements 2016" (EITI 2016a), which describe the requirements for EITI-implementing countries and cover all aspects of extractive industries, from exploration to closure. The EITI Standard Requirements underline the criticality of good financial management on the country's side, including the collection of appropriate revenues but also their allocation for social and economic improvement. Exploring the EITI framework, Hoffer argues that "intersecting transnational networks with complementary global norms facilitated construction of transparency as a solution for management of resource revenues" (2010). In this sense, the key concept of our analysis – long-term, broad based economic development – is at the centre of the EITI Standard Requirements.

While focusing on legal, economic, and social systems at the country level, EITI also reserves the possibility of suspending a country for critical breach of the requirements or even delisting it in situations of conflict or political instability. For the countries in our study, implementation of EITI has varied greatly. While Sierra Leone joined in 2008, the country has yet to be assessed against the 2016 Standard Requirements. Ghana was last assessed in 2018, and is deemed to have made meaningful progress. On the other side, though having been assessed in 2018, the Ethiopian mining and oil industries will not be examined in this study. As such, we will explore another framework, implemented by the UN Food and Agriculture Organisation (FAO), for the Ethiopian case.

The voluntary guidelines developed by the FAO on the responsible governance of land tenure, fisheries, and forests in the context of national food security (FAO 2012) will be an important tool to assess Ethiopia's land tenure system. Launched in 2012, the guidelines cover extensive requirements – from land tenure policy to the transfer of lands, and response to emergencies and climate change – and were created following regional consultations, including one in Ethiopia. Taking the example of Colombia, McKay, Rodriguez, and Fajardo argue that "the Tenure Guidelines can help trigger these virtuous cycles if they are used in a very proactive and pro-poor way." However, they also raise critical issues linked to certain inherent characteristics of the voluntary guidelines such that, inasmuch as they may inform policy, their usefulness depends "on how, by whom, where, why, and for what purposes they are used" (McKay, Rodriguez, and Fajardo 2016). These limitations are particularly compelling in situations that involve governments with limited democratic structures and traditions, where the guidelines may serve as a mechanism to justify destructive land policies.

The Need for an Innovative Framework for Natural Resource Governance Analysis

To remedy this knowledge gap, the three case study countries – Ghana, Ethiopia, and Sierra Leone – were selected so as to bring new research under the lens of the Political Economy of Natural Resource Governance framework (see Figure 1.1). This research examines how governance institutions and actors engage with foreign-owned private-sector actors in practice, the extent to which they contribute to the above objectives, and how natural resource governance and foreign investment actors interact in a dynamic way – the one feeding into the other.

This framework helps to classify and present knowledge on natural resource governance and foreign investment actors according to clearly defined country conditions (e.g., politically stable, post-conflict), thereby helping to discern how such conditions may determine the scope of foreign state-owned and private-sector activities. It also helps researchers to understand the potential of foreign actors to influence economic, social, and development outcomes, and how these outcomes and the influence of foreign investment actors affect the institutional reshaping of governance structures. The analytical framework builds on the structural political economy approach outlined by Hout (2015), in which the policies of development aid donors are examined by applying the sociological agent-structure problem.[3] Most importantly, the framework provides "an underpinning prism for the construction of explanations" (Stanley 2012).

Agency is the capacity of actors to make their own choices and act independently. Structures are the factors of influence that determine or limit an agent in making decisions, which in sociology include social class, religion, gender, ethnicity, and custom. The complementarity of agency and structure (a cyclical rather than a linear process) must be emphasized: structures influence actions, but agents can similarly influence structures. Different theories exist about the nature of the relationship between agency and structure. Berger and Luckmann (1966) posit that the relationship is dialectical – a continuous loop wherein structures form the actors, who in turn create the structures. Giddens (1979) supports this theory and notes that structures both enable and constrain agents. The debate about the agent-structure relationship changes according to its application

Understanding Conflict and Resource Management

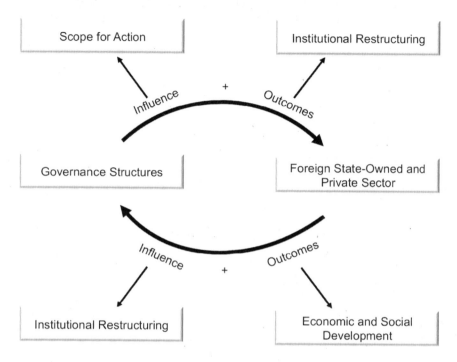

Figure 1.1 The Political Economy of Natural Resource Governance (PENRG) framework.

in particular cases; to apply it to structural political economy appears productive, given the complementarity of agency and structure evidenced in the three case studies and described by the cycle in Figure 1.1.

In this study, the analytical framework builds on the structural political economy approach but shifts its starting point away from "the identification of sets of elites in relation to the national structure of power" (Hout 2015, 89) to the existing governance arrangements, emphasizing the complementarity of governance structures, the actors that they govern, and the cyclical nature of governance. This approach provides a firm, ontological grounding for analysis that still enables discussion of elite-level politics but focuses on institutional restructuring in governance reform. The framework acknowledges the large-scale theoretical work done within the fields of functionalism and historical institutionalism, but distinguishes itself as a contribution to mid-range analytical framework building.

The PENRG framework captures the influence of governance structures on creating scope for action, which in turn can lead to institutional restructuring of investments by foreign state-owned and private-sector actors. The analytical framework considers this an outcome – if the restructuring occurs. These actors are the means by which economic, social, and development outcomes occur. As such, these outcomes can influence institutional restructuring, which in turn may accommodate further outcomes in governance arrangement, better enable foreign investment actors, or guide these actors differently. Such institutional restructuring leads to a changed scope for action – and the cycle repeats itself. Importantly, change can be incremental or characterized by punctuated equilibrium. With that said, time periods for the cycle cannot be assumed.

The objective of this analytical framework is to help orient thinking and discussion, which may take place at any level of governance and in any type of state, in order to develop solutions. The PENRG framework differs significantly from collecting and presenting best practices, though it enables the latter to be undertaken. It identifies junctures and entry points for variables to affect either the foreign investment actors or the structures that govern them. It can be used to generate questions and conclusions, and – importantly – to track changing linkages between natural resource governance and management, foreign state-owned and private-sector actors, and levels of stability, peace, and prosperity. The PENRG framework can help foster institutional change in resource-rich countries by identifying and addressing the critical gaps that limit or absorb the benefits of natural resources for long-term, broad-based economic growth.

The cases we explore in Ghana, Ethiopia, and Sierra Leone show the extent to which a lack of alignment of bureaucratic, administrative, and political structures can negatively impact a country's stability, peace, and development. From tax evasion to a lack of local beneficiation and capacity building, the destructive nature of the extractive industry's practices and structures can be devastating to a country's integrity. For academics and professionals alike, the PENRG framework will provide necessary lessons for introducing aligned systems that have proven their reliability for wealth redistribution in extractive industries. It can help any observer to understand the role of foreign investment actors and how that role may be enabled or constrained through institutional restructuring. Indeed, the tenets

Understanding Conflict and Resource Management

of PENRG are fundamental to investigate how governance structures (at both the resource sector and state levels) influence the nature and outcome of foreign-owned companies' and investors' involvement in the extractive and land resource sectors, and thereby contribute to greater economic growth, peace and political stability, and sustainable development.

CHAPTER 2

Studying Resource Management and the Role of Foreign Actors

By comparing the involvement of foreign-owned companies in the hydro-carbon, mining, and land sectors in three types of political states – stable (Ghana), post-conflict (Sierra Leone), and conflict-threatened (Ethiopia) – the analysis seeks to extrapolate the general trends and relationships that characterize Africa's new politics of natural resource governance and the actors that work to define its parameters and characteristics. Specifically, how governance structures (both sectoral and state) influence the nature and outcome of foreign-owned companies' and investors' involvement in the extractive and land resource sectors, and in the wider development process, and how these actors may contribute to the economic growth, peace and political stability, and sustainable development in such countries, is examined.

Methodological Overview

Methods used in field research conducted between February and April 2014, and between June and September 2015, included interviews, collection of oral histories, and analysis of government and foreign investors' documentation. Also undertaken was a review of secondary source materials and both historical analysis and personal observation of foreign investors' role and activities in the extractive and land sectors. The latter included the application of CSR mandates and internal policies aimed at promoting inclusive and local-level participatory development models. This research also relied on case studies, within- and cross-case analysis, as well as in-depth interviews and triangulation conducted under the aegis of its proposed theoretical framework, the Political Economy of Natural Resource Governance.

Extensive interviews, along with focus groups, were held in each country to identify relevant socioeconomic variables, as well as current challenges and opportunities related to foreign state-owned and private-sector involvement in natural resource industries. To allow for free and open discussion, in some cases the names and specific positions of those selected for interviews are not divulged.

Peace and stability, and economic growth, were operationalized through a number of concrete variables. For the former, evidence of adherence to the rule of law by government and private-sector entities, the absence of inter- and intra-state violence and conflict (especially conflict driven by natural resource extraction and exploitation), cooperative interaction among societal groups and between such groups and private-sector actors, and the harmonization of contract clauses with social values as defined by peace and reconciliation agreements, legal frameworks for protection resource rights, and free, prior, and informed consent. For economic growth, variables and indicators included:

- Resource contribution to small and medium-size enterprise (SME) creation and income levels
- Annual rate of positive change for GDP levels
- Annual rate of change in per capita income levels
- Significant private investment
- Distribution
- Creation and maintenance of a middle class
- Growth in access to social services, including education and healthcare
- Rates of foreign direct investment

While we recognize the limitations of economic growth–based studies, particularly at a time when much ink has been spilled over the need for degrowth (Hickel 2018), the goal of this book is to address the topic of extractive resources. This industry is based inherently on growth, not only in and of itself, but of the world around it as it ensures its survival. Tackling the issue of the extractive sector's benefits within a logic of degrowth would be unproductive and would likely comprise an unappealing environment for the economic actors themselves. In parallel, addressing the issue of beneficiation of extractive industries and linking it to economic growth does not necessarily signify an intolerable economic system. Focused on countries with economies considered weak to medium, the concept of economic growth also resonates in local discourses and, as such, should be accounted for.

Additional material was collected via policy-oriented research and dialogue with relevant stakeholders in the three selected countries. Desk research was conducted to triangulate information. Experiences and lessons learned that could be relevant to forming policy that promotes positive developmental outcomes in each country were selected from interviews and supported with existing literature on the topic. Key variables, isolated by the research, were incorporated into the new framework for conceptualizing and analyzing natural resource governance, sustainable development, and stability and instability in Africa.

Case Study Selection

Three countries – Ghana, Sierra Leone, and Ethiopia – were selected for case studies based on their representation of three categories: stable, post-conflict, and conflict-threatened resource-rich states.[1] The Seawright and Gerring discussion (2008) also helped to inform the selection process: as the researcher's objective is to construct or verify general causal theories about the social world on the basis of a few case studies, case selection aims to generate a sample that is representative of the population while exhibiting useful variation on the dimensions of theoretical interest – in this case, the stability classification of each country. Selecting diverse cases (the "diverse case" method of case selection) allows the investigation of variance along the relevant dimensions researched. Seawright and Gerring contend that "diverse cases are likely to be representative in the minimal sense of representing the full variation of the population … the diverse case method probably has stronger claims to representativeness than any other small N sample (including the typical case)" (2008, 297, 301). The different categories, the representativeness of the cases selected, and some

Case Study Methodology

In each case study, research techniques included limited process tracing, typological theorizing, and triangulation of sources. Due to its emphasis on the implications of case study findings for theory, and more specifically policy-relevant theory, this research follows the procedure for using case studies put forth by George and Bennett (2005). They outline how to design case study research that will produce results that could be useful to policymakers, which is one of the aims of this research project. In addition, this exploration of the impact of foreign-owned economic actors on natural resource governance uses within-case analysis to reduce the inferential errors that could arise from using only comparative methods.

George and Bennett (2005) also provide a detailed discussion of process tracing – understood in this context as attempting to track the links between possible causes and observed outcomes – which is applied throughout this research project. With regard to process tracing within cases, the method involves examining histories, documents, interview transcripts, and other sources to confirm the causal processes that a theory hypothesizes, while identifying variables and hypotheses based on sequences of events. This method helps to understand institutional decision making by enabling the analysis of the thought processeses involved in specific decision-making strategies – particularly useful when assessing elite-level politics. Process tracing, using the information generated from field research, was applied in each case study to generate the results outlined in the conclusion. As George and Bennett (2005) explain, typological theorizing provides a way to draw cases together in a single framework for more effective policymaking. In this context, such theorization forms the backbone of the present research, allowing for a comparative analysis of the three countries profiled.

Bennett and Elman (2006b) elaborate that both process tracing and typological theorizing help clarify forms of complexity, such as path dependency and multiple interaction effects. Path dependence refers to the situation in which current decisions are constrained by history, in the sense that they depend on past decisions and related trajectories. Bennett and Elman (2006a) indicate that process tracing and systematic case comparisons can assist in appraising path-dependent explanations by systematically considering causal possibility, contingency, closure of alternatives, and constraints upon the current path. The strength of case studies in appraising path dependence, they assert, is their suitability to provide a detailed, holistic analysis of sequences, to investigate rare events, to facilitate the search with regard to omitted variables, and to map interaction effects within one or several cases.

Case studies in this research will inevitably and importantly involve the triangulation of multiple sources to derive findings. Triangulation is used to examine the consistency of information across social groups and organizations with different viewpoints. A look at both data and information, as well as inductive reasoning, are used to arrive at conclusions. Triangulation is critical for increasing the authenticity and trustworthiness of findings, not to mention improving the comprehensiveness of narratives. The objective is to draw cases together in a single framework, with the triangulation of sources within cases, enabling the researcher to draw conclusions that may be used for cross-case comparisons.

This research primarily uses within-case methods, although its concluding chapter predominantly adopts cross-case approaches. The latter method is used to discuss illustrative experiences and lessons learned which could be relevant to policy making that promotes positive achievement of the project's selected dependent variables – peace, stability, and economic growth – and thereby contributes to an improved analytical framework. The present research is largely indebted to the work of Mahoney (2007), who discusses the strengths of within-case and cross-case methodology in the field of comparative politics.[2] Qualitative researchers, he explains, employ both within-case and cross-case methods of theory testing. Within-case techniques are particularly useful for identifying intervening mechanisms and testing multiple observable implications of theories. Cross-case methods, on the other hand, are useful for assessing hypotheses about necessary and applicable causes. As mentioned, each case study is structured thematically according to seven topics: legal/regulatory frameworks, beneficiation and value addition, inclusive economic transformation or the lack of it, conflict and security, local community development, sustainable energy solutions, and private-sector contribution to natural resource governance and management. The conclusion brings together the results according to themes in order to identify variables that are ultimately used to build the improved analytical framework.

Ethnographic Method

With regard to the concept of structure, Klotz and Lynch (2007) outline three complementary strategies, which are applied in the present research. The first of these, *micro-history*, involves the use of historiographies to address evidentiary errors appearing in macro-level histories. It concentrates on a single individual and community, and attempts, via study and analysis, to reach an understanding of wider issues at stake. For instance, a historiography is used in the Ghana case study to describe the plight of fishermen in coastal communities in relation to the oil industry. Generally speaking, historiographic methodology is not antagonistically opposed to the derivation from its use of generalized themes or conclusions, with Sreedharan describing it as an "unavoidable interpretative device" (2007, 87). Because the work deployed research methodologies to obtain micro-histories, it acknowledges several endemic pitfalls (which are considered throughout) when drawing wider hypotheses from the research. Generalizations should be considered as providing rough edges or guides for future study, rather than the final word on a particular matter (Sreedharan 2007, 89). As such, the project proposes that in the case of Ghana, generalizations are of a limited nature and are defined by the supposition that "in certain circumstances, the observed result can be achieved" (92). Therefore, while the work does make generalizations, in accordance with the best practices of history literature, it does so in recognition that beyond certain communities, regions, and countries, the breadth with which they may be applied has limits.

Accounts of African stakeholders and other insiders provide both a picture and interpretation of on-the-ground situations that sometimes complement, but often stand apart from, official statistics. This is partially a problem of government sourcing, but also of the academic study of Africa at large. Jerven, for example, argues that economists consistently misrepresent the continent's economic growth statistics by emphasizing poverty patterns of the 1970s and 1980s while largely ignoring the substantial growth of the 1950s and 1960s (2015). Economists and statisticians are also regularly reliant on what Jerven calls "poor numbers," off-the-shelf datasets that are not robustly and rigorously investigated for quality and content (2015). This research brings together stakeholders at various levels to generate new findings about the role of foreign-owned economic actors in affecting country stability. This was relevant in Sierra Leone where, for example, interviews revealed a stark divide in perceptions between community leaders ("chiefs") and youth group leaders regarding the impact of mining in the communities. Both groups relied on their own anecdotal evidence, with community leaders being perceived as siding with foreign investors. Ethiopia provided another example of this, whereby official statistics of recent and sustained high growth paint a picture of economic success that can easily mask vulnerabilities which become apparent when one engages with stakeholders on the ground.

Information and Data Collection

Qualitative Methodology

This project's research design is primarily qualitative. The use of extensive field research allowed for and enhanced personal contact with key stakeholders from different backgrounds and interests. In many cases, the collection of data and information, and the subsequent manipulation and publication of statistics, especially via official channels, can be political, especially on the African continent. This means that issues such as conflict, instability and corruption, and economic growth can easily remain obscured. Moreover, the role of foreign state-owned and private-sector actors in the natural resource sector is often guarded and simplified, with only some statistics relevant for analysis. This research project seeks to balance perspectives on foreign sector actors' influence on Africa's governance in general with perspectives on natural resource governance in particular, via an extensive survey of African stakeholders' perspectives.

Semi-structured interviews allow a picture to emerge rather than imposing it from the outside via the (mis)interpretation of statistics, such as macroeconomic statistics that often obscure conditions of poverty and inequality. An ethnographic understanding is possible by using various data sources. Interviews enabled the collection of targeted data and information by asking specific but open-ended questions (Leech 2002). This interview style allows the person or people being interviewed to answer without being limited to pre-defined choices. Such flexibility is a key difference between qualitative and quantitative approaches.

The field research was driven by the following overarching enquiries: what historical role did foreign-owned enterprises play in the governance and management of natural resources in these three states, and how have they affected peace, stability, and economic development in selected areas? What, including the political conditions unique to these countries, determines whether these actors play a positive or negative role in achieving peace, stability, and economic growth? How are these patterns and relationships evolving in the face of new investment flows, and how are governments and local communities reacting to these changes? And what concrete policy recommendations should be made so as to promote positive, impactful, successful, and meaningful development outcomes in each of these three country contexts? These questions framed the responses from interviewees in the field so as to elicit information on the impact of foreign-owned enterprises on dependent variables of peace, stability, and economic growth.

As qualitative, ethnographically oriented research, the third question receives special attention in the three case studies, as it concerns experiences and lessons learned by host governments, foreign state-owned and private-sector actors, affected communities, and international organizations, which could be relevant to designing policies to promote positive developmental outcomes. This is a crucial question, as it relates to core on-the-ground challenges to be addressed by policies and initiatives supported by governments, corporate actors, and non-governmental organizations (NGOs), at both the domestic and international levels, in the aim of promoting peace, stability, and economic growth in resource-rich African countries.

Challenges and difficulties encountered during field research included practical and logistical problems as well as cultural limitations. Major issues in undertaking the various case studies related to accessing the investment records and data of foreign state-owned and private-sector actors, as well as securing permission from the various authorities. Entrenched cultural obstacles to economic growth, especially in local communities, included isolation, self-sufficiency, and cultural constructions of gender. Information that remains incomplete includes details on interaction effects, which were too difficult to map given the scope of the research.

Institutes and Interviews

I travelled to Ethiopia, Sierra Leone, and Ghana between February and April 2014 to conduct field research and interview relevant stakeholders at governmental, private, and non-profit organizations. Subsequent exchanges with these stakeholders took place from January until September 2015. Additional field research was carried out in Ghana in August and September 2015. Details of my field visits are provided below.

Ghana

Mining, and more recently the hydrocarbon industry, has undoubtedly made a substantial contribution to Ghana's macroeconomic growth and stability over the past three decades, bringing the country to middle-income status. However, due to questionable business practices by foreign-owned enterprises and a lack of proper oversight by government, the natural resource economy has not resulted in improved living conditions in the majority of mining communities across the country.

Over two separate visits in March and April 2014, and August and September 2015, I met with leaders and/or staff members of the following organizations: Office of the President; World Bank; Ministry of Trade and Industry; Ministry of Lands and Natural Resources; Ministry of Energy; Petroleum Commission; Ghana Investment Promotion Centre (GIPC); Ghana Chamber of Mines; Kofi Annan International Peacekeeping Training Centre (KAIPTC); African Center for Economic Transformation (ACET); Kumasi Institute of Technology, Energy and the Environment

(KITE); IMANI Centre for Policy and Education; Natural Resource Governance Institute (NRGI); United Nations University Institute for Natural Resources in Africa (UNU/INRA); Ghana Information Services; European Union Delegation to Ghana; AngloGold Ashanti; Tullow Oil; Strategic Outlooks; Georgette Barnes Ltd; Ghana Center for Democratic Development (GCDD); Ministry of Energy and Petroleum; Third World Network (TWN); German Agency for International Cooperation (GIZ); university departments of political science, geography, and economics; and Institute of Statistical, Social and Economic Research (ISSER), University of Ghana.

I also spent two weeks in the mining communities of Busua, Takoradi, and Tarkwa, in the rural parts of western Ghana, where I conducted focus group discussions, interviews, and surveys of small-scale miners and villagers. In total, I conducted twenty-seven interviews in these communities, primarily with fishing community members affected by offshore oil and gas exploitation and exploration.

Sierra Leone

Over a period of one month in February and March 2014, I met with leaders or staff members of the following institutions/organizations: departments of economics, political science, and gender issues, University of Sierra Leone; Heifer International; Ministry of Trade and Industry; Sierra Leone Investment Promotion Agency; Centre for Development and Security Analysis (CDSA); National Mineral Agency (NMA); Sierra Leone Transformation Think Tank; German Agency for International Cooperation (GIZ); social and economic development departments, United Nations Development Programme (UNDP); African Development Bank (AfDB); World Bank; Sierra Rutile (mineral sands company); Network Movement for Justice and Development (NMJD); Ministry of Finance and Economic Development; IBIS in Sierra Leone; Office of the Vice-President, Development Assistance Coordination Office; Integrated Geo-Information and Environmental Management Services; CEMMATS Group; Chairperson's Office, Sierra Leone People's Party; London Mining; and Office of the President, National Commission for Privatisation.

I also spent two weeks in mining communities in rural parts of northern and eastern Sierra Leone, where I conducted interviews, focus group discussions, and surveys. Further information was procured from secondary sources such as white papers, policy briefs, government documents, and private company reports. My time in Sierra Leone concluded with field visits and interviews in Koidu Town in the diamond-rich Kono district, in Lunsar in Port Loko district, and in Makeni in Bombali district – all known for their gold and iron ore deposits, and all places where violence between mining communities, mining companies, and the police had escalated in recent years. In Lunsar, a group-based research discussion was held with community leaders.

In Koidu Town, a total of fifteen questionnaires were completed in a survey of mining communities. The questionnaires covered basic perceptions of the impact of mining in the community; positive and/or negative effects on the subject's livelihood and family; and the subject's relationship to, and support received from, local institutions in addressing mining-related grievances. These institutions included the local council, the local chief, community programs, civil society and donors, and government. Respondents were asked to state their wishes with regard to the mining sector in their community.

Ethiopia

In Ethiopia, natural resource investments primarily involve land acquisition. The country has some known gold deposits, and recent new discoveries of oil have raised expectations, but commercial drilling is many years away (Manek 2018). Recent investments and interest shown by Turkish companies in the apparel and textile industries (*Ethiopian Herald* 2018b), by Arab companies in the tourism, renewable energy, and agricultural sectors (*Ethiopian Herald* 2018a), and Indian companies interested in land acquisition (Anwar 2016) are important sources of revenue for the government, which is keen to attract foreign direct investment for infrastructure projects.

I conducted a large number of interviews with staff members at government institutions: Ministry of Agriculture, including its Agricultural Investment Land Administration Agency; Ministry of Foreign Affairs (which oversees many of the government's investment projects linked to foreign-owned entities); Ministry of Mines; Ethiopian Investment Agency;

and Addis Ababa Chamber of Commerce. Additionally, I spoke to individuals, including leading academics at various research bodies, think tanks, and universities doing work on land investments. In doing so, I built an extensive network of connections and partnerships: School of Natural Resources Management and Environmental Sciences, Haramaya University; University for Peace (UPEACE); Institute for Security Studies (ISS); Department of Political Science, University of Addis Ababa; Forum for Social Studies (FSS); and Center for International Forestry Research (CIFR). These institutions and their researchers provided insights into recent developments and challenges facing local farmers, local governments, and the national government in Addis Ababa. I also sought opinions on the outlook for the natural resource sector from representatives of several donor agencies: United Nations Economic Commission for Africa (UNECA); African Union; United Nations Development Program (UNDP); International Monetary Fund (IMF); European Union delegation; Frankfurt Zoological Society; World Bank; African Minerals Development Centre (AMDC); and embassies of Canada, Australia, and Qatar. In total, I conducted twenty-three interviews in Ethiopia.

The main challenge in Ethiopia was accessing foreign state-owned and private-sector actors' investment records and data relating to land investments. To obtain a list of interview contacts at companies operating in the field required obtaining special permission from the Ministry of Foreign Affairs prior to making a submission to the Agricultural Investment Land Administration Agency at the Ministry of Agriculture. I also needed to obtain special permission and official letters to interview contacts at these companies and undertake field visits to their sites of operation, many of which were situated hundreds of kilometres from the capital. I managed to receive the necessary documentation for the interviews and field visits, but time taken up in these bureaucratic processes affected the rest of the investigation.

Upon returning to Ethiopia in January 2015, my letter of permission from the Ministry of Foreign Affairs was considered invalid, which prohibited me from conducting field interviews with communities where land investments had taken place. As an alternative, I consulted members of two local research and advocacy institutions – the Forum for Social Studies and the Center for International Forestry Research, both of which had

70   GOVERNANCE, CONFLICT, AND NATURAL RESOURCES IN AFRICA

conducted field interviews with affected local communities in Gambella, a western province bordering South Sudan.

Challenges aside, the above methodology was helpful in developing the PENRG concept, isolating its key variables, and defining the parameters of its framework. Equally, it has sparked a novel contribution on how governance structures influence the nature and outcome of involvement by foreign-owned companies and investors operating in the extractive and land resource sectors, and specifically their contributions to economic growth, peace and political stability, and sustainable development. It is important to recall that these country case studies – two of them from the same sub-region with similar political systems, and concentrated on the extractive sector, and a third focused on land resources – and representing three distinct types of governance situation – politically stable, post-conflict, and conflict-threatened – provide a broad spectrum of opportunity for investigating the role of foreign-owned enterprises in natural resource governance.

Introduction to Case Studies

Ghana: The Transformative Potential of Hydrocarbon Resources

Since the 1980s, Ghana's economic growth has been increasingly tied to its mining sector, which is largely dominated by gold. The country is the second-largest gold producer in Africa and the eighth-largest globally. Gold accounts for over 95 per cent of the country's total mineral revenue (Ghana 2010). Ghana's real GDP increased by 15 per cent in 2011, when it began producing oil commercially, up from an average of 6.5 per cent in the 2000s (ICMM 2015).

Ghana's lucrative natural resources, stable political landscape, and increasingly diverse economy have seen it emerge as the second-largest economy in West Africa (after Nigeria). The country attained middle-income status in 2011, suggesting that its economic growth has had positive social impacts. Ghana's unemployment rate declined steadily from 10.4 per cent in 2000 to just 2.4 per cent in 2017 (World Bank, n.d.[g]). Moreover, its poverty headcount ratio (at the national poverty line)[3] declined from 31.9 per cent in 2005 to 24.2 per cent in 2012 (World Bank, n.d.[h]). As an indication of the social value of Ghana's mining sector, Toigo (2015) notes that new extractives revenues in Ghana could potentially fill the majority of the funding gap in its education sector. Ghana's natural resource wealth, stable political environment, and expanding economy could potentially encourage further change and have an enduringly positive and direct effect on capacity building in various sectors of its economy.

Ghana is also one of only a few African countries – though this group is rapidly growing – with a local content policy for its hydrocarbons industry. Petroleum regulations in the country, in the form of local content policies, were created to catalyze intersectoral linkages and facilitate the use of Ghanaian human and material capital, local expertise, goods and services, and financing (Ablo 2015). In addition, Ghana's local content policies seek to: develop local capacities through training, education, and skills transfer; achieve minimum levels of employment; increase the competitiveness of local businesses; create a petroleum industry that drives the country's sustainable development; and provide a degree of control over natural resource endowments on behalf of the Ghanaian people (Ablo 2015). Accra is placing great emphasis on ensuring that local content, beneficiation, and value addition are adhered to from the start, as the country develops its nascent hydrocarbons sector. The Ghanaian government established the Local Content Committee (LCC) to oversee, coordinate, and manage the overall implementation process. A minimum 5 per cent equity for local petroleum licences, permits, and contract operators – and at least 10 per cent equity for local providers of supplies and services – is supposed to ensure local participation by the Ghanaian private sector (MEP 2013).

The government has chosen this strategy to maximize value addition using local expertise, goods, and services to create jobs and skills, and keep them in the country. Despite these good intentions, however, the local content policies in Ghana appear to be weaker than similar provisions in other countries, such as Nigeria, as they fail to prevent locals from acting as fronts for multinational corporations; as Ovadia notes, "to stop companies sub-contracting services from foreign companies, does not require local companies in joint ventures to own any of the capital equipment, and does not address the issue of local companies importing goods manufactured abroad" (2016b). Indeed, there are concerns that at the rate that local involvement in hydrocarbon extraction is currently required under local content policies, the trickle-down impact for average Ghanaians will take decades to manifest (Ovadia 2016b).

The extractive sector may play a significant role in implementing the post-2015 development agenda in Ghana, pushing economic transformation, social development, and poverty reduction, as well as greater environmental protection. For this to occur, the country's development plan, as expressed in the "40-Year National Development Plan for Ghana" document, has to give the sector the attention it deserves, placing it at the core of Ghana's future and long-term development strategy and establishing the infrastructure needed for its development (Abubakari, Asamoah, and Agyemang 2018). This includes a well-planned and well-financed industrialization process for the in-country transformation of mining and mineral resources. Nevertheless, as shown in this chapter, this cannot happen if mining resources and transformation are not considered as tightly linked to agricultural development (agriculture being a key economic sector) and to downstream linkages between oil and construction, as well as between gold mining and other sectors of the economy. Along this interconnected chain, foreign investment actors, together with the Ghanaian government, will be key drivers of transformational change.

Sierra Leone: From Blood Minerals to Development Minerals?

Sierra Leone is undergoing post-conflict reconstruction and state building following brutal civil wars fuelled, in large part, by resource predation. Reconstruction efforts, particularly in the extractive sector, have focused heavily on private-sector growth (Del Castillo 2008; Andersen 2011). In Sierra Leone, diamond extraction by a variety of private-sector actors, via legal and illegal means, played a crucial role in destabilizing the country and provided a primary source of funding for armed rebel groups in the lead-up to and during the civil conflict. Recent efforts to resuscitate the economic livelihoods of communities devastated by the war have placed great emphasis on "good governance" in small-scale diamond-mining communities. Examples include certification schemes such as the KPCS, as well as CSR initiatives such as the EITI (Maconachie 2009). Nevertheless, resurrecting viable and transparent diamond- and gold-mining industries in the country has been problematic, as the "peace dividend" continues to elude many communities due to a lack of foreign investment and persistent corruption within political institutions, which hamper reconstruction and peacebuilding efforts.

As part of its post-conflict economic recovery processes and to allow substantial progress in attracting FDI, Freetown needs to reduce business constraints and bottlenecks to investment. Any unnecessary legal, bureaucratic, or financial constraints on the transfer of capital do not bode well for the business community's success. As highlighted by the World Bank's Doing Business ranking, the country particularly suffers from the lack of stability in business development, including access to credit, and the enforcement of contracts (World Bank, n.d.[b]). A more engaged private sector will help foster economic recovery, support the establishment of peace and stability, and prevent the country from slipping back into conflict. Aware of this, the government established a national privatization program, aiming to sell many state-owned enterprises and thereby provide greater opportunities to spur the development of the private extractive sector in particular (Sierra Leone 2002). This process represents a cornerstone in the Sierra Leonean government's overall strategy for national development. It promises to reduce public expenditure while stimulating the economy and providing jobs for the unemployed.

Although these steps are vital to encourage positive change, it is important to note that foreign natural resource investment does not guarantee that progress will be made in establishing equitable and mutually beneficial mineral community development agreements. It is also far from assured that peace, stability, and economic development will flow from such investments, particularly in the short-to-medium term. In the worst instance, investments could reinforce autocratic regimes or enrich mining companies at the expense of local communities and host countries, resulting in heightened corruption and nepotism. In the case of Sierra Leone, the government has arguably benefitted the least in the country's post-conflict reconstruction efforts. Domestic revenue collection reached a record high of 15.3 per cent of GDP following the end of the conflict in 2003, but has since dropped to 12 per cent due to a decrease in excise revenue and import duties (IMF 2011). In 2016, mining revenues collection reached $26 million and accounted for 7.3 per cent of GDP (EITI 2016b).

74 GOVERNANCE, CONFLICT, AND NATURAL RESOURCES IN AFRICA

Despite making progress in implementing mechanisms and regulatory institutions to help manage the country's extractive industry (this includes the creation of a Uniform Tax Code in 2000 and the National Revenue Authority in 2002, which brought together all revenue collection departments), resource revenue failed to reach the expected levels. Although corruption within Sierra Leone's National Revenue Authority has been largely to blame for this, a limited tax base and stagnating resource revenue have also been detrimental.

Ethiopia: Land Distribution as Developmental Tool

For Ethiopia, natural resource governance constitutes a crucial dimension of its development. The country serves as an excellent case study for this reason. Agriculture has long been the central axis of the Ethiopian economy: The Government of Ethiopia effectively owns all of the country's land (Ethiopia 1975). As of 2010, more than 80 per cent of Ethiopians lived in rural areas, while approximately 85 per cent of total employment was concentrated in the agricultural sector (Bues and Theesfeld 2012). Agriculture currently accounts for approximately 45 per cent of the country's GDP, 90 per cent of its exports, and 85 per cent of its foreign currency earnings (Bues and Theesfeld 2012). For these reasons, much of Ethiopia's political history has been defined by the control of agricultural land and the agro-economy to which this gives rise.

Though ultimately subject to the decisions of public-sector officials in Addis Ababa, the administration of land was decentralized in the mid-1990s and embedded in the new constitution, which was ushered in with the establishment of the Federal Democratic Republic of Ethiopia in 1995. The new constitution ensured that regional governments, formed along ethnic lines, would have a greater influence in land governance. In addition to enshrining an ethno-federalist model of governance and upholding an individual usufruct tenure system, the new constitution also explicitly acknowledged the land and property rights of pastoralists and women (Hagmann and Mulugeta 2008; Wanyeki 2003). Though the Ethiopian government, since 2003, has attempted to reduce land tenure insecurity by introducing a land certification program and complementary agricultural development policies in support of smallholder producers, the country has witnessed limited gains in agricultural growth, poverty reduction, and food security. Muted progress in these areas has been exacerbated by a lack of public funding and capital accumulation in the private sector. The economic arguments in favour of smallholder agriculture as the engine for Ethiopia's economic growth were thus increasingly questioned (Gebreselassie 2006). Eventually, senior Ethiopian policymakers became convinced that the government should take a broader approach to economic development.

In an attempt to kickstart the country's agricultural sector as an engine of growth, the new government began to expand its focus and laid emphasis on developing large-scale commercial agriculture, trade, and foreign investment. The earlier Agricultural Development Led Industrialization (ADLI) strategy became a component of a broader push to attract investment to usher in large-scale, mechanized, commercial agricultural output via Ethiopia's Growth and Transformation Plan (2010–15) and Growth and Transformation Plan II (2015–20) (MFED 2010; DAG 2016).

This revamped development strategy has offered generous investment incentives to foreign actors, including broad tax exemptions on imported capital goods and repatriated profits. Such inducements have led to an investment boom in Ethiopian land over the course of the last decade. Foreign investments now constitute nearly three-quarters of all land sought for large-scale agricultural production (Baumgartner 2012). The Ethiopian Investment Agency (EIA) maintains that three-and-a-half million hectares of land were subject to large-scale lease investments from 1996 to 2008 (interview, EIA, 17 April 2014).

In keeping with its revived commitment to the Comprehensive Africa Agriculture Development Programme (CAADP), which seeks to enhance efforts on the part of African governments to pursue pro-poor, agriculture-led growth during the 2005–10 period, the Ethiopian government drafted the Plan for Accelerated and Sustained Development to End Poverty (PASDEP). This plan underscored the importance of commercial agriculture and the critical role of large-scale investment to the development of Ethiopia's agricultural sector. Addis Ababa has argued that increased support for large-scale farming projects would ultimately have a positive, knock-on effect for the country's smallholder cultivators due to greater prospective employment opportunities, improvement of rural infrastructure, new sources of knowledge transfer, and lucrative opportunities for African agriculturalists looking to invest in other industries. Nevertheless, the commercialization of agricultural land results in its share of challenges, notably the government's failure to uphold the constitutional right of pastoralists and shifting cultivators not to be displaced from their land. Addis Ababa has yet to attain stable and inclusive growth, especially growth that benefits the country's small landholding producers. Such developments threaten one of the Horn of Africa's core states with growing political instability at a time when it already performs poorly on the Fund for Peace's Fragile States Index.

It is recognized that discrete classification systems do not properly capture the nuances, fluid nature, and multidimensional complexity of concepts such as fragility, conflict, and instability. The World Bank's Fragility, Conflict and Violence Group has released a "Harmonized List of Fragile Situations" on an annual basis since 2011; this was preceded by the Fragile States List in 2010, and the Low-Income Countries Under Stress List (LICUS) between 2006 and 2009. Since 2005, the OECD has produced its own reports on country fragility, which examine financial resource flows and general macroeconomic, political, and social trends in conflict-threatened countries. Ghana has not appeared on the World Bank's Harmonized List of Fragile Situations for more than ten years, and is therefore considered a stable country for the purposes of this research project. The most recent version of the Armed Conflict Dataset produced by the Uppsala Conflict Data Program at the department of Peace and Conflict Research, Uppsala University, and the Centre for the Study of Civil War, Peace Research Institute Oslo (UCDP/PRIO) describes post-conflict countries as those in which violent clashes ceased within the last fifteen years (Gleditsch et al. 2002). With this definition in mind, Sierra Leone is considered a post-conflict country. The OECD's *States of Fragility 2015* report considers Ethiopia to be one of the most fragile states in the world due to its potential for violence, the absence of credible rule of law, ineffective institutions, and limited adaptive capacity in the face of shocks (OECD 2015).

Case study country selection parameters also included a number of other important variables. All three countries have predominantly English-speaking populations, a situation that presented practical advantages for this study, such as speed of research and ease of interpretation of interview and archival data. In addition, each country is renowned for a particular natural resource: oil and other energy resources, and to some extent minerals (Ghana); minerals, more specifically diamonds (Sierra Leone); and agriculture (Ethiopia). The relative importance, in terms of GDP, of natural resource exploitation in each economy was also a consideration. Ghana, for its part, obtains over 25 per cent of its annual GDP from the industry sector, which includes oil and gas (Dontoh and Janse Van Vuuren 2017). For Ethiopia, agriculture (land) employs the vast majority of the country's population and accounted for 36.2 per cent of its total GDP as of 2016 (*Global Finance* 2017). While diamonds as a share of Sierra Leone's exports decreased from 15 to 10 per cent, the mining sector as a whole generates more than 28 per cent of its export earnings (Bertelsmann Stiftung 2016).

These three cases provide variation across levels of instability and stability, types and levels of natural resources, and the role played by private, and especially foreign, actors. By comparing the roles of actors in different natural resource sectors, the research isolated key variables and contributed to a broader framework for conceptualizing natural resource governance and stability in Africa.

CHAPTER 3

Ghana: The Transformative Potential of Hydrocarbon Resources

Introduction

With its stable political system and lucrative natural resources, Ghana managed to become one of the strongest economies in Africa until the recent financial instability crisis, although a change of government in 2000 has restored some degree of financial stability. About 28 per cent of Ghana's 25 million citizens – mostly those living in rural areas – still live below the international extreme poverty line of $1.25 per day (UNICEF 2013a). Ghana was ranked 142nd of 188 countries on the UNDP's 2019 Human Development Index (UNDP 2019; UNDP 2015a). The West African country attained middle-income status in 2011, with economic growth spurring positive social progress in terms of education and healthcare. However, despite a significant reduction in overall income poverty, challenges remain, including gender inequality, high unemployment, environmental mishaps, administrative fiscal bottlenecks, and disparities between the endowed South and impoverished North (Osei-Assibey 2014; Darimani 2013). Ghana's dynamic extractive sector, currently dominated by oil, has traditionally been based on gold, but its economic influence is decreasing.

Ghana has been praised by many for its use of natural resources and its ability to avoid the "resource curse." In a recent article, Adams et al. (2019) maintain that while the country's membership in the EITI and its progressive petroleum revenue management policies are steps in the right direction, Ghana's success in mitigating the negative impacts of the flow of revenues from the extractive industries is linked, at least in part, to macro-level institutional factors. According to the authors, these include "the quality of institutions, quality of governance, government effectiveness, accountability, corruption control mechanisms, natural resource sustainability and effective accounting practices" (Langdon 2009). Although it supports the broader thesis of this study, this approach also needs to be critically investigated, particularly its primary assumption that Ghana has successfully managed its natural resources extraction system.

To explore these limitations, Langdon's work on Indigenous knowledge and Gavin Hilson's study of artisanal extractive systems identify some of the pitfalls to avoid. Langdon's concept of *Indigenous* or *local* knowledge should be considered in opposition to the more typical approach, which presents global knowledge, and its Western, universalist underpinnings, as being somehow *above* local knowledge. Following this analysis, we have anchored the PENRG framework within local realities – as a tool inspired by localized issues but tackled at the macro level (in this example, the national level). The need for developmental discourses to learn from and become inspired by Indigenous forms of knowledge is at the core of Langdon's work. While taking examples from the health and education sectors, the validity of his approach can be extended to our concerns around the use and benefits of extractive industries, in particular those led by foreign-owned companies, for the country's broad-based and inclusive development.

Rooted in a similar desire to reconceptualize and adapt critical thinking to macro analysis, Hilson's focus on local artisanal communities, in Ghana and elsewhere, is enlightening for our own study (Hilson, Hilson, and Dauda 2019). Exploring the benefits of large-scale mining, often by foreign-owned companies, for communities' long-term well-being, the author highlights the disconnect between these mining enclaves and local-level economies.

When analyzing CSR practices, it often appears that these strategies are a "rebranding" of colonial practices aimed at pacifying and engaging local communities. In the case of Ghana, the similarity between development thinking and project financing today and during the colonial period is striking – the consequence of a pro-mining stance on the part of government officials leading to decreased expectations of engagement and revenue generation for local communities. Going further, the concept of "growth poles" is central for apprehending the challenges of large-scale mining and the creation of revenue-generating activities linked to the extraction of natural resources (Hilson 2018). The author argues that the stimulation of local economies through foreign investments in extractive and particularly large-scale mining in sub-Saharan Africa has largely failed to create a sustainable, long-term and broad-based development.

The orientation of what Hilson calls "booming resource enclaves" toward exports and the very limited added value of raw commodities restrain any economic benefits for communities. The concern around local content policies in the Ghanaian mining sector is profoundly linked to these debates. As such, the country's Mining Code establishes that "unskilled labour and clerical positions are reserved for Ghanaians only; for other jobs, the share of expatriate staffs should not exceed 10 per cent of total senior staff within the first 3 years and 6 per cent after 3 years" (Ramdoo 2016). However, in analyzing this issue at the national level, it is clear that the ease of revenue extraction through taxes, fees, and other payments is attractive for policy makers. From the standpoint of the companies, these policies are often very attractive, particularly compared to other regions where environmental, social, and economic requirements on extractive industries focus on repatriation of revenues to local communities.

Hilson's and Langdon's studies are critical to understanding the challenges to economic and social development in Ghana and, more broadly, across sub-Saharan Africa. While anchored in micro-level politics, their work will, in some respects, impact our analysis of the PENRG framework. However, it is critical to understand that our macro approach focuses on national systems of resource extraction governance and, as such, provides insights into the strategies used at the country level to retain added value and promote economic and social development through foreign-owned extractive enterprises.

This chapter analyzes how governance structures in Ghana, a politically stable state, have influenced the role and contribution of foreign-owned economic actors – specifically foreign investors and private extractive companies – in achieving peace, stability, and economic growth in the country. Democratic regimes such as Ghana (see: Gyimah-Boadi and Kwasi Prempeh 2012) are seen as the lower governance system risk for investment because the multiplicity of actors able to block legislative changes provides a stabilizing factor in the legal system (Tsebelis 2002). Similarly, and highly specific to Ghana, a critical factor for foreign actors' investments is the

Ghana: Hydrocarbon Resources

transparency of avenues available for corporations to influence the political sphere (Jensen 2008), a consideration linked closely to the transparency of political democratic regimes allowing companies to observe and anticipate changes in the legal framework (Rosendorff and Vreeland 2006).

This case study considers, in particular, how Ghana's natural resource governance systems have been effective in leveraging the private sector as a means of achieving beneficial outcomes from the mining and natural resource sectors. Subsequently, as this book investigates how governance structures (at both the industry and state levels) influence the nature and outcome of foreign-owned companies' and investors' involvement in the extractive and land resource sectors, this inquiry will be assessed in the wider development process and specifically through contribution to economic growth and political stability. Last, and with the goal of further developing the proposed PENRG framework, this chapter aims to provide ideas for optimizing the developmental impact of mining and oil extraction by laying out a vision for effective natural resource governance based on the Ghanaian case, specifically by leveraging the extractive sector for sustainable, pro-poor socioeconomic development and inclusive, broad-based economic transformation. This research considers the transformation of the mining sector and the emergence of the energy sector, comprised of the oil-and-gas industries, in the broader context of Ghana's political stability as well as the increasingly important role played by foreign-owned enterprises.

Natural Resource Governance

Since the 1980s, and following a shift away from Marxist rule and independence from Great Britain, Ghana's economic growth has been increasingly tied to the mining sector, largely dominated by gold. The country is the second-largest gold producer in Africa after South Africa, and the eighth-largest globally, and gold contributes more than 95 per cent of the country's total mineral revenue (Ghana 2010). Following the start of commercial oil production in December 2010, Ghana's real GDP growth jumped to 15 per cent in 2011, up from an average of 6.5 per cent in the 2000s (ICMM 2015). Despite a slowdown in 2013 and 2014, when real GDP growth decreased to 7.3 and 4 per cent, respectively (CIA 2015), analysts projected a recovery for 2016 and saw a three-year high of 9 per cent growth in 2017 (Okudzeto et al. 2015; *Trading Economics*, n.d.).[1] Ghana's overall GDP growth has been accompanied by a change in the structure of the economy, with the agricultural sector's contribution to GDP decreasing even though it still employs more than half of the country's workforce (FAO 2015). Agriculture remains a key sector, with cocoa remaining one of the country's largest exports (Tutu 2011). Notably, rural poverty in Ghana has fallen sharply since 2000, driven in part by cocoa cultivation expansion in labour-intensive small farms. This strategy enabled Ghana to become the first country to meet Millennium Development Goal 1 on reducing extreme poverty rates by half (UNDP 2015a).

The International Energy Agency (IEA 2014) states that taking three actions in the energy sector – so long as they are accompanied by favourable governance reforms – could bolster the size of the sub-Saharan African economy by 30 per cent within twenty-five years: investment of an additional $450 billion in the energy sector; deeper regional cooperation and integration; and improved management of hydrocarbon and other natural resources and revenues. Efficient and transparent licensing procedures and a reformed regulatory environment across sub-Saharan African countries would encourage the drafting and implementation of sound energy policies (Marandu and Kayo 2004; Kapika and Eberhard 2013). Improved consultation and transparency, and accountability measures to win stakeholders and public trust, would also help Africa gain considerably from the development of its hydrocarbon and other energy resources. But how would this ideal governance approach be achieved?

Ghana's Mineral Resources

Given Ghana's political stability, the country is generally considered to have a relatively attractive business environment. In 2019, it was ranked thirteenth in Africa and 118th globally by the World Bank in terms of ease of doing business (World Bank, n.d.[c]). Much of that political stability derives from the country's growing economy. In 2013, Ghana's mining sector contributed 10 per cent of the country's GDP (GHEITI 2012). The sector also accounted for 47 per cent of total exports in 2010, and employed

Ghana: Hydrocarbon Resources

about 15,000 people in large-scale mining (LSM); further, more than 500,000 people are engaged in legal and illegal small-scale gold, diamond, and sand mining and quarrying – referred to as "artisanal and small-scale" mining (ASM) (NRGI, n.d.). Only 2 per cent of all formal jobs in Ghana represent direct employment in large-scale mines, with most LSM workers on short-term contracts with limited labour rights (Darimani 2013).

AngloGold Ashanti, created in 2004 with the merger of AngloGold and Ashanti Goldfields Corporation, is currently owned by the world's third-largest mining company, Anglo American. The company owns two mines: an open pit at Iduapriem and an underground operation at Obuasi, both in western Ghana. With environmental permits received in June 2018, the mining giant is set to start construction and production. According to the Ghanaian government and company officials, an estimated $2.2 billion in state revenue will be received from this new exploitation, while local content is expected to reach $2.4 billion (interview with Mr Mark Morcombe, Senior Vice President, AngloGold Ashanti Ghana, 4 September 2015). On the other side, the oil sector is dominated by relatively small, foreign-owned companies. With revenues of $1.7 billion in 2017, Tullow Oil operates in sixteen countries, including in Ghana since 2006. In 2010, it extracted the first oil from its two licences and producing fields, and is currently developing the Jubilee field off the coast of western Ghana.

Other mineral resources, including diamonds and bauxite (IMANI Ghana 2010), account for a sizable part of the country's exports. Chromite, asbestos, andalusite, barite, mica, nepheline, syenite, cassiterite, columbite, monazite, beryl, spodumene, molybdenite, alluvial ilmenite, and rutile are also mined in the country. Given that there are no specific, comprehensive governance structures covering these other mineral resources, an analysis of the potential impact these might have on foreign-owned enterprises' contributions to peace, stability, and economic growth is limited to specific areas of the mining and energy sectors.

Ghana's legal and regulatory framework deserves special consideration, since the country has achieved stability and developed a substantial number of instruments for natural resource governance, including some that promote the aforementioned beneficial outcomes. Guidelines for policy implementation – specifically, of the country's laws and regulations – are relatively extensive compared to the frameworks of other countries on the continent. The legal and regulatory framework for the mining and energy sectors, as well as for natural resource governance more generally, includes: Internal Revenue Act, 2000 (Act 592) as amended and with associated regulations; Minerals and Mining Act, 2006 (Act 703) as amended; Minerals (Royalties) Amendment Act, 2010 (Act 794); Petroleum Commission Act, 2011; Petroleum Revenue Management Act, 2011 (Act 893) as amended; Minerals and Mining (General) Regulations, 2012 (LI 2173); Minerals and Mining (Support Services) Regulations, 2012 (LI 2174); Minerals and Mining (Compensation and Resettlement) Regulations, 2012 (LI 2175); Minerals and Mining (Licensing) Regulations, 2012 (LI 2176); Minerals and Mining (Explosives) Regulations, 2012 (LI 2177); Minerals and Mining (Health, Safety & Technical) Regulations, 2012 (LI 2182); Ghana Investment Promotion Centre (GIPC) Act, 2013 (Act 865); Petroleum Regulations, 2013 (LI 2204); Companies Amendment Act, 2016; and Petroleum (Exploration and Production) Act, 2016. The extensive legal basis for natural resource governance in Ghana, as well as associated policy guidelines for implementation and operationalization, provide immediate anchor conditions for the country to determine the limits of foreign-owned private-sector activities.

The Minerals Commission is responsible for regulating and managing mineral resources, and coordinating mining policies. However, as it stands, Ghana's extractive sector is highly susceptible to illicit financial flows, which amounted to $1.7 billion in 2013 (ACEP 2015a). Because of this, the country was ranked ninety-third among 145 developing countries in 2013 (ACEP 2015a) due to corruption, illegal exploitation, tax evasion by mining companies through various illegal deals (like transfer pricing), and resource smuggling. Lack of enforcement depreciates the capacity of a governance system to leverage foreign-owned private-sector actors as a facilitating force for peace, stability, and economic growth.

To begin to remedy some of these legislative and governance issues, Ghana signed on to the Extractive Industries Transparency Initiative (EITI), achieving compliant status in 2010 by establishing accountability and transparency in the local mining industry. According to the 2013 Resource Governance Index, Ghana ranked fifteenth of fifty-eight countries indexed – the highest-ranked African country and one of only a few African countries included in the Index. Because the government does not

Ghana: Hydrocarbon Resources

publish comprehensive information on key aspects of the mining industry, the most critical area for Ghana's governance of natural resources remains its reporting practices and publicly accessible information (RWI 2015). Notably, there is much donor interest in supporting the work of NGOs on transparency issues in oil-and-gas (interview, Third World Network, 4 March 2014).

Second, under the provisions of the Petroleum Revenue Management Act (PRMA) of 2011, Ghana's Public Interest and Accountability Committee is designed to enhance public participation by citizen organizations in the management of resource revenues (including hydrocarbons revenues), and to serve as a platform for public debate on how petroleum revenues should be spent. Its thirteen members are drawn from organized professional bodies, think tanks, advocacy groups, and traditional institutions (Ghana 2011). The Committee monitors and evaluates compliance with the law on the part of government, foreign enterprises, and other institutions, provides an independent assessment of petroleum production and payment of corporate taxes, and publishes its findings in annual and semi-annual reports.

In its 2012 and 2014 annual reports, for example, the Committee noted that oil revenues provided the government with considerable fiscal relief, and emphasized the urgent need for Accra to create a better budget to focus spending and improve the socioeconomic development of the country as a whole (Raji 2016). Unfortunately, in July 2014, crude oil prices began to drop from US$115 per barrel, eventually freefalling 55 per cent by January of the following year (IFS 2015). According to the Institute for Fiscal Studies, Ghana's real GDP growth dropped from a projected 4.0 to 3.5 per cent for 2015; budget contributions from oil extraction fell by 58 per cent; government capital expenditure dropped from 26 to 17 per cent; and the government pulled from stocks to help reduce budgetary shortfalls (IFS 2015).

Despite economic challenges, modern Ghana is a hallmark of political stability and democratic power transfer in Africa. PricewaterhouseCoopers (PwC) argues that Ghana's stable democratic institutions since 1992 make it a model for other countries, with democracy becoming deeply rooted in the fabric of the country (PwC 2015a; PwC 2015b). Deloitte adds that Ghana's political stability is further consolidated by a strong, independent media, active public dialogue, and guaranteed political rights, all of which placed it at number eight on the Ibrahim Index of African Governance in 2016 (Deloitte, n.d.). However, Ghana's political stability and the comfort afforded by regularized legislative regimes have not necessarily been translated to management of the natural resources sector.

Role of the Foreign-Owned Private Sector in Promoting Positive Change in Ghana's Mining Sector

The institutional milieu in Ghana is what dictates whether foreign-owned private-sector enterprises can play a positive or negative role in the country. Since the 1980s, Ghana has created a "good investment environment" as a preliminary step toward establishing sustainable economic growth – a macro-level positive outcome of the country's investment policies and extractive industry regulations. But impacts at the community level remain to be explored and assessed. As Hilson's work underlines, the lack of revenue retainer systems in extractive regions, and at the micro level, influences negatively the need for broad-based development through foreign-owned mining projects. Additionally, exploring the failure to translate resource extraction into broad-based development, Abdulai engages with Ghana's clientelist political system and maintains that the highly competitive feature of the country's electoral structure prevents long-term revenue generation in favour of short-term benefits that help maintain ruling coalitions (Abdulai 2017).

The Mining Fiscal Regime

The mining fiscal regime, which has been designed to capture resource rents from private, foreign-owned enterprises and to promote FDIS, has remained fairly stable since the mid-1980s. The mining sector's contribution to foreign exchange earnings stood at 14 per cent at the beginning of the 1990s, but since the mid-1990s has maintained, as a result of this stabilization, an average of 41 per cent (ACET 2014). According to the Ghana Revenue Authority and the Minerals Commission, the sector provided about 19 per cent of government direct tax revenues in 2013 and is one of the largest contributing sectors to government revenues, second only to the oil industry (ICMM 2015, 23). Moreover, purchases of local supplies by the mining sector were valued at over \$1.2 billion in 2012 (Aubynn, n.d.).[2] In terms of job creation, the sector employed about 21,000 people in the 1990s (Bank of Ghana 2003), but this figure fell to 15,000 by 2013 (ICMM 2015). Only 2 per cent of these employees are expatriates, and indirect and induced job creation accounts for six times the number of jobs as direct employment (each direct employee typically supports eight to ten family members). According to the ICMM's report on the Ghanaian mining industry's impact on employment, "over the period 2010–22, the sample of mining companies is estimated to support between 83,000 and 148,000 jobs, equivalent to an average of 111,000 jobs annually. In 2013, about 1.3 per cent of the Ghanaian labour force was supported by the sample of mining companies, a figure that is projected to decline to 0.6 per cent of the labour force in 2022" (ICMM 2015).

Even if the mining sector is governed properly, with sustainable, pro-poor policies and regulatory instruments that address challenges of revenue capitation and investment attraction, one of the pitfalls is that investment incentives have changed over time (Amponsah-Tawiah and Dartey-Baah 2011), and thereby failed to maximize the sector's potential to benefit local Ghanaians. For example, even as many incentives were put in place during the 1990s in the aim of boosting investment in the gold industry, they did not include additional policies on national or local participation. Understandably, governance structures will often include policy for incentivizing FDIs and foreign private-sector investment in a designated sector. But when this policy lacks transference protocols to distribute rents and revenues appropriately at a local level, the structures do not serve to encourage broad, multilevel economic growth. Indeed, as a politically stable country, Ghana should be transitioning away from simple FDI enticement and toward leveraging the sector for widespread economic sustainability, requiring an unabridged position on taxation and royalty collection suited to its middle-income economic status. Poor policy planning for mineral resource governance can contribute to class disparity, animosity, and antagonism between communities and companies – and ultimately instability.

Governance structures contribute to sustainable economic growth in politically stable countries when they include effective dispersal from national-level coffers to local communities. Mandated operationalization of community investment, as such, would entail a series of necessary organizational steps, to be undertaken by private-sector actors, to launch relevant and locally conducive community development projects based on community needs and in consultation with community leaders. Currently, the vast majority of mineral-related investment is tied to the gold industry, indicating an overdependence on one commodity. Little of this gold-derived income trickles down to communities, even those adjacent or associated with mine sites. This suggests that gaps in conditions of state governance institutions for natural resources can inhibit sustainable economic development, even in a politically stable country.

While there is a burgeoning literature on how to stimulate sustainable development in the mining sector (Hilson and Murck 2000; Janneh and Ping 2011; Boakye et al. 2012), a major challenge facing the Ghanaian government – and a lesson noted and incorporated into the PENRG framework – is the means by which one can change perceptions within the mining communities themselves in regard to how the private sector, especially foreign-owned corporations, might contribute to sustainable development. Akabzaa, Seyire, and Afriyie (2007) examine the effects of mining activities at the Ashanti Goldfields Company (AGC) mine located at Obuasi, the capital of Adansi West District – in the town itself and in surrounding communities, which constitute a major centre of mining activities in Ghana and for sub-Saharan Africa more widely. Since 2004, AGC merged with AngloGold to create AngloGold Ashanti, part of the Anglo American Group, a London- and Johannesburg-based multinational mining company and the world's second-largest gold producer (AngloGold Ashanti 2017). In 2017, AngloGold Ltd extracted 3.76 million ounces of gold, mainly from its facilities in Africa, the United States, and Brazil. The company's parent grouping, Anglo American, takes in annual revenues of US$26.24 billion, with operations in iron ore, diamonds, and base metals (Anglo American 2017). The Obuasi mine is an exemplary case study of unsustainable development: "There is no consensus on the true economic impact of mining by AGC on the local population. Industry backers use increased mine production and gross export value of mine products.

Ghana: Hydrocarbon Resources 89

However, increased negative environmental and social impacts on local communities and evasive foreign earnings from the sector as a result of the generous incentives to companies make the actual economic impact of the sector debatable" (Akabzaa, Seyire, and Afriyie 2007, 82).

The mine's social impacts were manifested as increases in the cost of living in the local communities due to company pricing practices that favoured the high incomes of mining workers and expatriates, violence and brutality on the part of private security agents against illegal artisanal gold miners, increases in mining-related respiratory diseases such as silico-tuberculosis, increased demographic pressures and food shortages due to workers abandoning agriculture for the mining sector, prevalence of prostitution among community members, and displacement of populations due to pollution. The environmental impacts included land and vegetation degradation, offsite migration of pollutants, and surface and underground water pollution caused by open-pit operations. What makes the Obuasi case unique is that the conflict between the private security agents and the illegal artisanal miners is not about grievances over land expropriation by locals, but an economically motivated conflict in which the artisanal miners are non-natives who have abandoned agriculture for mining and seek to obtain gold via their artisanal practices, and have formed an informal association that has been key to their survival (Okoh 2014; Akabzaa and Darimani 2001).

This example sheds light upon a persistent gap in the governance of natural resource systems in Ghana: the inability to influence, through policy and legislative mechanisms, the actions of private-sector and foreign-owned enterprises so as to remedy these issues. Indeed, Ghana should seek foreign direct investment for its mature mineral resources sector by leveraging the strength of its government and governance systems, respectively; stability and risk aversion matter deeply to private-sector actors, especially when operating in places deemed (erroneously, in many cases) to be frontier areas of the African continent.

The issue of illegal artisanal gold mining is at once contentious and ambiguous (Teschner 2012). Although at one point the Ghanaian government showed interest in formalizing and organizing the miners, it did not follow through, with the result that the government has lost control over the informal sector. Police tactics to eliminate ASM often involve violence and have largely been ineffective. In fact, artisanal miners provide significant amounts of sustained income to local communities, bridging the gaps left by deficiencies in the governance system, with the result that attempts to clamp down on them could lead to community abjection (Bush 2009). One observer argued that the only way forward is to work with artisanal gold miners to formalize the sector, which would minimize negative impacts while enhancing positive effects in the midst of an economy with a high unemployment rate (interview, Department of Geography, University of Ghana, 25 February 2014). Over the past decade, some transitory artisanal miners have forged strong bonds with host communities by sending pre-negotiation teams and arranging mutually beneficial agreements with local actors, indicating that some attempts to formalize their activities and contribute to community development have taken place (Nyame and Grant 2014).

Certain interviewees remarked that some artisanal miners have been panning for gold in abandoned mines, which also points to the need for more formalization (interview, Department of Political Science, University of Ghana, 28 February 2014). One observer suggested that improved relationships between small- and large-scale miners can only be achieved if the understaffed Minerals Commission is supplemented with assistance from other government institutions and international agencies such as the World Bank (Hilson 2002). When touring the Western Region bordering Côte d'Ivoire, Ghana's president mentioned that the government has been seeking World Bank support to register artisanal miners and support mining techniques dispersion, which would in turn create opportunities to cover mining holes and to recover and reclaim land through tree planting (interview, Department of Political Science, University of Ghana, 28 February 2014). To date, only one US$300,000 project has been approved, in June 2018, to provide technical assistance to the extractive industries (World Bank, n.d.[d]).

Another significant challenge is youth unemployment (interview, Kofi Annan International Peacekeeping Centre, 24 February 2014; interview, UN University Institute for Natural Resources in Africa, 24 February 2014). Ghanaian youth, who had hoped to secure some level of employment on the rigs, have become angry, frustrated, and resentful at the lack of opportunity and the fact that companies have hired expatriates or experienced

Ghana: Hydrocarbon Resources

Ghanaians from other regions. The Western Region's literacy and university enrolment levels are relatively low, which has translated to lower skills rates and fewer opportunities. Moreover, employed youths, such as carpenters, welders, and masons, have been disappointed by the lack of development projects such as construction of schools, hospitals, and roads. Since oil and gas were discovered offshore, that sector's products thus far have been transported by air such that companies have not needed to build infrastructure in local communities. The rigs, by their very presence, serve as a visible reminder of the challenges associated with using governance as a vehicle to achieve peace, stability and, in the case of Ghana, sustainable economic growth, where foreign-owned private-sector actors have been able to bypass the governance structure.

Indeed, at the macro level of analysis, local beneficiation and value addition in the natural resources sector should be primarily discussed within the context of the political economy of resource generation and transfer. In Ghana, value addition produced by mining companies' expenditures has great impact on both government and household income levels. The construction sector, local trades, manufacturing, and utilities receive most of the supplier expenditures (ICMM 2015). There are also opportunities outside of gold and oil. The Ghanaian government recently introduced a National Export Strategy for the Non-Traditional Sector (MTI 2016), which deals with processed foods, fish, lumber, and horticulture, among other products. The strategy aggressively promotes manufacturing, processing, and semi-processing, and aspires to move from $2 billion in non-traditional revenue in 2013 to $5 billion in 2017.

The Ghana Investment Promotion Centre, a government agency established in 2013, is an important governance vehicle for promoting investments that should lead to resource-based industrialization and expansion of the country's trade portfolio (Ghana 2013). Meanwhile, the Free Zone Act of 1995 was promulgated to promote economic development and job creation through a variety of incentives, including an exemption from payment of duties and levies on all imports for production with respect to imports and exports from free zones (designated areas within which goods may be received and stored without payment of duty) and an exemption from payment of income tax on profits for ten years with respect to international investors, with taxation thereafter at just 8 per cent (instead of the normal 25 per cent). To further promote investment and boost economic prospects, the government is considering the creation of special incentives for investors looking at the productive sector, particularly in regard to energy, adding value to extracted minerals, large-scale agricultural production, and manufacturing (interview, Ministry of Energy and Petroleum, 3 March 2014).

Other priority areas include building economic infrastructure to support investment (electric power supply, water access, telecommunications and transportation), reducing clearance times at ports, and streamlining the fiscal regime to reduce challenges associated with, among other things, taxes and interest rates (interview, Ministry of Energy and Petroleum, 3 March 2014). The Ghana Investment Promotion Centre has also established a land bank that encourages landowners to submit their land titles, whereupon they are made available to investors, including local investors. It also recognizes and awards the companies with the best CSR practices through the Ghana Club 100 annual listing in order to encourage further competition and improve products and services.

Appropriate governance of foreign-owned enterprises' investments would involve moving beyond the accrual of natural resource revenues and lacklustre attempts to stimulate sustainable economic growth and continued stability, and toward maximizing national value creation through local content, beneficiation, and value addition. Such a shift would be based on the revitalization of successful institutions like the Ghana Investment Promotion Centre and the Public Interest and Accountability Committee, as well as on addressing elite-level political issues. It is critical that the government does not serve the interests of foreign-owned enterprises alone, whether through intentional dismissal or ignorance of necessary implementation governance reforms, or outright preferential treatment. Such actions have the potential to give rise to social instability, unrest, and violence targeted at both the private sector and the government – consequences that could hinder sustainable economic growth and continuing peace.

Emergence of the Hydrocarbon Sector

While the mining sector has the potential to contribute to Ghana's future, the emerging hydrocarbon sector is set to shape the country through economic transformation, provided it is governed appropriately to promote positive contributions by foreign-owned enterprises. Ghana's oil reserves, the bulk of which are in the Jubilee field, are estimated at between 800 million and 1.8 billion barrels, and production, which began in 2010, is expected to continue for twenty years (NRGI, n.d.).[3] The Ghanaian government is currently drilling and producing oil under the terms of the 2016 Petroleum (Exploration and Production) Act, which creates a scope of action designed to encourage increased private participation and investment through an open, competitive public tendering process for the allocation of petroleum rights, as well as to clarify ground rules for operators and provide for "safe, secure, sustainable, and efficient petroleum activities in the country" (*Ghana Justice* 2016).

Earlier legislation from 1984, which the Act superseded, had established the Ghana National Petroleum Corporation (GNPC), a state-owned enterprise that commenced operations in 1985 and has broadly regulated the oil and gas industries. The Corporation is now involved in exploration, development, and production, and is looking to form joint ventures that leverage domestic and foreign investments with the objective of providing a reliable supply of petroleum products and reducing the country's dependence on crude oil imports through the development of native Ghanaian oil and gas resources.[4]

There are various contemporary discourses on how to manage Ghana's hydrocarbon resources to stimulate economic transformation and sustainable growth. Suggestions include altering governance structures and laws, boosting participation in the oil industry, creating oil and gas funds, implementing various investment strategies, focusing on upstream oil and gas strategies, and ensuring spatial development (Chitor 2012; Asamoah 2013a; Aryeetey, Osei, and Quartey 2014; Asante and Owasa 2014; Boatemah and Owusa 2014; Laryea 2014).[5] This section, however, focuses on governance, given the fact that the revenues from the oil and gas industries have already surpassed total mining receipts: indeed, they almost doubled – from $444 million in 2011 to $846 million in 2013 – as the oil companies began paying corporate income taxes (GHEITI 2012). The most recent data from the Bank of Ghana indicate that five years into commercial production, the country has generated approximately $3.285 billion in oil revenues, with the Annual Budget Funding Amount[6] receiving $1.4 billion.

The latter figure represents 43 per cent of oil revenues received (the Petroleum Revenue Management Act of 2011 set 70 per cent as the maximum). Yet, better transparency and accountability continue to be important natural resource governance issues in Ghana – issues that undergird all efforts toward economic transformation through partial participation in the sector by foreign-owned enterprises.

The Jubilee field is the starting point for an analysis of Ghana's hydrocarbon resource governance, and the similarities and differences of hydrocarbons to other natural resources. The field is operated by British-based Tullow Oil, which owns 35 per cent, with the remaining shares held by Kosmos, Anadarko, the GNPC, and Petro SA (interview, Tullow Ghana, 25 February 2014). The GNPC has praised the Jubilee field's development, but an independent review by the IMANI Center for Policy & Education (2012b) shows that "its development has been considerably scaled down to less than half of the projected capacity in order to fast-track the path to first oil, which has exaggerated the success rate of activities whilst undermining project resilience" (interview, Tullow Ghana, 25 February 2014). Despite this, companies operating in hydrocarbon resource extraction have simultaneously engaged in various CSR projects, with non-recoverable costs pulled from operational budgets (Tullow Oil 2015; Platform 2012; interview, Tullow Ghana, 25 February 2014). External independent monitoring of the Jubilee project, which included a site visit in April 2013 by an independent external monitoring group, identified many successful social components over the years, including grievance management that had been strengthened over time through training and communication facilities, with the top grievances concerning the safety zone restriction radius around the oil rigs, the gradual decrease in fish stocks, and the lack of employment opportunities (Motherwell 2010; Tullow Oil 2015; interview, Tullow Ghana, 25 February 2014).

Despite such positive evidence that foreign-owned enterprises have contributed to community development in the area, there are no guarantees that resource wealth will be used effectively to create sustainable growth. This points to a failure on the part of governance systems to establish a scope of action for the private sector that enables restructuring for the purpose of achieving sustainable growth.

In response to this challenge, the 2011 Petroleum Revenue Management Act established the Petroleum Holding Fund and Ghana Petroleum Funds, which include the Ghana Heritage Fund and the Ghana Stabilisation Fund.[7] These funds are intended to address intergenerational conflict created by exploitation of oil and gas resources, specifically by investing natural resource revenue into safe assets for the benefit of all Ghanaians (Oshionebo 2018). However, it could be argued that investing natural resource revenue now, rather than keeping it in the form of liquid financial assets, would be of benefit to current and future generations, especially as immediate investment would attract more capital. Amending the Act to use the Ghana Petroleum Funds as leverage to establish an infrastructure fund could also be beneficial (interview, Department of Geography, University of Ghana, 25 February 2014). According to a three-year review of petroleum revenues from 2011 to 2013, the budget allocated to the health sector over this period was limited, while the food and agriculture subsector budget was accorded more importance, with several projects targeting smallholder farmers. The significance of channelling petroleum revenues to the agricultural sector shows that the government is indeed willing to use revenues from the extractive sector for social development. Still, the review identified inefficiencies in the appropriation of petroleum revenues and criticized the choice of priority sectors and projects (ACEP 2015b).

Beyond generational funds, certain other fiscal arrangements might wring greater economic growth, as well as stability and peace outcome benefits, from oil and gas resources (Ayensu 2013; Van Gyampo 2016). Specifically, production-sharing agreements established as components of governance regimes would result in significant societal and economic transformation within fifteen years, with resulting socioeconomic effects that could enable Ghana to meet its domestic requirements for oil and gas for the duration of the Jubilee field's production life, export the surplus, and invest the gains in the Heritage Fund. Assuming a price of $60 per barrel over the next fifteen years, Ghana would earn $2.56 billion per year – instead of the $800 million per year projected by the Ministry of Finance under its existing royalty tax system – which could then be reinvested into much-needed infrastructure, such as access to drinking water for every community, and development of all-weather roads, educational facilities, affordable rental accommodations, and expanded healthcare facilities. The government could then afford to reduce tax levels on all commodities, including petroleum products, the multiplier effects of which would be large, leading to a much-improved standard of living for Ghanaians (Kwawukume 2012).

Natural gas is another important part of Ghana's discovered hydrocarbon resources. The state-owned Ghana National Gas Company (Ghana Gas) is central to industry operations, while the Chinese company Sinopec is engaged in a construction phase, although there has been some controversy surrounding project delays (IMANI 2013a; B&FT 2014). Providing exploration and exploitation services in Ghana's gas fields, Sinopec International Petroleum Services is part of the Sinopec Group, the world's largest oil, gas, and petrochemical conglomerate, generating $344 billion in operating income, with a profit of over $12 billion in 2017 (Sinopec Group 2018). The government is looking to increase the use – and reliability – of natural gas by building gas plants in Ghana to supplement the gas that is delivered from Nigeria, and inviting foreign-owned enterprises to enter the field through public-private partnership agreements (interview, Third World Network, 4 March 2014).

It appears that the troubling trends in the oil industry, which impact sustainable economic growth, are also evident in the gas industry. Despite initial high expectations, community members from existing project areas have reported issues with the level of awareness and access to information, compensation payments, environmental pollution, and number of employment opportunities, with limited reprieve available through existing governance mechanisms (Sakyi et al. 2012). Ishmael Edjekumhene, executive director at the Kumasi Institute of Technology and Environment (KITE), recommended paying more attention to the environmental impact assessment (EIA) process for future projects, being more realistic about projects' expected benefits, paying outstanding capitalization to the Ghana National Gas Company to enable it to pay outstanding community compensation, and establishing a special program for small and medium-size enterprises to enable them to take advantage of developments in their communities (interview, KITE, 5 March 2014). Other observers have identified challenges faced by Ghana Gas, such as projects falling behind schedule and shifting deadlines. These are major problems, since the number of gas fields – and thus the potential for gas extraction – is large, and the delays are resulting in missed opportunities for increased investment and sustainable economic growth (interview, Third World Network, 4 March 2014).

Comprehensive laws, regulations, and policies have been a prominent feature in Ghana's efforts to regulate and manage hydrocarbon resources. However, the government's focus on oil and gas at the expense of other sectors, including agriculture, can be economically dangerous, since global prices for the former have fluctuated severely over recent years. In fact, the Ghanaian government largely continues to see both the mining and energy sectors as endless sources of revenue (interview, IMANI Center for Policy & Education, 4 March 2014). As a result, to quote Debrah and Graham, Ghana is facing an "intellectual Dutch disease" (2015). Moreover, the national government's ability to positively influence economic and social outputs by foreign-owned enterprises participating in these sectors has been limited.

Research Results: A Case of Progress with Challenges

Effective natural resource governance can present opportunities for lasting political stability in terms of poverty alleviation, improvements to human capacities and physical infrastructure, and sustainable pro-poor socio-economic development, if conducted appropriately and in collaboration with all relevant groups. Private sector–led engagement in resource extraction could further stimulate positive change. Indeed, the ideal role of the private sector in natural resource governance in a stable country such as Ghana is to support efforts to establish sustainable economic development and political stability. Its ability to do so, however, hinges on effective governance at both the national and local levels that works to influence and encourage this type of outcome.

However, according to interviews conducted for this research, there has been little meaningful improvement in the sustainable development of mining communities as a result of national structures, as the Ghanaian government has so far failed to induce most foreign mining companies to contribute to improving living standards in the communities where they

98 GOVERNANCE, CONFLICT, AND NATURAL RESOURCES IN AFRICA

operate. Efforts to do this by some companies have been taken mostly out of self-interest (interview, Kofi Annan International Peacekeeping Centre, 24 February 2014). While some boards and chief executive officers feel morally and ethically bound to provide tangential and direct benefits to local communities, whether through directly funded projects and opportunities or via value addition, it would not be such a stretch to assume that social consciousness is considered by most to be just another means for achieving financial salience (Galant and Cadez 2017; Pan et al. 2014; Asmeri, Alvionita, and Gunardi 2017).

Host nations must work to establish a policy and legislative systems that will ensure value addition, economic sustainability, adherence to environmental standards, and beneficiation at all levels of society. In the case of Ghana, while the country has made strides in the regulation and governance of natural resource sectors in this regard, the traditional implementation gap continues to plague the country's ability to leverage those resources, and the private-sector actors exploiting them, for long-term sustainable economic growth and development.

Impact on Regulation and Governance

According to recent World Bank indicators, Ghana "continues to show good performance on democratic governance, arising from a strong multi-party political system, growing media pluralism and strong civil society activism" (Osei-Assibey 2014, 522). It could be said that the country's relative political, social, and economic stability may be linked in some respect to natural resource extraction. After all, the mining sector contributes somewhat to employment, and the mining and energy sectors contribute to government revenue through royalties and taxes, as well as improved living standards of Ghanaians (Aryee 2001). In 2005, Yelpaala and Ali determined that the deregulation of the Ghanaian diamond industry and the increased extractive practices from foreign and locally owned companies would "lead to a relatively reduced environmental burden in Akwatia [a diamond-producing area] and more revenue for the GCDD [the Ghana Center for Democratic Development] to invest in the human development needs of communities in the town" (2005). Furthermore, while government policy has helped to drive improvements in income levels and standards of living for some mining communities, it has also resulted in negative environmental impacts (Darimani 2013). Notably, democracy appears to increase political space for the autonomy of organized private capital, its access to the government, and policy influence (Kraus 2002).

The issue of participation – integral to effective governance – is one with which Ghana is still struggling, with an imbalance of power existing between the government, foreign-owned enterprises, and communities. Considering that changes have occurred over time in Ghana, the institutional and administrative environment may improve in the short term. The Ghanaian government pays attention to civil society and is willing to respond in certain cases, given how these can sometimes affect public perception. As an example, a public dispute over the China Development Bank's strict credit requirements demonstrated that the Ghanaian government responds to high-profile situations (*VibeGhana* 2012).

Ghana has a long and strong tradition of civil society participation in policy formulation, including in the extractive sector. For example, the Ghana Civil Society Platform on Oil and Gas, comprising 120 organized groups, individuals, and professional bodies (Hanson, D'Alessandro, and Owusu 2014), has tried to mitigate negative socioeconomic and environmental impacts, and advocated for the increased participation of local communities and stakeholders in oil management and governance. A second example: in 2015, in collaboration with government institutions, the African Centre for Energy Policy (ACEP) launched the online platform OurOilMoney (www.ouroilmoney.org). The platform was designed to improve transparency and accountability of oil management through the participation of relevant stakeholders. Given that it provides open access to the most up-to-date information and data on oil exploitation, revenues, and projects, together with mobile-based access integrated with WhatsApp and other social media, OurOilMoney is a powerful tool for mobilizing public support for advocacy initiatives, and has the potential to leverage Ghana's policy efforts for environmental protection related to the extractive sector.

For the mining sector to play a greater role in facilitating poverty reduction, social development, economic transformation, and environmental protection, its "40-Year National Development Plan" must include the implementation of regulatory systems that address corruption and infrastructure issues, and facilitate integration among the natural resource sectors. For instance, while the 2011 Petroleum Revenue Management Act set in place some of the most extensive accountability and transparency rules seen thus far on the continent for this sector, as well as a regulation to prioritize local jobs in oil and gas projects (Okpanachi and Andrews 2012), these rules have yet to include full contract disclosure and do not, at this point, apply to Ghana's mining sector. The Act should be considered as an innovative legal instrument for hydrocarbon resource taxation, as it outlines clear mechanisms for collecting and distributing petroleum revenue. (Conversely, the country's mining sector, a traditional mineral sector that inherits and progressively improves on previously existing regulations, is less innovative than the more recently created petroleum industry. Indeed, the latter's regulations are built upon the most up-to-date international rules on oil and gas.)

That said, Ghana's burgeoning hydrocarbon extraction industry faces similar implementation challenges, and the focus on consumption instead of investments is a major concern. Exemplifying this trend, one interviewee, an IMANI member who was invited to join a government committee, resigned after realizing that monies were being channelled into consumption-related areas instead of critical investment areas as outlined in the Act (interview, IMANI Center for Policy & Education, 3 March 2014).

Since 2010, the Ghanaian government has been cooperating with developed countries in the area of natural resource management to improve various aspects of governance, including transparency and accountability (Asamoah 2012; Twerefou 2014). Drawing on the experience of Norway's Oil for Development program and its principles of good governance, Ghana is striving to ensure economically, socially, and environmentally responsible management of its petroleum resources. Twinning arrangements between public-sector institutions in Ghana and their sister institutions in Norway have promoted continuity, sustainability, and a holistic approach with emphasis on the principles of transparency, accountability, and anti-corruption (GHEITI 2012). Furthermore, Star Ghana, a funding mechanism for private-sector actors that promotes good governance and accountability, is successfully gathering funds from donors, specifically the Netherlands, United States, and United Kingdom.

Ghana: Hydrocarbon Resources

In recent years, the Ghanaian government has made significant progress in terms of policy making, contributing to a political economy that is anchored in laws and regulations, and focused on wealth creation. Nonetheless, Ghana's economy has suffered the consequences of loose fiscal policy, high budgets and debts, and current account deficits, suggesting that natural resource governance should be improved if it is to establish a meaningful scope of action for facilitating restructuring. In addition, the issue of elite-level politics, perhaps the hardest problem to address, may emerge as the most critical. There is considerable pressure inside administrations to obtain a share of natural resource revenues, which has consequences for political decision making that could undermine the establishment of a culture of good governance (interview, Third World Network, 4 March 2014).

Although a large part of budget funding from natural resource revenues is allocated to capital expenditure projects – specifically infrastructure, agriculture, and capacity-building projects – these initiatives have not always produced the expected outcomes. A smaller part of the budget is reserved for future generations in form of the short-term Ghana Stabilisation Fund, which cushions the impact of oil-price shortfalls, and the longer-term Ghana Heritage Fund, which can only be accessed beginning in 2025 and is modelled on a similar Norwegian fund. Both funds form part of the Petroleum Account at the Bank of Ghana. Data from June 2016 indicate that, five years into the commercial production of oil, the Ghana Stabilisation Fund has so far received approximately US$618 million, representing 19 per cent of oil revenue, but currently stands at about $191 million due to a prolonged period of low oil prices and a lowering of the fund's cap. The Ghana Heritage Fund has received approximately $256 million over the same period, representing about 8 per cent of oil revenue, and currently has a balance of $268 million (reportingoilandgas.org 2016). Even together, these figures are modest compared to Botswana's Pula Fund, which in April 2015 had $7 billion in assets under management (Raji 2016). The economic challenges that Ghana faces are related to gaps in governance implementation, of which both public and private actors in the mining and energy sectors are guilty.

Impact on Community Development

The role of the private sector in promoting sustainable economic growth and continuing political stability is not only to incorporate sustainable economic development principles into their mainstream operations, but also to "chaperone the activities of all their associated companies – suppliers, joint ventures, foundations, and others – to make sure that they fall in line with a benign sustainability agenda" (Asamoah 2012, 55). Conducting efforts in a sustainable manner means that economic operations must meet environmental and social sustainability requirements and norms, specifically those related to health, safety, and environmental, social, and ethical responsibilities. In addition to the three pillars of sustainability (economic, social, and environmental), a governance dimension should be added as a fourth pillar – supporting the others and maintaining a balance between them, in particularl by ensuring that the correct trade-offs are made in business decisions (Asamoah 2012). Even if this is done, however, the private sector's successful participation in this endeavour still hinges on effective governance at both the national and local levels, where formal governance structures and informal governance arrangements overlap.

Ghana's experience with investment has primarily been with individual private extractive companies, not other governments (interview, Kumasi Institute of Technology and Environment, 27 February 2014). In many cases, companies simply compensate communities for their land, especially when crops and property are involved. Under their overall legislation and governance structures, the government expects companies to engage in csr activities by providing choice amenities to communities, but companies insist that it is not their responsibility to develop communities, especially as they pay taxes to the government (interview, Department of Political Science, University of Ghana, 28 February 2014). Even so, in 2012, companies voluntarily contributed $26 million to community sustainable development projects, such as trust funds, and economic development and community empowerment programs, with spillover effects in transportation, hospitality, and other sectors (Aubynn, n.d.). For instance, sponsored by the Global Fund, the private extractive company AngloGold is now involved in malaria control efforts in one district (in-

Ghana: Hydrocarbon Resources

terview with villagers, Tarkwa mining area, 6 March 201; interview, Anglo-Gold Ashanti Ghana, 4 September 2015).

Given that some communities have yet to see any social projects realized by mining and oil companies operating in their region, the argument can be made that Ghana's governance system is characterized by inconsistent application in all parts of the country (interview with villagers, Tarkwa mining area, 7 March 2014). Moreover, the environmental consequences of some projects should be underlined, as well as possible responses developed by the communities. One observer regarded the Wassa Association of Communities Affected by Mining to be the "best answer" to the failures of the government on mining-related issues, given that it is single-handedly taking on the government on behalf of certain communities, such as those whose water sources have been polluted by mining activities (interview, Department of Political Science, University of Ghana, 28 February 2014).

As it stands, only a handful of companies have built programs – mostly concerned with public relations – so that they may conduct business in harmony with the adjacent communities, but only because it serves their own interests; they are not compelled by the government to do so (interview, Kofi Annan International Peacekeeping Centre, 24 February 2014). This points to a deep chasm in Ghana's governance system – and to its scope of action – which continues to motivate or compel foreign-owned enterprises away from contributing to sustainable economic growth and stability. As a result, standards of living in mining communities with large-scale extractive activities have improved only modestly. If Ghana expects to use its mineral wealth to facilitate broad-based community development, which in turn drives political stability, it must ensure that CSR is included in governance regimes, and enforce subsequent compliance by private-sector actors, thereby closing the policy and legislative implementation gap and creating a robust scope of action that will lead to meaningful restructuring (Garvin et al. 2009). Further, it must achieve this through the junctures and entry points of change delineated above, whereby governance can be strengthened so as to improve effectiveness and impact. How to ensure such compliance without precipitating the abandonment of Ghana by those same extractive firms, however, is a challenge.

In the context of legal and illegal artisanal and small-scale mining (ASM), these activities may be a by-product of jobs from private-sector investment in the natural resource sector failing to materialize. As Osei-Tutu (2012) observes, in Ghana's Western Region, regarded as the breadbasket of the country, farming and fishing have suffered due to lost access to land and sea following the establishment of oil rigs, pipelines, and storage facilities, as well as fishing restrictions. In an ironic twist, while it is illegal for fishermen to travel within a one-mile radius of rigs, the rigs' power lights attract fish, reducing their prevalence elsewhere and creating further problems for fishermen.

Impact on Local Content Policies

Local content policies aim to leverage extractive value chains to generate sustained and inclusive growth through economic diversification and employment opportunities (Kusi-Sarpong et al. 2014). Existing mining regulations establish local content requirements for the mining sector and focus on three main areas: employment and promotion of local labour forces, procurement of locally produced goods and services, and additional licensing and reporting requirements. They require mining companies to hire a minimum proportion of nationals, while the percentage of expatriates must be reduced progressively to a maximum of 6 per cent of the company's total workforce in the country. With the aim of promoting local knowledge, each mining company must submit a comprehensive five-year plan to the Minerals Commission, which details the replacement of expatriates with Ghanaians and sets out training program parameters. A five-year procurement plan must also be produced, showing that preference is being given to local materials, products, and service providers. Penalties for violating local content provisions are provided. Having said this, however, local content could be greater if the Ghanaian government became more involved in the operations of mining companies – for example, by becoming a shareholder (interview, Ghana Chamber of Mines, 3 September 2015).

Despite these recent regulations, Ghana's local content policies mostly remain generic, preventing the application of an effective scope of action

Ghana: Hydrocarbon Resources

that would help to reshape governance structures and modify the actions of foreign-owned private-sector actors. The creation of enclaves, as described by Hilson (2012), around foreign-owned mining operations, focused on exports of raw commodities, does very little for revenue generation at the community level. Additionally, existing policies have not taken into consideration the views of the private sector. Foreign-owned enterprises would likely be more willing participants in programming that encourages sustainable growth and stability if they were treated as economic partners by the Ghanaian government, rather than simply sources of revenue. One entry point or juncture would be to ensure that the roles of stakeholders, including the government, the private sector, community service organizations (CSOs), and donors, are better outlined in Ghana's local content policies (Esteves, Coyne, and Moreno 2013). An added issue relates to the high degree of corruption and lack of government oversight. In Ghana, corruption is an endemic concern in all aspects of governance, driving up the costs and insecurity of doing business in the country (BMI Research 2015). As such, challenges at the policy level must be addressed: "The challenges are in the adequacy of the measures and in how to go about implementation, monitoring, and measuring achievements. On one hand, success depends on the procurement decisions of the large mining firms, which dominate the Ghanaian industry, on how much local procurement decisions are in the discretion of individual firms, and on the capacity of local supply firms. On another hand, success depends on the clarity and deliberate directions of government policies as well as on complementary government-industry relationships. Successful local content strategy must create a framework for learning and adaptation and should involve both government and industry" (ACET 2014, 42–3).

When it comes to the hydrocarbon sector, government tenders are reserved for local companies (interview, Georgette Barnes Ltd, 1 August 2015) and good governance structures have been introduced. The Petroleum Commission Act, the Local Content and Local Participation in Petroleum Activities Policy Framework, and the Petroleum Regulations (LI 2204) facilitate policy implementation in the sector and provide a comprehensive legal framework for local content. As oil is considered the key resource for short-term economic growth and transformation, if managed well, considerable effort has been made to ensure that the country does not suffer from the supposed "resource curse" (Kopinski, Polus, and Tycholiz 2013).

The African Centre for Energy Policy has lauded Ghana for its hydrocarbon sector legislation, which will, in its opinion, foster greater transparency in the sector; but ACEP also identified faults, such as the continued absence of penalties for conflict of interest by public officials (Adam 2016). Ghana is one of the few African countries with a local content framework for its petroleum industry. The framework targets job creation and value addition through the use of local expertise, goods, services, and businesses to ensure the retention of benefits within Ghana over the longer term. Senoo and Armah (2015), however, find that the alignment of the legislative content with the intended outcomes, the social, economic, and political context, the leadership of the Petroleum Commission (which regulates and manages upstream petroleum activities and coordinates associated policies), and the level of stakeholder involvement, do not support effective implementation.

The local content framework found in these legislative arrangements puts the onus on the government to take the necessary steps to ensure that value addition is given priority by the private-sector actors operating in the country (Arthur and Arthur 2014). While the government oversees the implementation process, a Local Content Committee – comprised of public- and private-sector stakeholders from government ministries, agencies, and departments, NGOs, and operators, contractors, and subcontractors – coordinates and manages this process. The intent is to ensure a minimum 5 per cent equity for local petroleum licences, permits, and contract operators, and at least 10 per cent equity for local providers of supplies and services. This should ensure local private-sector participation (MEP 2013). The framework also stipulates that within 10 years of a project's inception, 90 per cent of the required services and supplies must be provided by Ghanaian individuals or companies (Asamoah 2012). The government's intent is to maximize value addition using local expertise, goods, and services, thereby creating jobs and allowing skills to be retained in the country.

According to the local content framework, every stakeholder (contractor, subcontractor, authority, etc.) involved in the oil-and-gas sector must have an Annual Local Content Plan (similar to the five-year plans for the mining sector) for its projects, activities, operations, and transactions. Such a document must be updated and reviewed every year. The government provides fiscal incentives and rewards to stakeholders who exceed the goals laid out in their plan. The framework also encourages and promotes the participation of women in the sector, but does not provide further details or measures.

While Kayizzi-Mugerwa and Anyanwu (2015) argue that extractive companies would benefit from using local suppliers, five constraints hamper the latter's ability to be hired: 1) inability to produce goods and services at the required level of quality, 2) lack of access to credit, 3) an inadequate regulatory and institutional environment, 4) lack of required skills, and 5) substandard infrastructure. Therefore, governance implementation challenges are not limited to the exercise of will, but are equally hamstrung by practical, real-world challenges.

One of the main goals of the PENRG framework is to build skills capacity through education, technology transfer, and research and development – thereby helping to build institutional and organizational capacity, and competitiveness, of local businesses and industries related to the petroleum sector (MEP 2013). To support the capacity-building dimension of the policy, the framework recommends the establishment of a dedicated Oil and Gas Business Development and Local Content Fund under the Ministry of Energy, which oversees education, training, research, and development. The framework also explains how the fund should be financed and maintained over time.

While a recent assessment found that Ghanaian local content has moved in the right direction in terms of establishing and improving local polices, the absence of precise directions for local content policy implementation and operationalization, as well as the lack of a sound business environment for policies to be properly implemented, have contributed to policy implementation gaps (AfCOP 2016). Specifically, local human capacity and technological competencies remain inadequate to ensure meaningful participation by local companies. Further, a lack of financial capacity penalizes companies and local investment by forcing local companies to take on loans with high interest rates, averaging 20–30 per cent. As Abor and Quartey point out, development of Ghanaian SMEs is constrained by "a number of factors, such as lack of access to appropriate technology; limited access to international markets, the existence of laws, regulations and rules that impede the development of the sector; weak institutional capacity; lack of management skills and training; and most importantly finance" (Abor and Quartey 2010).

An assessment by the African Capacity Building Foundation concluded that local content requirements can play a positive role in driving economic transformation if they are aligned with the national development strategy and supported by capacity development efforts. Recommended opportunities for effecting change include incentivizing the private sector to assist in the design and implementation of local content policies, building capacity to encourage local specialized companies to merge and apply for contracts in the oil-and-gas sector, and implementing capacity-building initiatives that target financial gaps, human capital deficits, and environmental problems. Importantly, the local content framework must enable policies to be adapted to current contexts, and to local and external changes over time.

Technical Training and Education

To help build individual capacity, some scholarships exist to assist Ghanaians who wish to study abroad to gain specific skills in the oil-and-gas sector, but they are not well targeted (interview, Natural Resource Governance Institute, 3 September 2015). Beyond academic degrees, external investments of $6 million have been used to develop the Jubilee Technical Training Centre (JTTC) at Takoradi Technical University, targeting intermediate technical skills (Takoradi Technical University 2016). The JTTC is the first vocational training polytechnic in West Africa and offers accredited courses in technical subjects such as instrumentation, process, mechanical engineering, and electrical engineering. In 2014, sixteen students were enrolled at the JTTC.[8] These initiatives are certainly positive, but the number of Ghanaians trained locally is too limited to make a real impact on increasing local capacities in the sector (Oxford Analytica 2014). Outside of the oil-and-gas sector, Ghana's postsecondary education system produces a high number of science, engineering, manufacturing, and construction graduates when compared to regional standards. Neverthe-

Ghana: Hydrocarbon Resources 109

less, although these figures answer the requirements of the labour market, graduate unemployment remained at only around 50 per cent in 2015 (BMI Research 2015).

An additional, ongoing weakness in the local content framework is the vagueness of its monitoring and evaluation requirements. Arguably, the Ghanaian government has not made any effort to hold the private sector accountable because there is no comprehensive plan for meeting targets, especially regarding the broader objectives of sustainable economic growth and stability. This gap creates the danger that local communities will become resentful and angry when extractive companies do not fulfill promises. The Petroleum Commission's monitoring reports are not required to be public and, as indicated by the Ghana EITI, most information on the Ghanaian extractive sector is not directly available to the public. A way to solve this problem would be for Ghana to choose to include local content disclosures in its EITI reports. Ghana could draw on lessons from EITI's innovative multi-stakeholder approaches (such as the Bayelsa Expenditure and Income Transparency Initiative in Nigeria's Bayelsa state) to develop partnerships for local content monitoring and reporting. Ultimately, Ghana sits in the middle of the spectrum in terms of local content. In the future, it will be essential to ensure local content regulations are adhered to, especially in upstream activities. Also important is the promotion of backward linkages in Ghana's mining and energy sectors, specifically the local impact of downstream refining, transport, distribution, and sales marketing and processes, as well as mid-stream/side-stream sector activities from a holistic perspective. Bloch and Owusu (2012) argue that rather than being an enclave activity, as it is widely perceived, gold mining is deeply linked to the Ghanaian economy and backward linkages can likely be strengthened through policies and support.

The issue of land requires special attention, with tenure insecurity being a considerable problem (Arthur 2012). People continue to sell their agricultural land for ASM, hoping that they will get more money that way. As a consequence, that land cannot be restored and reclaimed at a later stage (interview, UN University Institute for Natural Resources in Africa, 24 February 2014). Moreover, young people who were engaged in illegal ASM have been displaced following land disputes that have resulted in the establishment of large farms (interview, Third World Network, 4 March

2014). Local chiefs have argued strongly that the government must review its communications on the subject (interview, UN University Institute for Natural Resources in Africa, 24 February 2014). Outright land grabs by the Ghanaian government have been known to happen, too, with the local chiefs being unaware of whose family land they were selling off. Even though land is communally owned, the chiefs manage it on behalf of their communities. Investors often negotiate directly with the community leaders and traditional authorities, and then move straight into initiating projects on the ground (interview, Kumasi Institute of Technology and Environment, 27 February 2014). Mining requires permits, and chiefs are not allowed to give land for mining – but in some cases, chiefs have applied for permits to conduct mining themselves (interview, Ghana Chamber of Mines, 3 September 2015).

Impact on Beneficiation and Value Addition

Beneficiation and value addition can also help ensure that profits from the hydrocarbon and mineral sectors are maximized and utilized to benefit the stability and economic growth of the country as a whole. *Beneficiation* refers to any process, such as smelting, that helps extract the maximum value from a given raw material, while *value addition* refers to processes, such as special processing, manufacturing, or marketing, that increase a product's value. Together, they can stimulate industrialization, employment creation, and economic growth, when processes are conducted in-country to maximize local economic contributions. According to the Ghana Chamber of Mines, building a smelting plant for the West African region would be an asset for Ghana, making it a regional hub for copper production. Ghana is therefore considering the importation of raw copper from Zambia to produce copper electric cables (interview, Ghana Chamber of Mines, 3 September 2015).

Similarly, the Precious Minerals Marketing Commission, the official authority for gold, diamonds, and silver, had been building a large gold refinery in partnership with the Russian company Geo Professional Services Ltd (interview, Ministry of Lands and Natural Resources, 2 September 2015). The company's managers were later arrested and the company shut down due to the illegal use of local mining licences (Ghana News

Ghana: Hydrocarbon Resources

Agency 2017). Today, two gold refineries in Ghana – the Sahara Royal Gold Refinery and the Gold Coast Gold Refinery – are smelting and refining raw minerals. For Ghana, this has already attracted international investors, while helping to decrease illegal traffic in gold. Experts have noticed that value addition in gold and diamonds offers greater prospects than other minerals (Amoako-Tuffour, Aubynn, and Atta-Quayson 2015).

Beneficiation and value addition could certainly progress faster in Ghana, but the process is led by the Ministry of Land and Natural Resources, while the Ministry of Trade and Industry is not directly involved, limiting the impact of policies (interview, Ghana Chamber of Mines, 3 September 2015). Consequently, efforts to advance private-sector development do not take into consideration beneficiation and local content requirements (interview, Natural Resource Governance Institute, 3 September 2015). Nevertheless, Ghana is developing a comprehensive program on artisanal mining that addresses local content and beneficiation (interview, African Centre for Economic Transformation, 4 September 2015). The government has recommended that mineral beneficiation should be part of its "40-Year National Development Plan" for the country, launched in 2017. Considering the weight and strategic importance of the sector for the country, this is crucial; but according to the Ghana Chamber of Mines, the sector's role is not properly recognized in the development plan (interview, Ghana Chamber of Mines, 3 September 2015). In fact, neither the Ghana Industrial Policy nor the Industrial Sector Support Programme focus on optimizing the potential of minerals at all. This is unfortunate, given that the mining and hydrocarbon sectors are not labour-intensive. Stimulating local content and, in turn, resource-based industrialization and economic growth that involves agriculture, manufacturing, services, and tourism would increase employment and, ultimately, result in socioeconomic benefits such as poverty reduction and political stability.

Impact on the Hydrocarbon Sector

Before oil extraction began in 2010, the government held many consultative meetings with chiefs and affected community members to seek permission to use their lands and offshore catchment areas. At the Western

Region House of Chiefs, chiefs requested that 10 per cent of natural resource revenues be given to the Western Region, as the resources in question were found in that region. However, the government explained that natural resources belong to the state and are to be used for the betterment of the entire country. A number of public consultations in the region outlined what would happen during the production phase: companies entering the area, fishermen prohibited from sailing within a one-mile radius of the rigs, and the navy patrolling the sea. These discussions were held during the presidential elections of 2008, during which all political parties redrafted their manifestos to link their messages to the promise and potential of natural resources, a tactic that generated grand expectations about jobs, incomes, and infrastructure across the country.

Since those elections, government communication initiatives have failed to manage people's unrealistic expectations of the possibilities offered by oil-and-gas (interview, Kofi Annan International Peacekeeping Centre, 24 February 2014). Indeed, despite drafting the Right to Information Bill in 2002, the bill has not yet been passed into law and stakeholders have repeatedly raised the issue of a lack of communication and information flow from the state (interview, Kumasi Institute of Technology and Environment, 27 February 2014). In addition, the government has failed to raise awareness about the continued reliance on oil-driven growth at the expense of other sectors of the economy, such as agriculture. The government's emphasis on oil-driven prosperity has been detrimental to the agricultural sector, with Ghanaians leaving the sector to seek jobs in the energy industry (interview with Dr Elias Ayuk, UN University Institute for Natural Resources in Africa, 24 February 2014).

In parallel, when the Ghanaian government established its oil-and-gas sector, it had neither the capital nor the expertise to effectively establish legislative arrangements that could facilitate added value and local development, limiting its ability to create a scope of action from the outset of extraction. As a result, concessions in contracts were generous for those who were willing to risk the investment. Moreover, the imperative among political elites to win elections, together with structural inequalities between investors and the government, resulted in the negotiation of oil licences on terms favouring foreign-owned oil companies. Thus, longer-term planning decisions were deprioritized in favour of shorter-term gains

(Mohan and Asante 2015). Now that Ghana is a bona fide oil-producing country, the risk element has been significantly reduced. For the time being, few Ghanaian private-sector entities have the risk-taking capacity to partner with foreign companies in the energy sector, which has resulted in the interim solution to promote the Ghana National Petroleum Corporation (GNPC). One observer noted that almost half of the funds received between 2011 and 2014 – a critical infrastructure-building period – have been devoted to capacity building within the GNPC (interview, IMANI Center for Policy & Education, 4 March 2014).

Unfortunately, efforts by donors to improve governance, transparency, and accountability of both the Ghanaian government and private-sector actors are being duplicated, possibly establishing overlapping scopes of action when ushering in restructuring: the World Bank, Switzerland, Norway, the United States, and the United Kingdom all provide government-oriented support in Ghana, but have not coordinated their efforts. For example, the German Agency for International Cooperation (GIZ), the World Bank, and the United Kingdom provided $38 million to build institutional and human capacity in Ghana's natural resource sectors. Unfortunately, these funders had only put in place a roadmap, not a strategic plan, and this was insufficient to carry out effective capacity-building initiatives. The United States, on the other hand, brought in advisers to be attached to Ghanaian ministries to guide the development of natural resource governance. One observer suggested that as a result of these initiatives, Ghana's government institutions have become complacent after being given significant amounts of funding by donors (interview, GIZ, 26 August 2015).

Alongside oil-and-gas, the Ghanaian government has also committed to renewable energy development. The 1997 Energy Commission Act (Act 541) established the Energy Commission, which has overseen the regulation, management, development, and utilization of energy resources, specifically acting as the technical regulator of Ghana's electricity, natural gas, and renewable energy industries, and as an advisor to the government on energy matters. Notably, it introduced the Strategic National Energy Plan 2006–2020, which outlines Ghana's plan for sustainable energy production in a context of development-oriented policies (Arthur, Baidoo, and Antwi 2011; Gyamfi, Modjinou, and Djordjevic 2015). The 2011 Renewable Energy

Act (Act 832) established the country's renewable energy regime, which includes obligatory schemes and provisions such as feeding tariffs.

The regime seeks to create an enabling environment for investors through fiscal frameworks, and this has resulted in an oversubscription of interest in solar initiatives. Renewable energy – particularly solar options such as subsidized solar lanterns – offers the best decentralized approaches to electricity generation for communities that cannot currently be reached by grid extension. Ghana has already committed itself to the development and integration of renewable energy into its energy mix, with renewables currently accounting for more than 70 per cent of the whole through the use of biomass, mainly from wood fuels, and hydroelectric power, which generates approximately 70 per cent of Ghana's electricity. Hydroelectricity is a priority option, since it has additional benefits such as supporting river transport, fishing, agriculture, and irrigation. However, from a microeconomic perspective, the adoption of renewable energy has been hindered by the relatively high cost of certain products and the inability of end users to pay such fees. This has led to the introduction of grant facilities and loan schemes to offset risks for the private sector (interview, Department of Renewable Energy, Ministry of Energy and Petroleum, 4 March 2014).

Future Opportunities

Corporate Social Responsibility and Local Content

Governments have an obligation to their citizens to hold companies and, in particular, foreign-owned enterprises accountable to good corporate practices as defined through a governance-created scope of action in relation to a country's specific context and needs. Today, oil revenues do not always contribute to poverty alleviation and sustainable growth (interview, UN University Institute for Natural Resources in Africa, 24 February 2014). Because natural resources have the potential for promoting sustainable development, peace, and stability for broad segments of the population, given the right political balance, meaningful collaboration in resource governance is critical. The resource curse does not need to be the norm. Rather, as in Ghana, resource extraction can lead to economic growth and contribute to achieving a country's economic priorities – there are "resource blessings," after all. Of course, Ghana is by no means a perfect example, as corruption, mismanagement, and poor practices have been and continue to be a hindrance. Under a functional and effective natural resource governance system that encourages a sense of obligation to practice sustainable economic development, foreign-owned enterprises may affect growth through taxes, royalties, and so on. But transforming an economy fully and pulling people out of poverty can only happen when there is a critical effort to promote secondary industries that rely on or feed into the mining and hydrocarbon sectors to generate employment opportunities for communities and revenues for the country.

Foreign-owned enterprises have a responsibility to contribute to the national well-being of resource-rich countries. Indeed, emergent literature argues that private-sector actors, especially mining companies, are becoming key partners and leaders in promoting and facilitating development, often assuming this responsibility from ill-equipped government or traditional donors (Black and O'Bright 2016; Ite 2005).

To the contrary, mining companies and certain observers have argued that it is the responsibility of the Ghanaian government, not the private extractive sector, to invest in and improve the livelihoods of communities through sustainable economic growth. Arguably, the government should be assigning royalty revenues for community development, but this is currently lacking. Royalties that are routed back to communities are usually channelled to community leaders, district chiefs, or local chiefs, who use such monies for private expenditures and not necessarily for the benefit of their communities. To increase oversight, linkages, and integration, mining companies should also get a say in how the government assigns royalties. For instance, the mining sector could have a positive and direct effect on building individual human capacity. Indeed, research findings by the African Development Bank show that new revenues from the extractive sector in Ghana could close up much of the funding gap in the country's education sector (Toigo 2015).

Thanks to improved legislation and governance, all Ghanaian mining companies now have CSR agreements, outlining community-driven sustainable development projects in regard to employment, infrastructure, protection of natural resources, and cultural heritage. Gold-mining companies are involved in public-private partnerships and multi-stakeholder initiatives that include community representatives, NGOs, traditional authorities, political leaders, and youth (ACET 2014). But these arrangements remain weak and should not be left to mining companies alone (Andrews 2016). The social and economic activities produced under these agreements should be aligned with broad national development plans as much as possible. Hoping to transform the CSR landscape, the Ghanaian government is currently preparing a CSR policy that challenges, but does not compel, companies to respond to these imperatives (MTI 2014), but currently the policy does not have any legal power (interview, Ministry of Energy and Petroleum, 3 March 2014). CSR is important, but it is crucial to move from voluntary to mandatory initiatives to make companies more accountable.

Given its generous fiscal and other incentives for the mining sector, the government has come under increased scrutiny to institute sustainable resource management policies – the institutionalization of a scope of action. To promote accountable business practices at both the national and local levels, and to maintain stable relations between community members and the private sector, the Ghanaian government must effect change. It can do this by signing more advantageous contracts and engaging in tough negotiations to ensure social and human security, and compliance with progressive environmental laws to protect communities from unforeseen circumstances. The government must also demonstrate to communities that Accra will stand up for them when corporations, foreign or local, break the law. Calls for reform in this regard have come amid unacceptable socioeconomic and environmental impacts linked to mining companies' operations, such as high poverty rates and loss of land in ASM communities (Hilson 2002). In this vein, some observers have suggested establishing a Mining Common Fund to support and develop mining-affected areas, putting in place inclusive planning and decision-making structures, and introducing a sound mining policy framework (Boon and Ababio 2009).

Stakeholders have also discussed the possibility of developing CSR guidelines for Ghana as a whole (interview, Kumasi Institute of Technology and Environment, 27 February 2014). One observer argued that the government should make a conscious effort to communicate how oil revenues are being used to implement development initiatives and to limit Ghana's borrowing dependency (interview, Department of Political Science, University of Ghana, 28 February 2014). The approach would help generate information about local content, beneficiation, and value-addition potential, provide options for sustainable development, and reveal why resources and development activities are not producing the expected outcomes. In addition, it would place further pressure, from a governance perspective, on foreign-owned enterprises to contribute more readily to these outcomes. It is important to identify and address binding constraints on both sectors, specifically within their value chains. Importantly, limiting negative socioeconomic and environmental impacts requires that all stakeholders embrace the responsibility to enforce human rights standards (Owusu-Koranteng 2005), gender diversity (Osei-Assibey 2014), and labour and environmental norms and standards.

In light of the fact that private-sector actors are the drivers of economic activity and development in developing countries, Asamoah (2012) states that local content policies, in conjunction with stronger CSR frameworks for external private-sector actors, particularly foreign-owned ones, typically include the development of local skills, technology transfer, employment of local workers, and local manufacturing in the aim of building a skilled labour force that can compete as a supplier base. Local content policies that promote capacity building, spur the creation of small and medium-size enterprises (SMEs), and promote local products and services, help to provide jobs to local populations and retain wealth within the country. They also generate opportunities for regional integration and trade, thereby gradually reducing dependence on external aid. Barriers to local content development can include lack of infrastructure, inefficient business licensing, pre-qualification and certification procedures, skill shortages and strict regulations on labour migration, and a lack of access to credit, all of which increase costs for local enterprises. In this vein, the Ghanaian government has introduced local content policies for both the mining and energy sectors – but more could be done.

Georgette Barnes Ltd (GBL) provides an example of local content in the Ghanaian mining context and more widely in West Africa. GBL is a drilling supply company created in Accra in 2009 by its CEO, Georgette Barnes Sakyi-Addo, and currently operating in West Africa. GBL supplies drilling muds and consumables to the exploration industry. These are industry-specific products that cannot be used for other purposes, and such locally owned businesses have great value in promoting local content. This leads to increased beneficiation, as Ghanaians learn procedures and develop skills while experimenting with progressive business practices. In sum, as a juncture or entry point, local content adds considerably to the mining industry in terms of training. It also generates employment and income. According to Sakyi-Addo, local content should be supported by the private sector, including foreign-owned companies. The government needs to empower local mining supply companies like GBL and compel foreign-owned mining companies to source their products from them, even at a premium cost, rather than directly from the global market.

The poor state of infrastructure – an obstacle to investment in the country – will likely be at the core of the Ghanaian government's Long-Term National Development Plan for Ghana (2018–57) (Abubakari, Asamoah, and Agyemang 2018). As part of its strategic drive toward industrialization, the government is looking to ensure that the country's energy requirements are met by 2018 (interview, Ministry of Trade, 2 September 2015). In regard to the Ghana Infrastructure Fund's board, opening up the membership to include the private sector would help to increase infrastructure financing, as companies appear unwilling to invest when they have no say in project management.

The World Bank has acknowledged in interviews that Ghana's laws are very positive, but underlined the lack of implementation. Overall, Ghana's security and political stability provide a safe environment for investment, but institutional reforms are deeply needed. Given this situation, the diversification of commodities would be beneficial (interview, World Bank, 1 September 2015). Improvements should also be made by other actors, including international agencies – for instance, the International Finance Corporation (IFC) should revisit its Environmental, Health, and Safety Guidelines to enhance the level of protection in offshore deepwater oil-and-gas exploration (CAO 2010; IFC 2015).

Development outcomes depend largely on how national and local government actors in resource-rich countries manage their relations with the private sector, especially foreign-owned enterprises. The private sector has the potential to be the primary engine of growth in stable, resource-rich

Ghana: Hydrocarbon Resources

African democracies. However, this can only be fulfilled by imposing strong, coherent, and strategic national and local governance structures that clearly define the role of foreign-owned enterprises in facilitating sustainable economic growth, peace, and stability, and outline their responsibilities to all stakeholders, including mining communities.

Overall, the Ghanaian government has been working to promote peace and social cohesion in resource-rich communities by respecting local beliefs, attempting to produce clear communication strategies, and creating incentives for the private sector to act in a socially responsible manner. However, policy implementation gaps remain an issue. Much more time should be spent on identifying gaps in policies and regulations, and initiating actions to remedy the problems. A larger issue, here, is simply the lack of political will (interview, Kofi Annan International Peacekeeping Centre, 24 February 2014; interview, UN University Institute for Natural Resources in Africa, 24 February 2014).

In this context, it is also critical to consider implementing new ideas from the bottom up, drawing on the expertise of on-the-ground experts in Ghana, specifically in regard to advocacy, community participation in decision making, and monitoring frameworks (Owusu-Koranteng 2013). Importantly, community service organizations (CSOs) lack the necessary substantial support, specifically in terms of resources and technical knowledge, to participate effectively in natural resource governance. One promising avenue is that donors identify credible local NGOs and CSOs, design working documents collaboratively, discuss concepts and ideas, and then implement them. Such collaboration could begin as a pilot program and then be scaled up (interview, GIZ, 27 August 2015). Within civil society, top-down and bottom-up strategies could be proposed by community groups and research institutions. CSOs and NGOs should have a greater voice in governance so that such strategies can receive more attention.

Conclusion

When it comes to Ghana's performance in both the mining and hydrocarbon sectors, the national government could improve efforts to turn natural resource revenues into sustainable economic growth, human development, and political stability through management of resources and institutional processes, channelling funds to regions and various actors, and transferring funds into other forms of capital that are measurable assets to help build human capacity. Moreover, beyond looking at extractive revenues nationwide, Accra should create evaluation tools to assess, every year, the impacts and shortfalls of its various initiatives and efforts. Specifically, when considering its initiatives, the government needs to evaluate their effectiveness and analyze whether they are meeting national priorities in line with national strategies. This is crucial, given the mounting evidence that initiatives have not been effective and priorities are not being met (see, for instance, IMANI 2013b). At the moment, political parties introduce their own manifestos and objectives, and use these as benchmarks for deciding how to channel resources.

Another major problem in Ghana – one that negatively affects priority spending by government on established national issues – is that public-sector expenditures are very high. An unsustainable percentage of government revenue is spent on salaries in line with increased revenues from oil, while reform efforts have slowed down despite ongoing development challenges and high internal and external unpaid debts (IMANI Ghana 2012). For example, the IMANI Center for Policy & Education (2010a) advocated unsuccessfully against the introduction of the Single Spine Pay Policy in 2010, arguing that it ignores the economic situation and simply rewards employees according to their level of education. Channelling money into salaries also facilitates consumption rather than investment in much-needed human capacity building and infrastructure. Further, there is low capacity for revenue collection. While corruption and lack of transparency in contracts can be problematic, the government is failing to collect revenue, and foreign-owned enterprises are taking advantage of loopholes and leakages in the revenue collection system; both of these developments are reducing revenue and need to be addressed at the national and local levels (interview, United Nations University Institute of Natural Resources in Africa, 24 February 2014). The government's contracts with foreign oil companies need to be publicized, and Accra should prevent further secrecy in contracts, opaque revenue payments, and any increase in spending when it enters into negotiations with foreign partners (Asamoah 2013b). Moving forward, and drawing on examples from other

Ghana: Hydrocarbon Resources

countries, research should be initiated to determine the effectiveness, to date, of decentralization and CSOs in Ghana.[9]

Decentralization should be evaluated in terms of the legal/political structure, expenditure responsibilities, and revenue access (Dafflon and Madiès 2013). Given how much power the government has in policy enforcement, it may be difficult to measure the performance of CSOs in terms of policy implementation. However, CSO performance could be categorized into various levels, such as contribution to knowledge generation and contribution of relevant resources during the deliberative and analytical stages of policy formation. Looking at the process, and at the outcomes of law and policy implementation with the findings in mind, could be fruitful (interview, Kumasi Institute of Technology and Environment, 27 February 2014). At the same time, some CSOs, such as the Wassa Association of Communities Affected by Mining, focus on how Indigenous populations relate to mining companies and promote human rights education and advocacy. Their contributions should also be noted and evaluated at the outset.

Even in a politically stable country such as Ghana, foreign-owned enterprises initiate conflicts in the natural resource sector; these should be addressed by including the people who live in the affected communities in creating a solution. Issues such as conducting EIAs and paying adequate compensation to community members, when necessary, will be important. The government must remain vigilant when holding private-sector actors to account with regard to adhering to existing governance protocols and ensuring the quality of their interactions with communities. Issues around Free Prior Informed Consent Protocols need to be examined closely to assess whether or not private-sector actors are continually and adequately informing and securing the consent of resource-rich local communities for their investments and extractive activities. Equally important, government needs to assess to what extent these actors support the goals of the Political Economy of Natural Resource Governance framework – namely sustainable economic growth in social, economic, and environmental terms.

NGO observers recommend establishing guidelines, based on community size, to regulate interactions between those communities and the public and private sectors, as well as which representatives are to be involved in such interactions. This must be done to ensure genuine exchange with a relevant sample size within each community (interview, Kumasi Institute of Technology and Environment, 27 February 2014). This issue of participation – which is at the centre of the new concepts presented here – should be emphasized by the Ghanaian authorities to ensure that the impact of governance in the natural resources sphere are strong and positive.

Funding of social projects and activities at the local community level, coupled with mechanisms to ensure that resource revenues are channelled to nationwide social and economic initiatives, are critically important for establishing a positive corporate reputation, and creating elevated brand recognition and opportunities to boost sales. To date, mining companies have failed to recognize that CSR essentially points to their role as development partners rather than profit-making strategies, or that their mining activities may positively or negatively affect the environment, society, and economy.

The ideal role of the private sector in natural resource governance in a stable country such as Ghana is to support efforts to establish sustainable economic development and political stability. However, Ghana falls short on many aspects, including the provision of a strong Political Economy of Natural Resource Governance framework that promotes sustainable, broad-based development.

CHAPTER 4

Sierra Leone: From Blood Minerals to Development Minerals?

Introduction

With a population of approximately six million, Sierra Leone remains one of the world's poorest countries in the world, ranking 181/188 on the UNDP's 2019 Human Development Index (UNDP 2019). Decades of economic decline – massive inflation climbed dramatically from 1.9 per cent in 1967 to 14.7 in 1983, with annual GDP growth declining from 3.7 to 1.9 per cent by 1983 – along with more than ten years of civil war have had a dramatic negative impact on the economy. More than half the population lives below the $1.90-per-day international poverty line, earning less than $1.25 per day (Luke and Riley 1989, 141; UNICEF 2013b; Davies 2003).

Following independence in 1961, Sierra Leone soon fell under the authoritarian rule of Siaka Stevens. As its first president from 1971 to 1985, Stevens, having already served as prime minister from 1967 to 1971, increased his authority by transferring parliamentary rule to a presidential republic (Chege 2002). Today, Sierra Leone's struggle to rebuild its democratic political system contrasts sharply with the two other case studies. Themnér and Sjöstedt (2020) discuss the challenges of creating a democratic regime under what they describe as "warlord democrats." As such, the governance risk for investment remains high, mostly due to the lack of legislative process and, more importantly, the limited transparency of avenues for corporations to influence the political sphere.

While the country experienced moderate per capita GDP growth of 2.5 per cent between 1961 and 1970, the global oil crisis, combined with a negative balance of payments and rising inflation, resulted in a reversal of fortunes. At the time of Stevens's retirement, Sierra Leone's economy was in unstoppable decline. The Sierra Leonean civil war would begin in 1991, as an insurgent army, the Revolutionary United Front (RUF), initiated an uprising against the ruling government of Joseph Saidu Momoh, Stevens's successor as president.

Illicit Mining

Under Stevens's rule, mining rights were used as a strategic tool to ensure the loyalty of supporters. The Stevens presidency also saw the formation of illicit, armed diamond-mining groups, comprised mostly of unemployed youths, which served as "presidential forces" and intimidated political opponents as deemed necessary (Reno 2003). The diamond-mining industry, the country's most important economic driver, peaked between 1960 and 1970, a period when only about half of the country's diamond output was exported legally (Smillie, Gberie, and Hazleton 2000).

The Stevens autocracy led to the emergence of the Revolutionary United Front. Led by Foday Sankoh, the RUF was a loosely organized rebel group supported by several external actors, including the former Liberian president, Charles Taylor. In supporting the RUF, Taylor aimed to overthrow the All People's Congress government – the APC was Stevens' political party – and gain control of the country's diamond-producing regions (Lancaster 2007). Throughout the 1980s, continued economic troubles, including a highly overvalued domestic currency, fuelled illegality within the mineral sector. During this time, state licensing of private diamond exports generated a payoff system between Stevens's government and traders with foreign connections (Chege 2002). Indeed, widespread corruption and economic mismanagement, which reduced the government's ability to deliver social services, provide access to basic necessities, and create jobs, were the key triggers for the civil war (Gberie 2005). Since 1985, which saw the covert sale by the incoming Momoh government of mineral prospecting rights to its supporters, there has been even less regulation of the diamond industry, with government revenues consequently declining even more, and a deepening of the economic crisis (Davies 2003).

The civil war – a particularly violent conflict which saw the widespread use of child soldiers (Richard 1996; Hoffman 2011) and much political turbulence – resulted in the deaths of an estimated 70,000 people and the

Sierra Leone: Blood Minerals

displacement of approximately 2.6 million (approximately half of the population). Following the war's end, in January 2002, general elections were held (Kaldor and Vincent 2006). Under the leadership of Ahmad Tejan Kabbah, the Sierra Leone People's Party (SLPP) won a landslide victory, taking 83 of the parliament's 112 seats (African Elections Database 2012). While the SLPP government was credited for its efforts to end the country's civil war, it was also blamed for widespread corruption and economic mismanagement, particularly in the mineral and mining sector. Disappointment with the state once again became widespread, with concerns raised about the viability of sustained peace. Ernest Bai Koroma of the APC, a businessman turned politician, narrowly won the 2007 general election with a slight majority in parliament, his party securing 59 seats out of 112, compared to the SLPP's 43 (African Elections Database 2012). Despite widespread remobilization of former combatants as political tools, security was maintained in the country during the elections (Christensen and Utas 2008).

The period of APC rule was characterized by a dynamic increase in economic growth and transformation marked by a reduction in poverty and a shift to a market economy, which brought widespread support for Koroma. These changes were made possible by restoring relations with the International Monetary Fund (IMF) and other international donors, which led to a resumption of development assistance and increased technical support. This occurred despite the government's problems in satisfying donor and IMF conditionalities, especially in terms of enacting governance and macroeconomic reforms based on free-market principles such as moving toward a strong investment climate and limiting the government's economic role (Bertelsmann Stiftung 2014). The government instituted a new FDI policy, particularly in the mineral, hydrocarbon, and agricultural sectors, which emphasized these sectors and promoted the country as a stable investment destination relative to other, more conflict-prone states in the region (Bertelsmann Stiftung 2014). Sierra Leone's economic reforms advanced despite the bitter rivalry between Koroma's APC and the SLPP. Owing to the rise in his personal popularity and his party's standing among the electorate, Koroma consolidated his grip on power by winning re-election in 2012, the APC obtaining 69 seats against the SLPP's 42 (Suffragio 2012).

The Quest for an Inclusive Economic Transformation from Mining Extraction

Although post-conflict Sierra Leone has not yet been able to convert its natural resources into sustained economic growth and development, effective governance of its natural resources presents an opportunity for positive change – as it did with Ghana – and lasting peace and stability. With respect to natural resource extraction, foreign-owned enterprises can play an important role in facilitating and contributing to post-conflict reconstruction, economic transformation, and socioeconomic development, and in enhancing governance capacity.

Starting in 2003, the Government of Sierra Leone embarked on its first post-conflict development program, Sierra Leone Vision 2025. It established an ambitious long-term framework for post-conflict reconstruction efforts aimed at sustained economic growth and human development within the context of a peaceful political landscape and stable macroeconomic environment. In so doing, the government established a link between economic growth and private-sector actors, and acknowledged the need for a robust scope of action (UNIPSIL 2003). From a consultation process, strategic areas of focus were developed in concert with all relevant stakeholders (including the private sector and foreign-owned enterprises); these were meant to constitute the building blocks for future government policies. Having laid the foundations with its Poverty Reduction Strategy Papers I (2003–07) and II (2008–12), which, together with the 2002 National Recovery Strategy, focused on promoting post-conflict economic resilience, human rights, and service provision, in 2013 the government embarked on the country's next five-year economic transformation program.[1] PRSP III (2013–18), popularly referred to as the "Agenda for Prosperity," established clear goals and targets for the period, as well as an overall goal of obtaining middle-income status by 2035.

The Agenda for Prosperity consists of eight central pillars: 1) diversified economic growth, 2) management of natural resources, 3) accelerating human development, 4) international competitiveness, 5) labour and employment, 6) social protections, 7) governance and public-sector reform, and 8) gender and women's empowerment (Sierra Leone 2013). Integral to achieving the Agenda's goals is a rapid growth in mineral production

Sierra Leone: Blood Minerals

and exports, to be led by the private sector, in order to meet high global demand and garner favourable prices for the country's precious minerals. The National Minerals Agency (NMA), established in 2012, is expected to take the lead in applying strategies aimed at maximizing the benefits accrued from mineral resource exploitation while minimizing the negative social, political, and environmental effects – in effect, actualizing and operationalizing Vision 2025 within the mining sector.

In terms of promoting diversified economic growth, the government has acknowledged that while mining activities are vital to the country's reconstruction efforts and poverty reduction strategies, as are commodity exports, these alone will not fuel economic growth indefinitely, particularly if governance efforts are unable to manage private-sector activities. The country would need to diversify (Sierra Leone 2013). Therefore, the government aims to promote small-scale, large-scale, subsistence, and cash crop agriculture, as well as develop the tourism and manufacturing sectors. Efforts to date have included providing a wider range of financial services to small entrepreneurs, improving infrastructure, and increasing the participation of women in the economy (Sierra Leone 2013).

Economic indicators for Sierra Leone are promising. Since the end of the civil war, Sierra Leone has experienced one of the highest GDP growth rates in West Africa, including growth of more than 7 per cent between 2004 and 2007, stable growth of 5.5 and 4 per cent in 2008 and 2009, respectively, and growth of 15.2 per cent in 2012, 16.3 per cent in 2013, and 13.8 per cent in 2014 (World Bank, n.d.[f]; AfDB et al. 2014). The country's GDP increased from $635.9 million in 2000 to $4.1 billion in 2013, but slid to $3.6 billion by 2016. Today, GDP growth is stabilized at around 6 per cent (World Bank, n.d.[f]). Gross national savings as a percentage of GDP increased from -7.5 per cent in 1999 to 13 per cent in 2012 but have yet to reach the country's prewar levels of over 15 per cent (World Bank, n.d.[f]; 2011; 2015). Gross national income per capita increased as well, from $150 in 2000 to $660 in 2013 (World Bank, n.d.[f]).

Yet, despite these successes, Sierra Leone's Human Development Index valuation of 0.420 in 2014 – a slight increase from 0.336 in 2011 – remained below the sub-Saharan regional average of 0.502 (UNDP 2014). Challenges include continued socioeconomic marginalization of youth, economic mismanagement, and stagnation of government performance in various areas, including control of corruption (Kaufmann, Kraay, and Mastruzzi 2007). This suggests that the country's relatively strong economic performance over the past decade has failed to meaningfully improve the livelihoods of Sierra Leoneans, at least in the context of sustainable development – a key factor outlined in the Political Economy of Natural Resource Governance (PENRG) framework. The country appears to be a victim of the resource curse – unable to develop adequate governance structures that would enable it to benefit from the wealth of its natural resources and having failed either to restructure or manage the actions of the private sector with regard to natural resource extraction.

Evidently, the capture of mineral rents has helped the Government of Sierra Leone to operate, but the informalization of the mining sector, coupled with the lingering effects of the civil war, have hampered expansion of the private sector (an engine of economic growth) in the extractive industries – and thus, too, the sector's ability to contribute to sustainable growth, economic transformation, and post-conflict reconstruction. Stalled development aside, sociopolitical relations in Sierra Leone, in the form of free and fair democratic elections and new development programs since 2002, have greatly improved in spite of the sordid legacy of more than a decade of armed conflict (Berghs 2012). The removal of administrative barriers is a further attempt by the government to attract foreign investment, particularly in the natural resource, agricultural, manufacturing, and tourism sectors (Sierra Leone 2013). However, while attempts have been made to make it easier to conduct business in the country – elevating Sierra Leone's position on the World Bank's "Doing Business Index" to 141 (out of 183 countries) in 2012 from 160 in 2008 – these advances have been short-lived, with the country downgraded back to 160th place in 2017 (World Bank, n.d.[b]).

Overall, the political landscape continues to be a challenge for foreign-owned enterprises. Sierra Leone's potential to develop socially and economically is inexorably tied not only to political stability but to its ability to govern its natural resources in such a way as to encourage the involvement of foreign-owned enterprises in ongoing peacebuilding and reconstruction efforts.

Role of the Private Sector in Peacebuilding and Reconstruction Efforts

Since the end of the civil war, Sierra Leone's government has made progress in removing administrative obstacles in an attempt to attract foreign investment. This is reflected in the country making the "Doing Business Index" list of top-ten business reformers for 2010–11 (World Bank, n.d.[b]).

Much work remains to be done, however, in the post-conflict environment to eliminate obstacles that seriously hamper both the level of investment that can be leveraged from foreign-owned enterprises and the country's long-term economic stability. Obstacles that continue to deter foreign investors include a severe shortage of skilled workers and managers, rampant corruption, minimal infrastructure, cumbersome customs procedures, a weak judiciary, the absence of an effective land titles system, and an underdeveloped banking system (Collier and Duponchel 2013), not to mention a nationwide lack of electricity and telecommunications infrastructure, and a poor national water supply (US Embassy, Freetown 2011). Another problem arises when corporations that operate and invest in Sierra Leone do not live up to their potential. According to civil society reports, many foreign-owned enterprises neither engage with civil society nor contribute to ongoing conflict resolution efforts that could foster mutual trust and social capital among workers in the communities in which they operate (CIVICUS 2006). Tax revenue from mining activities in particular has the potential to strengthen the government's ability to provide services, but could lead to dependency on the mining industry at the expense of growth in other sectors. On the domestic front, a lack of infrastructure (road, rail, electricity, and water systems), inadequate capital reserves and access to credit, and a lack of capacity necessary for tapping into investment opportunities all hamper private-sector investment.

Efforts to improve the investment climate should focus on political stability, prudent fiscal discipline, greater personal security, and liberalization of the economy. These goals should be pursued alongside macroeconomic reforms that impose greater transparency and accountability on public servants and foreign-owned companies. Such reforms are needed to ensure proper governance procedures as well as post-conflict reconstruction –

which, altogether, are integral to the successful management of Sierra Leone's economy. In light of Sierra Leone's politically fragile and economically vulnerable state, the need exists for external financial and technical support, including from private-sector actors, to sustain peacebuilding and reconstruction efforts. To answer the IMF conditionalities, the Koroma government launched a national program to privatize many state-owned enterprises; this measure may well serve to spur private sector development (Bertelsmann Stiftung 2018). The process represents a cornerstone of the government's strategy for national development, which will lighten the burden on government finances while stimulating the economy and creating jobs. However, any effort at resource governance must link liberalization and investor-friendly policies with corporate social responsibility so as to encourage local beneficiation and value addition, domestic retention of revenues, localized development, and environmental sustainability (Campbell 2012).

Interviews with key policy makers, donor community members, and private-sector actors, conducted between March and April 2014, underlined the challenges the government faces in mobilizing international and domestic private-sector resources to promote sustainable, broad-based growth and poverty reduction. The necessary measures include:

- Strengthening domestic resource mobilization and absorption capacity with regard to foreign direct investment (FDI), remittances, and development assistance. Specifically, the government needs to address issues pertaining to the capture, retention, and effective use of national savings through tax revenues, investment by foreign-owned enterprises in local economies, and higher tax revenues from the mining sector.
- Boosting capital inflows, especially from the mining sector, and ensuring that this revenue yields economic transformation, post-conflict reconstruction, and developmental impacts, particularly in the areas of value addition, beneficiation, and the provision of decent work comprising safe working conditions and appropriate levels of payment.
- Strengthening aid effectiveness and promoting trade and market access for actors within the domestic private sector.

Sierra Leone: Blood Minerals

- Instituting steps to manage debt in an efficient and effective manner.

These challenges are linked to Sierra Leone's continued dependence on government and international institutional development assistance for its reconstruction agenda – and are the reasons behind the government's emphasis on promoting FDI and private-sector development. In 2012, approximately 44 per cent of the estimated $1.92 billion required for implementing PRSP II was sourced from donors via budgetary support and other developmental assistance initiatives (Sierra Leone 2009a). This continued reliance on development assistance for budgetary support constitutes a risk for Sierra Leone, as the country cannot depend on donors given the unpredictability associated with multilateral development cooperation, donor fatigue, and changes in donors' bilateral policies and agendas (Kanyako 2016). In this climate of uncertainty, opportunities exist for foreign-owned enterprises to play an active role as partners in sustainable development, economic transformation, and reconstruction. Using public-private partnerships, for example, the Government of Sierra Leone has been looking at setting up a public-sector-mandated unit charged with vetting some $1.7 billion in unsolicited private-sector proposals (IMC Worldwide 2016).

Opportunities to expand the role of foreign investors and the domestic private sector are largely hindered by weaknesses and inaction at the governmental level due to limited financial resources and slow implementation of policies aimed at stamping out corruption. Legislation crafted to attract foreign investment, as well as measures such as the national privatization program, are designed to promote private-sector involvement, but don't go far enough to address current challenges, such as skilled worker shortages, insufficiently developed institutions and infrastructure, inadequate capital reserves and access to credit, and continued dependence on development assistance (Kargbo and Adamu 2009; Johnson 2011). Concrete policy options would help to improve natural resource governance in a way that increases the ability of foreign-owned enterprises to drive broad-based sustainable development, peace, and stability.

Sierra Leone's Mining Sector

Conflict and Security

Diamonds helped perpetuate decades of turmoil, civil unrest, smuggling, conflict, corruption, and environmental degradation in Sierra Leone. Although Collier (2000) did not factor diamonds into the econometric analysis that informed his "resource curse" argument, other scholars such as Lujala, Gleditsch, and Gilmore (2005) contend that there is a direct link between diamonds and violent conflict. They also indicate that the mining of primary diamonds (particularly kimberlite, most common in South Africa and Botswana) has had a smaller impact on the onset and prevalence of violent conflict, as primary diamonds are usually linked to more stable state systems and institutional support from government and private-sector actors. Le Billon (2001) presents a typology on the political economy of natural resources and specific types of conflict, suggesting that

> a point resource may be more easily monopolised than a diffuse resource, but that its desirability usually makes it vulnerable to contestation and often depends on international recognition for mobilising investors, hence the likelihood of coup d'état or secession as a function of relative proximity. Rewards from resource control are maximised by insurgents when resources are easily accessible and marketable and sufficiently valuable, such as distant diffuse resources, hence the association with warlordism. Finally, proximate diffuse resources involving large number of producers would be more likely to lead to rebellion or rioting in nearby centres of power. (2001, 572–3)

The author also suggested that resource rents in dependent countries are the ultimate prize for achieving political control, sparking violent attempts at overthrowing existing regimes, as in the case of Charles Taylor in Liberia. Undoubtedly, resources can equally exacerbate greed among political elites (574). Finally, Le Billon argues that resources can promote secession conflicts, motivating regions rich in natural resources to split from the larger geopolitical entity (574). Secondary diamonds, such as alluvial diamonds, play a significant role in the occurrence of certain types of civil war, such as the one that beset Sierra Leone (Lujala, Gleditsch, and Gilmore 2005). They are easy for ordinary people and militias to retrieve and sell for purposes of acquiring arms, fuelling violent conflict.

However, according to one interviewee, a lesser known cause of Sierra Leone's war was the collapse of the central authority and its "inability to deliver development," which alienated young people and led to them being used by those in power to extend the conflict and promote destabilization (interview, Director, Economic Policy and Research Unit, Sierra Leone, 27 February 2014). This respondent also indicated that the government failed to meet the mounting expectations placed upon it by the country's large youth population, which was engulfed in a vicious cycle of unemployment and economic insecurity without any prospects for escaping abject poverty (interview, Director, Economic Policy and Research Unit, Sierra Leone, 27 February 2014).

In the years following the war, various donor agencies flooded the country with development assistance and foreign-owned enterprises staked claims in the diamond sector, fuelling hope. However, the expected development did not materialize, an outcome often blamed on a loss of confidence in development on the part of the government and donors. One interviewee argued that blame can be laid on the donors, who displayed overcautious attitudes and failed to address immediate, pressing issues such as the need to restore electricity production (interview, Development Assistance Coordination Office, Office of the Vice President of Sierra Leone, 27 February 2014). With respect to oil, little movement has been made on drilling and production contracts (interview, African Development Bank Sierra Leone, 25 February 2014; interview, African Development Bank Sierra Leone, 26 February 2016) and, given the decline in oil prices, it is now doubtful whether extraction and export of these offshore discoveries will be commercially viable or profitable to investors.

The mining sector has historically held a central position in Sierra Leone's economy since the discovery of diamonds in the 1930s. Prior to the civil war, the sector accounted for 25 per cent of the country's GDP on average (Maconachie and Binns 2007) and constituted some 70 per cent of foreign exchange earnings and 15 per cent of fiscal revenue (RWI 2011). Decades of poor natural resource governance, however, resulted in a broad-based failure to restructure private-sector activities, leading to lost government revenues, a decline in living standards (particularly in mining communities), and environmental degradation. During the 1990s, the illicit sale of diamonds was a key source of funding for several warring factions. The RUF relied on the diamond trade to sustain its war campaign, while both government forces and rebels battled over diamond-abundant areas (Keen 2005). Rebel commanders are believed to have profited immensely from the illegal diamond trade, pocketing approximately $200 million per year over the course of the war (Alao 2007, 144).

Today, about 14 per cent of the total workforce – artisanal mining alone accounts for some 250,000 workers (McMahon and CEMMATS Group 2007) – depends on the mining sector for its livelihood (World Bank 2008). After subsistence farming, the mining sector is the second-largest employer in the country and Sierra Leone's largest source of foreign exchange (McMahon and CEMMATS Group 2007).

Following years of misappropriation, exploitation, and mismanagement in the extractive sector, the government, in conjunction with donors, multilateral institutions, and private-sector actors, has begun to implement measures aimed at promoting improved governance, transparency, and accountability. These include the introduction of a suite of measures, rules, regulations, and policies designed to eliminate the factors that have destabilized the economy and perpetuated conflict (Kawamoto 2012). However, progress has been hampered by the government's continued emphasis on increasing revenue generated by the mining sector, which has only resulted in policies and legislation that have increased unregulated investment and activities – including by those same private-sector actors. (In fact, a growing number of African countries have relinquished control over their mining industries in favour of policies beneficial to private, and particularly foreign, investment.)

In this vein, Sierra Leone's Ministry of Mines and Mineral Resources (MMMR) – previously the Ministry of Mineral Resources and Political Affairs (MMRPA) – has been accused of issuing licences that carry few

Sierra Leone: Blood Minerals

regulatory restrictions. Even with a strengthened scope of action, and mostly due to capacity constraints and infighting, the MMMR has been unable to fully restructure the activities of private-sector actors in the mining sector.

Despite these challenges, diamonds will likely remain central to post-conflict reconstruction efforts underway in Sierra Leone, especially given their role in funding the civil war in the first place (Reno 1997; Smillie, Gberie, and Hazleton 2000; Hirsch 2001; Maconachie and Binns 2007). According to a report compiled by the World Bank (2009), the country's post-conflict management framework was established on three major pillars: 1) the Kimberley Process Certification Scheme (KPCS), aimed at halting the trade in conflict diamonds and ensuring that diamonds do not finance rebel groups that might undermine the rule of law and legitimately elected governments; 2) the diamond area community development fund (DACDF), established in 2001, aimed at reallocating 0.7 per cent of the total export value of artisanal diamonds for distribution among chiefdoms across the country's mining communities; and 3) the surge in deep-shaft kimberlite mining, which is encouraged by the government and expected to accelerate sustainable development.

Recognizing that diamonds remain a conflict-sensitive resource, Sierra Leone has begun to encourage diversification in the mining sector, particularly in the production of iron ore, ilmenite, rutile, zircon, and gold, along with a shift from artisanal to large-scale mining. Currently, five large-scale mining companies are operating in the country, along with two more that are near commencing considerable gold-mining operations. There are also 186 companies engaged in exploration-phase work, as well as twelve small-scale mining companies in operation. One major sector player is Tonkolili Iron Ore Ltd, formerly owned by London-based African Minerals Ltd and now the property of the Chinese Shandong Iron and Steel Group Co Ltd, one of the world's largest steel producers. Tonkolili is building a major 200-kilometre railway between the extractive site and the port at Pepel at a cost of US$1.5 billion (Cornish 2013; *Guardian* 2018; Bloomberg 2018).

As a result of increased investment by foreign enterprises in these other raw commodities, total diamond exports dropped from 41 per cent in 2006 to 29 per cent in 2011. In nominal terms, diamond exports dropped to $80 million in 2009, down from $125 million in 2006 and $140 million in 2007 (MMMR, n.d.[b]), before increasing to $221 million in 2014 and $158 million in 2016 (Kimberley Process 2018). This decline resulted in significantly reduced government revenues, such that most earnings now derive from a 3 per cent export duty (MMMR, n.d.[b]). Meanwhile, total exports of titanium ore and concentrate rose to 29 per cent from 11 per cent over the same 2006–11 period (Sierra Leone 2013).

Increased global demand and favourable commodity prices have helped to promote the exploration and production of minerals other than diamonds, with the mineral sector now accounting for approximately 60 per cent of the country's export revenue (Sierra Leone 2013). The short- and medium-term economic potential of the mining sector is greater than that of any other sector. If the conduct and contributions of foreign-owned enterprises are governed appropriately, the sector will undoubtedly have the most immediate and most widespread impact on poverty reduction over the medium term.

The government has made it a priority to revisit mining agreements and policies in order to generate more revenue – a key factor in achieving sustainable economic growth, peace, and stability (Sierra Leone 2012; interview, Development Assistance Coordination Office, Office of the Vice President of Sierra Leone, 27 February 2014; interview, Fourah Bay College, University of Sierra Leone, 3 March 2014). The government established a task force in 2008 to examine the mining sector and generate recommendations, which included the revision of its Mining Law and the establishment of the National Mining Agency (NMA). Approval of a transformation plan to restructure institutional arrangements for the sector will result in better-organized institutions aimed at building capacity, improved governance, accountability and transparency, and greater facilitation of investment. In March 2018, Sierra Leone's newly elected president, Julius Maada Bio, criticized the lack of transparency on the part of his predecessor, Ernest Bai Koroma, and called for an immediate review of the 2009 Mines and Minerals Act as well as the mining company licences (Cooper 2018).

Sierra Leone: Blood Minerals

Legal and Regulatory Framework

Currently, the Ministry of Trade and Industry provides policy direction, while the NMA implements and sets standards for the regulatory framework. One interviewee noted that the framework remains weak and is easily exploited (interview, Coordinator, Enhanced Integrated Framework National Implementation Unit, Ministry of Trade and Industry, 25 February 2014). The same individual also asserted that bribery is common, given that low-paid officials handle large sums of money and are constantly tempted with payoffs from companies to turn a blind eye to their failures to meet contractual obligations. This view is supported by the World Bank in its 2013 report *The Political Economy of Extractives Governance in Sierra Leone*, which notes that the heads of Sierra Leone's directorships of mines and geological surveys are presently housed within the NMA and have seats on the country's Minerals Advisory Board (MAB). In what is a significant conflict of interest, technical advice provided by NMA officials, who are charged with upholding and enforcing the regulatory framework, is subject to being overturned by political appointees to the MAB. Correspondingly, the report notes that even though one of the NMA's functions is to promote the needs of communities, including the sound administration of Community Development Agreements (CDAS), the NMA does not have resources or staff dedicated to delivering that portion of its mandate (Fanthorpe and Gabelle 2013).

Despite this, several interviewees perceived the NMA in a positive light (interview, CEMMATS Group, 25 February 2014). One official called for more ingenuity in policy making that opens doors to other sectors and avenues for revenue (interview, NMA, 25 February 2014). Interviewees also claimed that in order to further improve policies and negotiation positions vis-à-vis mining companies, the government needs to perform detailed land surveys to confirm which resources are available, where they are located, and who owns the relevant land (interviews, MMMR, 26 and 28 February 2014). This point plays into a wider analysis of what must be done to ensure sustainable and broadly beneficial economic development in Sierra Leone. Better land surveying by the government would complement certain conditions identified in the African Development Bank's 2013 report *Green Growth Sierra Leone*, which notes that clarifying land tenure

138   GOVERNANCE, CONFLICT, AND NATURAL RESOURCES IN AFRICA

and land rights, strengthening public procurement, and providing improved, publicly available social, economic, geographic, and environmental data and information sources are essential to implementing socially and economically beneficial growth policies (AfDB 2013a).

Interviews with academics, civil society representatives, and policy makers also yielded positive views of President Koroma, who, in light of his private-sector background, promised to lead the country "like a business" (interview, Investment Promotion, Sierra Leone Investment and Export Promotion Agency, 26 February 2014; interview, Sierra Leone Port Authority, 27 February 2014). Interviewees pointed to several positive presidential projects, including the restoration of electricity to Freetown after a disruption caused by a broken shaft in the Bumbuna hydroelectric dam, the introduction of solar-powered streetlights in provincial towns, and free healthcare for lactating and pregnant women, and for children under five (interview, Economic, Trade and Regional Cooperation Section, EU Delegation to Sierra Leone, 27 February 2014).

Working with donors and multilateral institutions like the IMF, the government formulated the Extractive Industries Revenue Bill, which is designed to establish a new taxation regime for extractive industries. Tax and non-tax rules have been combined into a single legal instrument, and a resource rent tax on all windfall profits has been introduced. This Bill has generated positive results. In 2011, the government reported earnings of $27.6 million, amounting to approximately 11 per cent of total natural resource exports, compared to an annual average of 4.2 per cent between 2006 and 2010 (SLEITI 2010). Revenues amounted to $7.2 million in 2006, and increased to $10.2 million the following year (SLEITI 2010).

Although this would seem to be a positive step toward maximizing the potential of the mining sector and its contribution to the country's economic reconstruction efforts, natural resource revenue is still well below what mining communities and civil society groups have called. Indeed, the proportion of total government revenue from mining amounts to a mere 5 per cent. For a resource-rich country that requires significant revenue to finance post-conflict reconstruction, this is far from optimal (NACE 2011).

The private sector – foreign-owned enterprises in particular – continues to be blamed for not doing enough to advance the government's socio-

Sierra Leone: Blood Minerals

economic development plans, and is viewed with suspicion by both civil society and some government officials. Part of this problem stems from continuing legislative and regulatory challenges associated with revenue generation from the natural resource sector. While the government is attempting to introduce new transparent regulations for companies interested in investing in the country, existing agreements must be allowed to run their course (interview, IBIS Sierra Leone, 26 February 2014). Having many different, concurrent standards for companies operating in Sierra Leone has placed the country in a precarious situation. Consequently, not only is the government facing strong opposition from certain foreign-owned enterprises, but there is also the risk that such companies may migrate to other resource-rich countries.

Another issue involves corporate income taxes. Tax losses are estimated to be as high as \$240–\$270 million (interview, World Bank Sierra Leone, 26 February 2014; interview with Mr Alvin Hilaire, Resident Representative, IMF Sierra Leone, 27 February 2014) due to tax evasion and the informal market for artisanal mining (Steinweg and Römgens 2015, 13; Sidi Bah, Mosioma, and McNair 2010; interview, Institute for Governance Reform, 25 February 2014). Since the beginning of 2015, companies have been required to pay a 30 per cent corporate income tax (interview, Department for International Development (UK) Sierra Leone, 26 February 2014). Property tax evasion is also common, and misunderstandings are frequent when local councils, to which property taxes are owed, are not informed of companies' property tax exemption agreements with the national government (interview, EIF-NIU, Ministry of Trade and Industry, 26 February 2014).

Mining companies, mostly foreign, are also being accused of environmental degradation associated with large-scale formal mining. They have been implicated in contributing to socioeconomic dislocation in the mining communities in which they operate, and in areas of resettlement, leading to loss of livelihood for farmers who lose their land, and to increasing surface rents. Mining community members argue that surface rents have been disproportionately distributed among a select few stakeholders, including local councils, paramount chiefs,[2] and national government agencies, with but little filtering down to community members. Indeed, interviewees in mining communities complain about the misuse of these funds by such stakeholders in the form of kickbacks (interviews with mining communities, Kono, Tonkolili, and Port Loko districts, 3–6 March 2014). Another argument is that the paramount chiefs' share of surface rent is too large, and exact amounts have often been either hidden or inaccurately reported.

Meanwhile, other mining community members believe that local councils often receive the lion's share of surface rents paid by foreign-owned enterprises. This is particularly troubling, given that in the eyes of many community members, these local councils have little influence in their communities and often are not accountable to their constituencies. They are viewed with great suspicion by community members – which is troubling given the increased likelihood of dissatisfaction, instability, and reversal of post-conflict reconciliation among members of mining communities, where tensions have been rising and opportunities for increased violence are deemed to be high. Although the distribution of surface rent takes place via a process that involves the national government, paramount chiefs, and local councils, community leaders appear not to be involved. Furthermore, no clear procedure could be determined that might explain how final decisions on the distribution of surface rents are made, giving rise to concerns about the opaque nature of the entire process.

In light of the lack of social services and the poor quality of infrastructure, as well as the government's inability to create sufficient employment opportunities for the thousands of young people entering the workforce (Enria 2018). Calls for accountability in CSR were also frequent, with one respondent suggesting the need for an independent monitoring organization. Community representatives noted that mining companies have destroyed buildings; furthermore, when asked for help in transporting children to school after a company created difficulties by rerouting roads, the company provided no help (interview with mining community leaders, Lunsar, 26 February 2014).

This is particularly relevant given the foreign-owned private sector's failure to meet such community expectations, a failure due to the limitations of the existing operating requirements and shareholder and legislative obligations. Before the enactment of the Mines and Minerals Act in 2009, there were no rules in place to require foreign-owned enterprises to adhere to CSR principles relating to social service delivery or infrastructure development projects in the communities in which they operated. Often, companies were free to formulate their own CSR commitments with little or no oversight, and to limit the amount of funding and technical support that could be funnelled directly toward sustainable economic transformation and post-conflict reconstruction and stabilization. Despite the fact that the legislation contains terms obliging such companies to adhere to CSR and related initiatives, there appears to be no enforcement from the government when it comes to unfulfilled commitments or promises made by the private sector to mining communities.

These limitations have been corroborated by Kaldor and Vincent (2006), Maconachie (2012), and Fanthorpe and Gabelle (2013). Furthermore, there is no monitoring by or coordination with donors or national government agencies such as the NMA, and CSR programs are not necessarily linked to community development initiatives and local needs at all – in fact, they are often divorced from national development priorities. Moreover, many companies operating in Sierra Leone appear intent on reducing or removing legally binding terms that compel them to adhere to CSR initiatives, and are increasingly demanding involvement in the creation of new legislation (interview, Network Movement for Justice and Development, 26 February 2014).

When it comes to how mining revenue is managed, community development funds (CDFs) administered by the MMMR are often mishandled, with money instead channelled to government or mining community elites (interview, IBIS West Africa, 25 February 2014). According to the United Nations Development Programme, despite ambitious initiatives in mining governance, Sierra Leone has been mired in administrative mismanagement and corruption since the civil war. This has led to a distrust of politics among the citizens, making adherence to mining codes and legislation all the more imperative (Kaldor and Vincent 2007). Linked to the failure of CDFS, recently mining companies have also come under heavy criticism for insufficient local content (interview, Institute for Governance Reform, Sierra Leone, 25 February 2014) and for not producing enough positive impacts on communities (interview, Institute for Governance Reform, Sierra Leone, 25 February 2014). In cases where opportunities have been created, local people's skills did not meet the professional requirements due to education gaps (interview, UNDP, 25 February 2014).

In an attempt to rectify this situation, the government recruited the services of the United Kingdom's Department for International Development (DFID), the German Agency for International Cooperation (GIZ), and the International Finance Corporation (IFC) to study how Sierra Leone's Local Content Policy is being applied. Although concrete figures were not provided, the government's intent is to increase local content significantly, on an economy-wide basis, by 2018 (DFID 2012). According to a representative of the Sierra Leone Chamber of Commerce, Industry and Agriculture, mining companies need to broaden CSR beyond philanthropic activities to include more tangible development initiatives identified by mining communities, including local content (interview, Sierra Leone Chamber of Commerce, Industry and Agriculture, 25 February 2014). These initiatives should align with communities' development, health, and education needs, and address government priorities as outlined in economic agendas. Despite the foregoing, however, the potential and expected effects of the mining sector on the national economy remain a key subject of debate.

The Potential of Iron Ore Companies to Eradicate Extreme Poverty

The recent discovery of approximately 10.5 billion tonnes of high-grade iron ore deposits in the country's Marampa, Tonkolili, and Bembeye mines portends a significant increase in government revenue for the coming decades (Sierra Leone 2013). The expected economic impact of increased mining production and exports has spurred the government's initiative to promote higher FDI and foreign-owned enterprise involvement in mining communities. Statistics indicate that by 2020, the country could be expected to export approximately $1.2 billion in mineral resources and retain approximately 7 per cent of their value. If this money is used correctly, some 900,000 Sierra Leoneans could be lifted out of extreme poverty. Although this is an optimistic projection for the mining sector and a positive development with respect to mining companies' contribution to economic growth and development, mining community leaders and civil society groups associated with the sector have been comparing Sierra Leone's situation to those of other countries in Africa. For example, mining revenues in countries such as Tanzania and Ghana account for approximately 10 per cent of total government revenue (NACE 2009). Revised assessments of revenue derived from minerals are needed in light of the recent collapse in world commodity prices, the suspension of iron ore mining following the Ebola outbreak in 2014, and the healthcare costs and economic losses associated with that outbreak.

Sierra Leone's mining sector has undergone significant changes since the civil war, with new minerals gaining ground on alluvial diamonds following the enactment of the Mines and Minerals Act in 2009. Yet these changes cannot disguise the ongoing development and security challenges that hinder sustainable development in the country. The mining sector still lags on key governance indicators despite improved sociopolitical relations in the country and the enactment of progressive legislation. Indeed, the challenges appear to dwarf the opportunities created by expanding the role of foreign-owned enterprises, with stakeholders providing insights into socioeconomic dislocation, the failure of CSR to provide tangible development outcomes, and various interviewees revealing community resentment to the point of creating a potential for violence (Peligal 2014). Given that subnational governance and related CSR initiatives are voluntary, government intervention may be the deciding factor on whether the private sector plays a positive or negative role in driving sustainable economic growth, peace, and stability.

There is clearly a need for more financing to support natural resource governance, but better oversight is a prerequisite for funding provision. It is also imperative that the government address corruption at various levels, as any changes in legal and regulatory frameworks have yet to meaningfully effect substantive change.

Community Development Agreements in Mining Communities: An Entry Point for Restructuring Action

Despite being deeply affected by mining operations, mining communities see very few dividends from extractive industries. As a result, these communities are increasingly putting pressure on the government to require the private foreign-owned sector to implement long-term local CSR initiatives as part of their business and sustainability strategies.

Information gleaned from interviews with IBIS Sierra Leone, the CEMMATS Group, the Network Movement for Justice and Development, and the German Agency for International Cooperation (GIZ) suggests there is still much work to be done to address the concerns of mining communities, local councils, and civil society regarding the lack of direct economic impacts of CSR practices in Sierra Leone (interview, Extractive Resource Governance, GIZ, 4 March 2014). In its recent report on the Ebola response, the UNDP notes that foreign-owned enterprise assistance in developing sustainable economic opportunities in communities throughout Sierra Leone has been muted due to inadequate promotion of public-private partnerships and other CSR-related activities (UNDP 2015b). However, it is important to note that this is not a uniform conclusion, as some businesses in Sierra Leone, including mining companies, have endeavoured to deliver direct, socioeconomic benefits to local communities.

Ultimately, critics associated with the problems of mining communities in Sierra Leone, including academics, development partners, civil society groups, mining communities, local mining community administrators, and government officials, complain of a lack of definition of CSR. They also note that CSR is typically practised when it is most convenient for a company to do so, which does not lead to sustainable progress (interview, Institute for Gender Research and Documentation, Fourah Bay College, University of Sierra Leone, 2 March 2014; interview, African Development Bank Sierra Leone, 23 February 2014; interview, NMA, 25 February 2014). If CSR is poorly defined, might this be seen as a wholesale failure of governance structures to determine the scope of action for the private sector, and instead allowing the latter to dictate terms?

Examining the function of community development agreements (CDA) is a fruitful starting point to answer this question. CDAs are linked to voluntary principles of CSR, and function as a company-defined corporate responsibility arrangement for an area in which a company operates (O'Faircheallaigh 2013; O'Faircheallaigh 2015; Dupuy 2014). They aim to promote greater transparency and accountability in the area of corporate practice, while allowing the private sector to develop a positive standing among its domestic and international stakeholders, and maintain a social

Sierra Leone: Blood Minerals

licence to operate within mining communities (Yakovleva 2005; ICMM 2012; World Bank 2009). CDAs have two fundamental principles: 1) gradual strengthening of relationships between mining communities, mining companies, and civil society groups, and 2) support for and encouragement of mutually beneficial dividends from mining activities, including schemes designed to empower mining communities and provide them with alternate sources of income that may fall outside the immediate scope of a mining project (World Bank 2009).

To date, CDAs represent the most ambitious attempt to hold mining companies accountable for their social responsibilities and for leveraging their technical and material resources to achieve sustainable economic development, peace, and stability. These agreements also facilitate foreign-owned enterprises' contributions to Sierra Leone's post-conflict peacebuilding and reconstruction efforts, particularly with respect to advancing pro-poor sustainable development initiatives in mining communities.

There is an understanding on the part of the government that Sierra Leone's fragile peacebuilding and reconstruction efforts could be jeopardized if adequate steps are not taken to address the grievances of mining communities. Indeed, at the community level, the promised benefits of natural resource exploitation have often failed to materialize, with governance systems being either unwilling or unable to require foreign-owned enterprises to contribute meaningfully to communities via CSR schemes or CDAs. Governance structures are only as effective as their implementation mechanisms. As such, the role of mining companies, particularly foreign-owned ones, in the country's current transformation process is paramount given their fragile relationship with mining communities, and considering how these communities have become increasingly emboldened with the passage of new mining legislations. There remain, however, many shortcomings and challenges regarding the successful implementation of CDAs in Sierra Leone. For example, while the Mines and Minerals Act aims to empower mining communities entering into CDAs with mining companies, the legislation does not clearly indicate when and how such agreements should be constituted (Otto 2017). As mining companies generate larger profits, citizens are increasingly demanding that the government legislate for "more equitable revenue-sharing codes and ... a larger developmental role for the state" (Besada and Martin 2013).

The government has an interest in ensuring that mining revenue is shared and that mining companies provide social services and public goods – not only to retain power, but also to ensure peace and stability, all of which is cyclically reinforced through economic sustainability and growth (Hilson 2012; Maconachie and Hilson 2013; interview, Local Governance and Economic Development, UNDP Sierra Leone, 4 March 2014). As an illustration of this trend, structured and unstructured interviews in ten mineral-rich chiefdoms in the Kono, Port Loko, and Tonkolili districts found that mining communities considered the diamond area community development fund (DACDF) to be their communities' most important source of revenue.

CDAS cover all minerals. In contrast, DACDFS are restricted to diamond-producing areas (i.e., excluding other minerals important to Sierra Leone's economy such as bauxite, gold, and iron ore). But most importantly, the DACDF structure dictates that all small- and large-scale mining companies must enter into agreements with mining communities to promote local development projects that community members have decided to support (Maconachie 2011; 2012). Under this structure, of the 3 per cent in export taxes levied on artisanal diamonds each year by the state, 25 per cent is allocated to the DACDF to facilitate community-run development projects. Direct cash transfers to diamond-mining communities are presented formally by local government officials, and a representative from MMMR, to those assembled at a chiefdom meeting.

Specifically, DACDFS are disbursed to district and chiefdom councils as follows: 20 per cent of monies collected in a given period are distributed among diamondiferous district councils;[3] 20 per cent to diamond-mining chiefdoms with artisanal mining licences, based on a flat rate and irrespective of the number of licenses held; and the remaining 60 per cent to chiefdom councils according to the number of artisanal mining licences they hold (World Bank 2009). By 2007, the Sierra Leone government had received approximately $4.25 million in diamond-mining revenue, of which the DACDF distributed about $3.5 million to mining communities (Temple 2008).

According to the government's DACDF operational guidelines, allocated monies are not to be distributed to chiefdoms automatically. Projects must

Sierra Leone: Blood Minerals 147

be defined and approved prior to fund dispersal (MMRPA and MLG 2008, 3). Chiefdoms must meet the following requirements:

1 Each chiefdom must form a project committee with at least five residents elected at an annual general meeting.
2 The committee solicits project ideas from the community, with priority given to those that demonstrate effectiveness, impact, sustainability, feasibility, partnership with other funding sources, and a balanced portfolio.
3 The project committee then completes and submits a project proposal to a chiefdom committee for consideration against broader appraisal criteria and specific development plans.
4 The chiefdom committee sends selected project proposals to a district-based review committee for approval or rejection.
5 Once summary reports from district committees have been received and vetted by relevant government departments, cheques are issued from the DACDF.
6 Projects are monitored and audited. (MMRPA and MLG 2008, 3–15)

Although participants interviewed for this study credited some paramount chiefs and local councils with sound management of funds and financing of important local development projects, the initiative has been hindered and compromised somewhat by reported incidents of cronyism, bribery, and fraud (Maconachie 2012). Allegations of fund misspending and misappropriation, and the refusal of national government officials to accept responsibility, resulted in the suspension of funds disbursement in December 2006 (MMRPA and MLG 2008; interview, Heifer International West Africa, 5 March 2014). A lack of citizen participation in the decision-making process with regard to fund allocations, as well as a lack of community awareness about the nature of the fund and its intended uses, may also explain, in part, the challenges that have accompanied the management of the DACDF.

It is also important to note that mining companies operating in Sierra Leone have taken issue with what they see as unfair expectations levied upon them by mining communities and the various levels of government. This is particularly true of small-scale mining firms, which believe that their obligations to local communities should consist of adhering to laws, paying lawfully authorized fees and taxes, providing employment opportunities alongside other indirect economic benefits (e.g., the emergence of local businesses that support mining operations), and undertaking environmental reclamation. Many of these companies believe they should not have to provide infrastructure and social services to communities, arguing that these are the purview of the government. Such differences in opinion can lead to enmity between these stakeholders as well as longer-term instability. It can also create operational difficulties for small-scale mining companies that fail to engage in greater CSR activities. Looking forward, the government should distinguish between small- and large-scale mining companies in terms of its CDA expectations, so that it may better satisfy its national development priorities (World Bank 2008).

Interviews with mining community leaders and the National Mining Agency reveal three major issues that have undermined the monitoring and evaluation process. First, communities do not have the necessary technical capacity and institutional structures to negotiate effectively with mining companies, and especially foreign-owned enterprises, for improved developmental programming. Second, the NMA does not have the resources to send field inspectors to mining communities across the country on a regular basis, since its budget is tightly controlled by the MMMR (Fanthorpe and Gabelle 2013; interview, Regional Resource Governance in West Africa, GIZ, Sierra Leone, 5 March 2014). Third, the competition between the NMA and the MMMR is intense, despite their different (albeit complementary) mandates (Fanthorpe and Gabelle 2013; interview, London Mining, 5 March 2014).

A further regulatory failing pointed out by respondents is the absence of a mutually agreed-upon reporting framework between foreign-owned mining companies and mining communities, as well as the lack of an oversight mechanism, particularly with regard to the use of funds distributed under CDAs. Although the MMMR has overall responsibility for ensuring the implementation of CDFs in cooperation with the NMA, the demarcation of roles and responsibilities between these two entities is unclear, which effectively undermines the entire process and leaves mining com-

Sierra Leone: Blood Minerals 149

munities feeling frustrated and, at times, helpless (Fanthorpe and Gabelle 2013; interview, Sustainable Energy, Oil, Gas and Mining, World Bank, 6 March 2014). Ambiguity surrounding CDAS in the 2009 Mines and Minerals Act only adds to the problem.

Although the law accords the MMMR discretionary power to make the final decision on appropriate allocation of resources and implementation of development projects in disputes between mining communities and mining companies, there appears to be a lack of clarity regarding the monetary value of the penalties that can be imposed on mining companies accused of reneging on their responsibilities to communities. To the detriment of mining communities, the ad hoc administration of CDFs between communities and mining companies means that communities do not receive the support they need to drive sustainable growth (Kanu 2010; interviews with mining communities, Kono, Tonkolili, and Port Loko districts, 3–6 March 2014).

According to reports from civic groups, many corporations – particularly those involved in resource extraction – still do not engage them in their operations, particularly with respect to development agreements, nor do they have a conflict resolution strategy that would help foster mutual trust among workers and develop social capital within the communities in which they operate (CIVICUS 2006).

London Mining Company

In 2012, the London Mining Company's operations flooded several communities, destroying crops and pumping water from fishing areas, and thereby reducing the communities' ability to sustain themselves. Exemplifying its lack of CSR policies, the company pressured the Manonkoh communities to sign off on agreements whereunder London Mining would provide the communities with a few hundred machetes and hoes, leaving them with very few resources. In October 2014, the UK company's shares dropped by more than 70 per cent, while its value for 2014 decreased by 99 per cent. Operating in Ebola-hit Sierra Leone and employing approximately 1,400 people, and having failed to find a buyer to plug a funding gap, London Mining faced collapse. On 16 October 2014, the company appointed PricewaterhouseCoopers (PwC) as its joint administrator (Fastmarkets MB 2015).

While tax revenue has the potential to strengthen public services and moderate aid dependency, Sierra Leone has also sought to create new opportunities using the CDA mechanism. These development agreements are an improvement upon CSR initiatives, as they are formally engineered by donors with the consent and participation of the government, the private sector, and mining communities. To strengthen the management of CDAS and CDFS, interviewees suggested an array of policy options: evaluating and harmonizing policies on mineral rents and allocated resources to mining communities; developing documentation on the calculation and distribution of mining revenues; publishing mining-related revenues and payments; promoting community participation at the local level; and fostering multi-stakeholder engagement on the administration, monitoring, and evaluation of CDAS. In this sense, global initiatives, such as the EITI, appear to be a productive start for countries like Sierra Leone to address the revenue repartition of extractive industries and to promote inclusive policies aimed at long-term development (Aaronson 2011).

Although CDAS represent a progressive step toward sustainable development via foreign-owned enterprises, if corruption issues linked to their administration are not addressed, then expectations as to sustainable development, stability, and post-conflict reconstruction will not be met.

Research Results: Hope and Unfulfilled Potential

Impact of Governance and Regulation

The government – specifically the MMMR – has taken major steps to establish legal, regulatory, and institutional capacities with a view to increasing the effectiveness and sustainability of the sector's management as well as its contributions to economic growth, peace, and stability. The first of these steps was passing the Mines and Minerals Act in 2009 (interview, MMMR, 4 March 2014). Civil society, donors, and local councils have all lauded the Act as a step forward toward establishing a regulatory framework to allow the private sector, in particular foreign-owned en-

Sierra Leone: Blood Minerals

terprises, to play a role in the country's economic growth and development programs, which contribute to ongoing peace, stability, and post-conflict reconstruction (Akiwumi 2011). But the Act does not adequately address environmental protection, health and safety, and community development – deficiencies that could undermine such peace process efforts. However, to the government's credit, the legislation permits the Minister of Mines and Mineral Resources to develop a framework for transparency in the reporting and disclosure of revenues that mining companies pay to the government. The Act also makes EITI implementation compulsory for mining companies, provides for the resettlement of mining communities affected by mining operations, and articulates the mining companies' responsibilities toward mining community members affected by mineral exploration and development. With regard to environmental protection, the legislation requires mining companies to undertake environmental impact assessments, apply for environmental impact assessment licenses, and put in place environmental management plans (Sierra Leone 2009b).

The government's second major step was to close the regulatory gaps related to the environmental, social, and operational management of the mining sector. How the sector is to protect the economic, social, and cultural interests of workers, communities, and the environment is now specified in new regulations covering workplace health and safety, waste disposal, storage and transportation of minerals, explosives and blasting, dredging, underground mining, and mine closure – the first time in seventy years of mining operations in Sierra Leone (Sierra Leone 2009b; interview, NMA, 4 March 2014). New environmental and social regulations ensure that mining activities are carried out in a sustainable manner by minimizing or eliminating negative impacts on the environment and communities. The regulations also specify how the environmental and social risks of mining will be identified and mitigated. This is a major achievement toward building goodwill and partnership between foreign-owned enterprises operating in the mineral sector, mining communities, and governments (national, provincial, local, and traditional).

The third major step concerned the operationalization of a world-class Mining Cadastre Office (MCO) to process, record, and monitor applications, licences, and revenues. In a significant step toward full transparency, the government launched an online repository in 2011 to share licensing and revenue information online (interview, NMA, 3 March 2014).[4] The MCO is fully operational throughout the country, and revenues from all fees and taxes are transparently calculated, collected, and reported. Geological maps, together with satellite imagery for detailed analysis, allow for a geographical view on mining and exploration concessions. Such visualizations can help with other land uses as well – for example, to review information pertinent to potential disputes. The government's online repository lists, by company, all licences and applications; and payments can be viewed by licence, company, or year, and downloaded for further analysis. Integration of the repository with the National Revenue Authority and the Gold and Diamond Office covers most revenue streams required to be monitored under EITI specifications (interview, NMA, 5 March 2014).

The fourth major step was institutional reform designed to deliver better-organized oversight institutions with a mandate to manage and enforce legislative requirements for private-sector contributions to economic sustainability. Critical, here, was the establishment of the NMA, which is responsible for the day-to-day implementation of the Mines and Minerals Act and related regulations. The NMA is also responsible for managing mineral rights, collecting and disseminating geological information, and regulating the trade in precious minerals. The principles underpinning the new institutional model for the mining sector are founded upon best practices in natural resource governance and public-sector reform from around the world, including those adopted by various African countries such as Namibia and Botswana. Specialization has resulted in increased efficiency, while a well-managed professional agency gives the private sector the confidence to make long-term investment decisions.

In 2014, the government reached yet another milestone in its efforts to reform its natural resource governance system. A suspension of Sierra Leone from the EITI in February 2013 came about as a result of the government's inability to account for more than $1 million in mining licence fees paid by African Minerals Ltd in 2010. In April 2014, however, the EITI International Board recognized Sierra Leone as EITI-compliant, signalling that the country's publication of revenues derived from its natural resources was sufficient. As a result of renewed confidence engendered by

Sierra Leone: Blood Minerals

government reforms, the mining sector has attracted new investment and expanded existing operations.

Despite these successes, the MMMR still faces a number of immediate, critical challenges that limit its capacity. These include budget uncertainty surrounding its ability to support the Mines and Minerals Act, the limited capacity of the Geological Survey Division to provide accurate data to encourage inward investment, and ineffective monitoring and compliance of precious mineral trading. Additional constraints include a weak investment climate, which hinders Sierra Leone's ability to compete in the highly competitive world of mineral exploration; a lack of exploration opportunities, as a small number of companies controls the great majority of the resource base, making it unattractive to reputable global mining companies; and the smuggling of precious minerals, a continual challenge given the prominence of artisanal mining. Similar issues have been raised in other African countries, where regulators struggle with issues such as the ease of smuggling precious minerals.[5] Gold and diamonds in particular are easy commodities to smuggle.

The Government of Sierra Leone views the private sector as a pillar of sustainable economic growth, stability, and a vehicle through which postconflict recovery programs can be implemented. In response to the last period of global austerity and decreasing donor support for developing countries (since 2008), coupled with the fact that mining sector investments have accounted for a substantial proportion of the country's economic growth in recent years, the government has taken steps to improve the investment climate – a measure aimed at growing the private sector and strengthening the economy. Positive change can only occur when government interventions are designed to improve the country's investment climate and curb corruption, all while reducing the costs of doing business. The government must develop a strong partnership with foreignowned enterprises if it is to generate employment and reduce poverty.

In recent years, the government has taken various steps to attract FDI through legislation such as the Investment Promotion Act (2004), the Investment Code (2005), the Business Registration Act (2007), the Investment Promotion Agency Act (2007), the Companies Act (2009), the Bankruptcy Act (2009), and the National Private Sector Development

Plan, which came into effect in 2009 (US Embassy, Freetown 2011). These reforms were enacted to provide greater protection for companies investing in Sierra Leone, to streamline the business engagement process, and to create more opportunities for private ownership and control. Following a decade-long decline in FDI during the civil war, which saw foreign investment averaging less than $7 million annually between 1990 and 2000, FDI grew to $97 million by 2007, dropped to $33 million in 2009, and then slowly increased again to $36 million in 2011 thanks to Chinese investment (UNCTAD 2011; US Embassy, Freetown 2011).

Investors can play a crucial role in providing economic opportunity and related stability via job creation, infrastructure development, and provision of social services such as schools and healthcare, which would simultaneously support ongoing peacebuilding efforts. Given that foreign aid and debt relief – the traditional remedies offered to overcome Africa's dependency and underdevelopment issues – have been ineffective, the private sector is increasingly viewed as the missing link in the push to improve Sierra Leone's competitiveness. As such, there is a need for an investment-friendly, enabling environment to attract FDI and encourage the growth of small and medium-size domestic enterprises. Sierra Leonean legislators must nevertheless balance these considerations with the need to implement policies that prevent opportunistic, predatory rent seeking while fostering effective forward and backward linkages between foreign private investors and the country's domestic enterprises.

Impact of Private Sector and Local Community Development

Community groups, NGOs, and donors continue to express concerns that decisions are made arbitrarily, often in favour of the private sector and at the expense of local sustainable development initiatives, which creates unhealthy animosity between potential development partners. An interview with Mr Jinnah Ibrahim, the NMA's director of precious minerals trading (27 February 2014), revealed a continued distrust of the private sector by mining communities; he accused the corruption-plagued private sector, particularly foreign-owned companies, of backtracking on promises to provide leadership and promote developmental outcomes that benefit the broader population. Mining companies have been hesitant to negotiate

Sierra Leone: Blood Minerals

and consult with communities themselves, with one interviewee noting that a manager from African Minerals Ltd, who participated in a community meeting, was later penalized by the company (interview with Mr Patrick Tongu, Program Officer, NMJD, 26 February 2014). The same informant observed that people living in areas into which companies are only just entering are becoming more vocal as they feel that they are not being compensated appropriately, with some in the Chiefdom of Tonkolili even demanding to negotiate on their own behalf. Where companies negotiate directly with community members, promises – sometimes expressed as verbal agreements – are often not kept, creating instability.

The government has also failed to provide a detailed, holistic account of the total revenue it receives from the mining sector, instead producing irregular and incomplete data on mineral production, revenue, and taxation. This creates conditions in which a scope of action for effecting restructuring cannot be appropriately implemented. In the past, Sierra Leoneans have complained that they have not received many benefits from the sale of diamonds, given that business remained in the hands of artisanal miners and illegal traders, while exporters and traders made purchases with hard currency (Wilson 2011). Such trade was problematic for the government, which was eager for the proceeds to be used to help generate employment and kickstart secondary industries that are dependent on, or contribute to, the mining sector. Interviewees pointed out that export taxes of 3 per cent did little to generate revenue for poverty alleviation programs or to promote sustainable development projects (interview with Mr Joseph Rahall, Executive Director, Green Scenery, 27 February 2014). As well, foreign-owned enterprises continue to be criticized for their unwillingness and (in some cases) inability to provide detailed accounting of taxes and payments made to the government and the mining communities in which they operate. To the disappointment of mining communities, donors, and civil society, Sierra Leone's parliament does not have the technical, administrative, or financial capacity to examine and inspect government-company revenues, tax payments, and agreements (interview with Ms Christine Sheckler, Country Program Manager, USAID, 3 March 2014).

When the government fails in its role to provide a meaningful degree of transparency for its natural resource sector revenues, foreign-owned companies will often limit their contribution to CSR activities, particularly when governance systems and institutions are poorly enforced. Indeed, the World Bank (2008) notes that mining company contributions to social service provision in Sierra Leonean mining communities has been limited. In addition, there appears to be an absence of official figures to corroborate how many job positions have been added to the country's mining sector since the end of the civil war, while an International Labour Organization report from 2010 suggests that unskilled positions are relatively easy to come by, while surveyors and geologists are largely recruited from abroad. Local engineers are often overlooked for such positions on the grounds that they lack the practical experience or specialized knowledge required by the mining companies. The document also notes that mining companies' CSR initiatives have tended not to target youth employment as the corporations consider employment in Sierra Leone, irrespective of age, to be a national problem and a primary responsibility of the government (Arai, Cissé, and Sock 2010).

Interviews with community members highlighted this division in the population with regard to positive and negative views on the private sector. On the one hand, representatives of mining companies, diamond dealers, and local and paramount chiefs were pleased with the economic impacts of mining in affected communities, citing employment opportunities and reduced crime rates. However, one town chief did note that expected employment numbers do not always materialize (interviews with mining communities, Kono, Tonkolili, and Port Loko districts, 3–6 March 2014). On the other hand, the majority of women's and youth group representatives expressed more negative opinions, with youth groups having a particularly negative view of mining companies. Concerns included disruption of lives and destruction of dwellings, displacement, lack of water and arable land, increased dropout rates in schools, and blasting, seen as especially disruptive.

Indeed, youth unemployment has to be an important issue in a country where young people comprise above 30 per cent of the population, but it gains extra importance considering that youth unemployment, in the context of state delinquency rates, was one of the major factors in the recent civil war (Peters 2011; Ferme 2001). Youth employment remains a pressing issue in Sierra Leone, with an estimated 60 per cent of men and women

Sierra Leone: Blood Minerals 157

between the ages of 15 and 35 unemployed as of 2012 (Sierra Leone 2012).

Interestingly, criticisms from women's groups were more balanced and mentioned both positive and negative impacts, noting challenges such as the relocation of schools, deprivation of agricultural land that women use to provide for their families, and the dangers of blasting. Representatives from the clergy and the education sector criticized the lack of prioritization of schooling for children, deforestation, uncovered pits, and displacement, although teachers who were interviewed acknowledged the benefits of increased mining company taxes, higher salaries, and CSR activities.

A lack of institutional structure and coordination has meant that little effective progress has been made in decreasing youth unemployment (Sierra Leone 2012; interview with Prof. Ekundayo Thompson, Director, Directorate of Planning, Research and Development, and Coordinator, Peace and Development Studies program, Njala University, 25 February 2014).

Impact of Value Addition and Beneficiation

Mineral beneficiation and value addition have great potential to advance Sierra Leone's economic transformation, sustainable growth, and stability. As the authors of the Political Economy of Natural Resource Governance framework state, value addition and beneficiation play a crucial role in stabilizing a post-conflict country like Sierra Leone. A comprehensive study examining and promoting backward linkages in Sierra Leone's mining sector could improve local economic prospects for mining communities and the broader public. The goal for Sierra Leone should be to establish a systemic approach to identify binding constraints on the country's industries, thereby creating a direct portal for bottom-up information transfer between communities and government actors. The key to this is the ability to study the entire mineral value chains in order to identify the obstacles to beneficiation and value addition in the country. Awareness and understanding will help to tailor actions and make policy adjustments over time to utilize mining revenue effectively and generate optimal sustainable development outcomes.

A "Local Content Assessment Report" commissioned by Sierra Leone's Ministry of Trade and Industry and the UK Department for International

Development (DFID) presented startling revelations about the extent of local content in the country's mining sector (Adam Smith International 2013). It identified that the use of local supply had reached only a mere 5.8 per cent, which was mainly blamed on low capacity in the local market. One of the reasons behind the low rate is the lack of knowledge about the government's Local Content Policy and its application with regard to foreign-owned private-sector actors. Private companies have argued that local service providers have poor operating capacities and lack technical expertise and knowledge, and that distorted tax agreements favour foreign investors by contributing to loopholes and reducing tax burdens. Local enterprises are often part of a lower value chain and do not contribute to the strengthening of local secondary industries or beneficiation. The report emphasized the fact that respondents perceived the public procurement process as unfair, with most respondents stating that local firms do not receive preferential treatment. Respondents strongly argued for the country's education system to be overhauled to include technical vocational training and courses catering to industry requirements.

The mining sector is expected to account for nearly 30 per cent of governmental revenues by early 2016 (interview with Mr Dominic Hope, Investor Relations Associate, Sierra Rutile, 5 March 2014), and the state is grappling with how to ensure that the sector does not continue to serve the interests of public and private elites above those of average citizens. Currently, local beneficiation and value addition in Sierra Leone's mining sector are limited and forward-facing only, with the average Sierra Leonean not benefitting from mineral proceeds, increased investment, or economic growth. This situation has given rise to social instability, unrest, and sometimes violence, which could slow the government's efforts to promote the private sector and foreign-owned enterprises as partners in generating sustainable economic growth, stability, and peace.

Recent efforts have been made to address the potential risks associated with the mining sector's inefficiencies, as well as to capitalize on increased investments to spur economic growth. By enacting its Local Content Policy in May 2012, the government aimed to "promote strong linkages between multinational private sector actors and the local economy" (Adam Smith International 2013) by encouraging private sector and foreign-owned enterprises to play a greater developmental role in

Sierra Leone: Blood Minerals

the country's transformation process. The policy sets out expectations with regard to employment generation, beneficiation, value addition, promotion of secondary industries reliant on the mining sector, and supply chain development. Similar to continental and regional efforts led by the African Union and various regional organizations, the policy is also designed to increase the capacities and technical abilities of Sierra Leonean service providers by promoting linkages between local service providers and foreign entities operating in the country, training Sierra Leoneans, and stipulating that 50 per cent of intermediate positions and 20 per cent of managerial positions at foreign-owned companies must be held by Sierra Leoneans (Fanthorpe and Gabelle 2013). Much hope has been placed in the Local Content Policy, although it has had little effect thus far (interview with Mr Herbert M'Cleod, senior governance specialist, 27 February 2014).

Based on interviews conducted with government officials and representatives from the private sector in March 2014, the local private sector's weak productive capacity to meet local and external market demands is a major challenge. Even the larger foreign mining companies that operate in the country have complained that they are forced to import from markets outside the Economic Community of West African States (ECOWAS) due to weak manufacturing capacity in the country. DFID (2012) echoes these sentiments, noting the limited number of domestic businesses capable of offering suitable goods and services to mining companies in Sierra Leone. The report also states that data on supply and demand for the sector is limited, as local output figures are predominantly based on anecdotal accounts, while mining firms' supply requirements are unknown. In addition, mining companies appear to lack comprehension or understanding of the local content requirements.

The business operating environment is expected to improve in the long term as a result of the 2013 Finance Act, which is designed to help promote FDI, simplify tax administration, and boost mineral revenues. However, current and prospective investors are worried that the policy may undermine business operations and negatively affect future profits, impeding their ability to be partners in sustainable development given the difficulties in sourcing skilled labour locally (interview with Mr Claude Perras, Head of Sustainability, London Mining PLC, 25 February 2014).

In an effort to address these concerns, the government agreed in November 2013 to a Local Content Compact with the private sector. A dialogue with foreign-owned enterprises is expected to lead to a robust national compact on local content development and governance. The planned consultative process will involve government members from the National Ministerial Committee who deal with local content, major foreign-owned private-sector actors, industry associations, civil society groups, and development partners such as GIZ, the World Bank, the EU, and DFID. Only time will tell if this compact will remedy the remaining endemic ills afflicting this post-conflict country's natural resource sector and help drive sustainable development and growth.

Future Opportunities

Possible Approaches to an Effective Governance Framework

Sierra Leone's challenges are somewhat unique to its environment, resource deposits, governance systems, and context. The country's Mines and Minerals Act stipulates a comprehensive overhaul of CSR activities, with priority on the promotion of community development initiatives. First, mining companies are required to obtain a land lease for any mining activities (Sierra Leone 2009b). The terms of the lease include payment of rents to landowners in mining communities. Second, mining companies are expected to compensate landowners and other lawful occupants of mining communities for any damage to their livelihoods, vegetation, crops, or infrastructure (Sierra Leone 2009b). Third, mining companies are required to implement community development agreements (CDAs) to be financed by no less than 1 per cent of their gross mining revenue of the previous year.[6] According to the Act, the primary host community expected to reap these benefits is a "single community of persons mutually agreed [upon] by the holder of the small-scale or large-scale mining license and the local council" (Sierra Leone 2009b). In the event that no such communities exist within a thirty-kilometre radius of any boundary encompassing a large-scale mining licensing area, CDA funds would be provided to the local council. The Minister of Mines and

Sierra Leone: Blood Minerals 161

Mineral Resources is accorded the power to resolve disputes that may arise involving mining communities, while the Director of Mines has the legal authority to approve a CDA in any given mining community (Fanthorpe and Gabelle 2013).

Interviews with seventy-five community members from the Kono, Tonkolili, and Port Loko districts pointed to a broad, general lack of knowledge about CDAs. After a brief explanation, respondents indicated that CDAs should be based upon community-wide consensus and previously agreed-upon objectives, while the respective roles and responsibilities of mining companies and mining communities should be clarified, in consultation with the government. Respondents also suggested that timelines for development projects should be timely and transparent, progress in regard to development outcomes in the community should be impartially assessed, and conflicts and disputes between communities and mining companies should be resolved with the government acting as an impartial arbitrator. CDAs should be drafted with the mining companies by (in this order) local chiefs, paramount chiefs, artisanal miners, traders, women's group leaders, youth leaders, civil society groups representing mining communities, local government officials, religious leaders, and farmers within the prescribed thirty-kilometre radius.

In an effort to strengthen the management of CDAs and CDFs, members of donor communities and mining communities presented the following recommendations for leveraging foreign-owned enterprises as active contributors to sustainable economic growth, peace, and stability:

- Evaluate and harmonize various policies related to mineral rents and resources allocated to mining communities.
- Develop detailed and all-inclusive documentation on guidelines for calculating and distributing mining revenue locally and nationally.
- Publish mining-related revenues and payments, and make these available to mining communities.
- Promote community participation at the local level.
- Foster multi-stakeholder engagement between civil society, government, and mining companies to improve the administration, management, coordination, monitoring, and evaluation

of CDAS. (interviews with mining communities, Kono, Tonko-lili, and Port Loko districts, 3–6 March 2014)

Respondents also expressed interest in the creation of a CDA monitoring body consisting of members of mining communities, civil society groups involved in community development programs, donors, government officials, and mining companies. This body would oversee budgets and fund disbursement, and evaluate impacts in communities. Funds should be deposited into a special, audited account, accessible only to designated signatories representing the national, district, and community-level governments, and audited financial statements from mining communities be made available.

Respondents also called for the establishment of Community Natural Resource Management Committee (CNRMC), a District Natural Resource Management Committee (DNRMC), and a National Natural Resource Management Committee (NNRMC) to oversee CDA funds disbursement and project completion at the local level. These committees would be organized and tasked as follows:

1 CNRMC (consisting of eight local individuals, including chiefs, representing different community groups – i.e., women's groups, youth groups, artisanal mining associations, farmers' associations): manage CDA projects and processes at the local or community level; oversee the successful completion of CDA projects and submission of comprehensive reports to the DNRMC prior to submission to the NNRMC; organize meetings and engage in consultations with representatives of mining communities pertaining to the receipt and expenditure of funds earmarked for development projects; solicit input, ideas, and feedback from mining communities regarding development projects that might benefit from CDA funding.

2 DNRMC (consisting of a district council chairperson, representatives of mining companies, members of civil society groups, donor community members, district mining engineers, and elected community representatives): develop, implement, and evaluate CDA activities in communities within the thirty-kilo-

metre radius specified in the Mines and Minerals Act; register communities that are expected to benefit from a CDA and funding; review community applications and proposals submitted by the CNRMC and make recommendations to the NNRMC; ensure compliance with the provisions of a CDA and the Act.

3 NNRMC (consisting of members of civil society groups representing mining communities, members of Parliament, a representative of mining companies operating in the district, and the Director of Mines): review decisions on CDAS received by the DNRMC; make decisions on funding, distribution, deadlines, and criteria for implementation; monitor and evaluate projects; consult with and inform communities on outcomes of approved projects and allocation of required resources.

Interview results also indicated that many resource-rich communities view diamond area community development funds (DACDFS) as a better alternative to CDAS, citing benefits such as road improvements, agricultural investment, establishment of trading routes, road construction and maintenance, construction of clinics, provision of scholarships for secondary school students to study in Freetown, financial support for local and traditional administrations, vocational training, law enforcement, and provision of basic services such as water and electricity (Kanu 2010). However, the reality is that DACDF projects in the three districts were badly constructed or abandoned halfway through, with some failing to take into consideration the needs of various interest groups, particularly children, the disabled, and the elderly. With respect to CDAS, many mining communities in the three districts have yet to reap any benefits, although a few chiefdoms, particularly in the diamond-rich Kono District, have recorded substantial gains from the use of funds ceded to them by mining companies. The great majority of these development projects were built using CDFS. In the three districts, concerns remain that ceded mining revenues allocated from CDAS and the DACDF is not being used effectively (Dupuy 2017).

In light of the continuing opportunities and challenges regarding both CDAS and DACDFS, a comprehensive study should be undertaken to examine and promote backward linkages, specifically with respect to the local impact and response (current and prospective) of downstream refining, transport, distribution, marketing and sales processes, and mid-stream or side-stream sector activities. Such a study would improve understanding of local content identification and inclusion, resource value chains, national procurement institutions, the influence of emerging technologies, and contemporary transnational business practices.

Furthermore, backward and sideways linkages need to be enhanced – a key objective of the African Union's Africa Mining Vision (AMV) policy framework. This proposed study would help to establish a systemic framework, which could be used to assist Sierra Leone in identifying constraints affecting its industries. It could also take specific action to improve and strengthen its industries, while becoming a direct portal for bottom-up information transfer between communities and government actors. A systems approach would also allow stakeholders to study the entire mineral value chain from exploration through extraction, processing, fabrication, and marketing, and thereby identify the obstacles to beneficiation and value addition in Sierra Leone. A necessary starting point would be to map AMV-compliant participatory policies and mechanisms in both the public and private sectors. The information could then be made available via online platforms. The proposed study should also consider the following documents:

1 The UNDP's multilevel "Strategy for Supporting Sustainable and Equitable Management of the Extractive Sector for Human Development" (UNDP 2012) focuses on strengthening the capacities of subnational governments and civil society by leveraging analytical and research capabilities to develop participatory legislation, policy and planning, and people-centred extractive practices.
2 Operationalization of the Africa Mining Vision and Country Mining Vision frameworks would constitute a selection of specific guidelines related to leveraging natural resources for development and economic growth (UNECA 2014).
3 The OECD's "Policy Dialogue on Natural Resources-based Development" framework (OECD, n.d.), to which the AMV is

party, argues for establishing an operational framework for public-private collaboration on resource-based value creation by building an empirical basis for decision making. It is aimed at inclusive participatory processes, leveraging opportunity areas for "quick wins" and long-term collaboration, creating an enabling environment for business while ensuring sustainable action and meaningful local engagement, and establishing a monitoring and evaluation process.

4 The High-level Expert Group Meeting report "Towards the Post-2015 Development Agenda and the African Agenda 2063" (UN 2015) provides, among other things, an assessment of the AMV implementation progress, a selection of best practices and lessons learned for local beneficiation and inclusivity, and recommendations aimed at contributing to implementation of the AMV and building new partnerships among all key stakeholders.

A holistic, locally driven, and upgraded Sierra Leonean mineral value chain also requires careful consideration of the following issues:

1 Limited local beneficiation and value in the current mineral value chain should be discussed within the political economy of resource generation and transfer. Such a political economy has implications for the transparency of the extractive industry (including the mining sector), particularly in regard to combatting the high incidence of illicit financial flows out of Africa that occur on several fronts, such as abusive transfer pricing; trade mispricing and unequal contracts, for purposes of tax evasion; aggressive tax avoidance; and the illegal export of foreign exchange (ACEP 2015a). Bond (2008) sees such activities as the output of Africa being linked into systems of global power, accumulation, and state-based class disputes that facilitate the looting of the continent as a whole, maintaining its levels of poverty so as to enrich the North.

2 Promoting natural resource–based industrialization (including

166 GOVERNANCE, CONFLICT, AND NATURAL RESOURCES IN AFRICA

minerals) requires the harmonization of fiscal and mineral policies and regulatory frameworks, all of which form the cornerstones of regional integration programs and proposed development corridors across the continent.

3 An in-depth understanding of the interests and the relationships among relevant stakeholders will help considerably to align interests, build trust, establish transparency, determine suitable incentives for making the value chain work better, and promote the fair distribution of benefits among stakeholders.

Sierra Leone is in a unique position to take advantage of contemporary global economic patterns that have increased demand for its mineral resources, but a decline in the commodity price supercycle, which had contributed to the country's impressive recent economic growth rate, has negatively affected commodity prices. This means that diversification alternatives must be explored along the value chain, and regional market opportunities must be considered. Minimizing the socioeconomic and environmental impacts of mining requires that stakeholders outside the private sector accept responsibility for enforcing human rights and gender protections, as well as labour and environmental norms and standards.

Collaborative governance, especially in the form of CDAS and DACDFS, has great potential to leverage private-sector actors and foreign-owned enterprises as partners in advancing Sierra Leone's economic transformation, post-conflict reconstruction and, as a result, stability and peace. The country's citizens would benefit from the Political Economy of Natural Resource Governance framework, whereby strong governance systems promote development and stability in the social, economic, and political spheres. It has been proposed that a comprehensive study to examine and promote backward linkages in Sierra Leone's mining sector be undertaken, which could improve local economic prospects for mining communities and the broader public.

The goal is to identify binding constraints on Sierra Leone's industries and suggest specific actions to improve and strengthen them, thereby creating a direct portal for bottom-up information transfer between communities and government actors. The key is the ability to study the entire mineral value chain in order to identify obstacles to beneficiation and value addition in the country. Awareness and understanding will help tailor actions and make policy adjustments over time to use mining revenues effectively and generate optimal sustainable development outcomes. In line with CDAs, mineral beneficiation and value addition could unlock Sierra Leone's social and economic potential if the infrastructure undergirding natural resource governance functions efficiently and is able to adapt to changing needs and circumstances.

CHAPTER 5

Ethiopia: Land Distribution as Developmental Tool

Introduction

Over the past decade, Ethiopia has achieved and sustained a relatively high level of economic growth, with an average annual GDP growth rate between 2004 and 2014 of around 9 per cent (World DataBank 2016b). This is remarkable given the low-income status of the 102 million people who live there, and where the guaranteed national income per capital is $1,719.40. Notable gains have also been made in human development (World Bank, n.d.[e]), helping to elevate Ethiopia to among the top ten countries globally to attain the largest absolute gains with regard to its human development index (HDI) in recent years. For example, between 1990 and 2015, life expectancy rose from 47 to 65 years, infant mortality rates dropped from 121 to 41 per thousand births, and labour productivity grew from 1.7 to 5.5 per cent (World Bank, n.d.[g]; World Bank, n.d.[h]).

Despite this impressive economic performance over the past decade, not all Ethiopians appear to have benefitted from this growth. Livelihoods of Ethiopian farmers and pastoralists, who account for above 80 per cent of the population (Ali, Dercon, and Gautam 2007), have remained precarious due to a lack of transformation in the smallholder agricultural sector.[1] In 2016, droughts across the country caused 10.2 million Ethiopians to require emergency food relief (WFP 2016), up roughly 65 per cent from the 6.2 million Ethiopians in need of food assistance in 2009 (Bues and Theesfeld 2012; Rahmato 2011). The average wage for unskilled agricultural labour in Ethiopia was reported to be $0.80 per day in 2008 (Shepherd 2013).

Ethiopia: Land Distribution 169

Food insecurity remains a perennial threat to the well-being of the majority of Ethiopians, who live in poverty due to lack of access to productive resources, particularly arable land, and economic opportunities. The country's economic growth has yet to be leveraged to deliver inclusive and sustained economic gains for all Ethiopians.

This state of affairs, compounded by the inherently inequitable outcomes of the country's economic growth, underline a growing fragility in terms of brewing ethnic tensions, which in turn undermine political and social stability, prompting the characterization of Ethiopia as a conflict-threatened country (Kefale 2013). Since Ethiopia's first national multiparty elections in 1995, the central government's policies have become increasingly authoritarian and ethnically based – and even divisive – which has created dissatisfaction among several of the country's ethnic groups in recent years (Erk 2017). Human Rights Watch reported that in 2015 and 2016, Ethiopia experienced widespread ethnic-based protests against the existing political order, which allegedly resulted in the killings of some 500 people by internal security forces (HRW 2017). Indeed, the 547-seat House of People's Representatives is overwhelmingly controlled by the ruling party, which currently occupies 502 seats. This situation creates a de facto one-party state with a tendency toward dictatorship-style government, which has been facilitated by persistent crackdowns on independent media and civil liberties (HRW 2017).

The state of democracy within the Ethiopian regime has been widely criticized, mostly due to Addis Ababa's harsh responses to any opposition (for more information, see Svensson 2019). As such, the lack of diversity in political actors is a critical challenge for foreign investment as it threatens the stability of the democratic political system. Nevertheless, the election of Abiy Ahmed as prime minister in 2018 has produced some positive changes, but much remains to be done. Clashes took place between Ethiopian Somalis and Oromians in mid-2017 following major anti-government protests across the country a year earlier (BBC 2017; Gaffey 2017). For many years now, the Oromia region has been the site of large-scale anti-government marches, clashes, and the like since the Ethiopian People's Revolutionary Democratic Front (EPRDF) came to power in 1995 (africanews.com 2019). In October 2017, the Ethiopian Human Rights

Commission, which also characterized the country as conflict-threatened after studying violence in Oromia, Somali, Gambella, and the Southern Nations, Nationalities, and Peoples' Region (SNNPR), concluded that security forces and traditional leadership have been unable to stem the growing tide of crisis and called for a national policy on conflict prevention (africanews.com 2017).

At the same time, opposition parties have argued that "people are fed up with what the regime has been doing for a quarter of a century, hence, they're protesting against land grabs, reparations, stolen elections, and the rising cost of living (Hayden 2016). Some argue that if the government continues to repress the people even as millions are demanding their rights, civil war is one likely scenario. Anti-government protests have revolved around access to and use of land, specifically what the protesters perceive as unabashed land grabs, repatriations of wealth, and the reduction of land rights for average Ethiopians – conditions which, taken together, may be setting the stage for civil war (Hayden 2016). This situation is further exacerbated by what is becoming widely known as a quintessential example of climate-induced conflict, with violence along the Sudanese border, particularly in the Nile River region, becoming increasingly likely as farmers and pastoralists, negatively affected by climate change and desertification, cross borders in search of water and farmland (Aton 2017). Using the metrics defined in the OECD's *States of Fragility 2015* report noted earlier in Chapter 2, Ethiopia's current situation demonstrates a number of relevant features: prospects for violence; absence of the rule of law, especially in regard to security forces; and a limited capacity to adapt in the face of unrest or challenges to existing government structures. Collectively, these features suggest that the designation "conflict-threatened" is an appropriate usage in the case of Ethiopia.

Research has shown that large foreign land investments have had disastrous consequences at the local level in Ethiopia. Wolford et al. have addressed the issue of global land grabbing at length, and argue that "new land acquisitions are drawing upon, restructuring and challenging the nature of both governance and government" (2013). In the same vein, Borras's work on the capitalistic features of foreign investment in land – i.e., that it serves as a mechanism of dispossession – is very much at stake in the Ethiopian case (2012). Borras's book on land grabbing, co-edited with Mar-

Ethiopia: Land Distribution 171

gulis and McKeon, underlines the multipolarity and complexities involved in governing acquisitions of land by foreign-owned economic actors – a line of questioning at the heart of this chapter (Margulis, McKeon, and Borras 2014). At play here is the inability, in an increasingly densely populated region where agriculture and forest-based work are at the centre of the economic structure, to combine the two systems of production. Shete and Rutten's work on this issue highlights the link between the development of large farming and decreased food security and loss of income for local communities (2015). This reality has frequently been identified by scholars who explain the Ethiopian government's strategy as sacrificing food security for local communities in favour of increased foreign exchange earnings (Lavers 2012a). As such, while this manuscript focuses on macro-level analysis of national politics and policies aimed at promoting broad-based development through foreign-owned investments in natural resources, it is critical also to remind the reader that micro-level politics and systems of governance ought to be at the centre of efforts to support revenue beneficiation for communities. All over sub-Saharan Africa, strategies to re-localize the land tenure process – through means such as land registration and surveying – have revealed both benefits and risks, and may inform the Ethiopian system as well (Toulmin 2009).

Land Administration and Tenure in Ethiopia

Agriculture has long been a central pillar of the Ethiopian economy, with more than 80 per cent of the Ethiopian population still living in rural areas (Ali, Dercon, and Gautam 2007). The sector contributes about 45 per cent of the country's GDP and accounts for 90 per cent of export earnings and 85 per cent of foreign currency earnings. Consequently, much of Ethiopia's current politics and political history revolve around access to and control of arable land (Ensene 2018).

Unlike most African countries, Ethiopia never experienced colonial rule. Instead, it had been governed for many centuries by an imperial regime, under which land ownership was administered according to a quasi-feudal structure. In 1974, following a popular uprising that overthrew the last emperor, Haile Selassie, a left-wing military regime called the Derg took power and reconfigured the country's land and agriculture frameworks. In view of the uprising's premise – to eliminate the land-holding elite – the new government redistributed land to smallholder farmers through newly created local peasant associations. With the enactment of the Public Ownership of Rural Lands Proclamation in 1975, all land was nationalized and redistributed. Peasant associations – each of which was accorded an area of at least 800 hectares – were granted the power to redistribute land on the principle that peasants should be able to access land parcels of up to ten hectares per household (Ethiopia 1975). Land was redistributed at various points thereafter to appease new claimants as the country's population increased (Holden and Yohannes 2002). Under this new arrangement, Ethiopians were given individualized and usufruct rights, meaning that lands were granted by the government on a household basis, and could not be legally transferred via sale, lease, rental, or mortgage (Ethiopia 1975).

The intent of this policy reform was to create a land system that would empower Ethiopian smallholder producers. This did, in fact, happen – in large part for those in the southern peripheries, where land ownership had previously been concentrated among an elite minority. In practice, however, it also served to create widespread tenure insecurity due to the requirement for regular redistributions of landholdings as the population increased. In turn, this insecurity discouraged private smallholder agricultural investments, as peasants had no guarantee that their land, and any improvements they made to it, would not be reallocated to others in the future. Additionally, due to its individualistic nature, with land being granted on a household basis, this policy reform alienated peasants in the northern highlands from their customary, quasi-communal land arrangements. In summary, the 1975 Proclamation, in combination with later agricultural directives such as the failed promotion of producers' cooperatives, increased public investments in state farms, which led in turn to the forced resettlement of various populations and completely debilitated local smallholder production (Belete, Dillon, and Anderson 1991).

In the fifteen years following the 1975 Proclamation, the Derg regime – later known as the People's Democratic Republic of Ethiopia – failed to stay true to the political underpinnings of the social movement that had brought it to power. The central demand embedded within the 1970s up-

Ethiopia: Land Distribution 173

risings had been the call to redistribute land and power from the imperial elites to the peasantry (Makki 2012). While the subsequent policy reforms facilitated this redistribution, the Derg's rule in Ethiopia became progressively dictatorial and created another oppressive form of centralist governance. As a result, in the decade and a half following the 1975 Proclamation, Ethiopia experienced a 70 per cent decline in agricultural output (Makki 2012). In light of the country's slide into authoritarianism, the regime's leader, Mengistu Haile Mariam, was ousted in 1991 by a coalition of rebel forces led by the Tigray People's Liberation Front (TPLF). Once in power, this new group established the Transitional Government of Ethiopia (TGE), which eventually adopted a new constitution and became the Federal Democratic Republic of Ethiopia in 1994. The TGE was later elected as the Ethiopian People's Revolutionary Democratic Front (EPRDF) in the country's first national elections in 1995. Two major policies enacted during this state-building process were the continuation of state ownership of land and the establishment of a new ethno-federal system that devolved land administration to ethnically delineated regional governments (Donham 1999).[2]

Although other African countries have actively avoided accommodating ethnicity as a formal political element due to its tendency to provoke interethnic conflicts and state fragility, in the case of Ethiopia this nation-building strategy was essential to the formation of an stable government, given the process by which the TPLF came to power (Abbink 2011). In fact, the TPLF was able to mobilize a significant amount of support, and eventually took power by building a sense of unity out of the various ethnic groups' grievances against the (chiefly Amharic) Derg (Soule 2016). Some ethnic organizations, such as the Oromo Liberation Front, portions of the Southern Ethiopia Peoples' Democratic Coalition, and the Eritrean People's Liberation Front, which had all been sidelined under the largely Amharic imperial regime, were further marginalized during the Derg's rule. Given this history, the EPRDF, once in power, confronted a critical need to impose a governance structure that would empower aggrieved ethnic groups and unite them under a shared political agenda.

As a result, the new government hailed the creation of an ethnic-based federalist model, whereby nine regional territories and governments were assigned based along ethnic lines as a means of allowing ethnic self-determination (Abbink 2011). By creating ethnically delineated regional governments, especially those governing the more marginalized populations, the government argued there was room for greater ethnic equality in terms of government representation and, perhaps more importantly, access to resources (Aalen 2006). One of the most notable responsibilities of these new regional governments was the administration of land within their territories. While land legislation remained under the mandate of the federal government, corresponding laws and detailed guidelines on how federal laws, proclamations, regulations, and directives were to be implemented now fell under the purview of its regional counterparts (Benin and Pender 2001).

In contrast to this significant political evolution in land administration, land tenure remained unchanged. The new regime proceeded to implement and codify two major land-related policies in Ethiopia's 1995 constitution (Ethiopia 1995). In addition to implementing an ethno-federalist framework and upholding an individual usufruct tenure system, the new constitution also upheld and increased the focus on land rights for vulnerable agricultural groups. Article 40 (5) entitled Ethiopian pastoralists to "the right to free land for grazing and cultivation as well as the right not to be displaced from their own lands," while Article 35 (7) granted women "equal rights with men with respect to use, transfer, administration and control of land" and "equal treatment in the inheritance of property." The decision to maintain the Derg's land tenure model of state control over the allocation and use of land was likely made with the legacy of the earlier imperial regime in mind. Although land rights had been usufructs for many years under previous emperors, when Emperor Haile Selassie returned from exile in 1942, he established rules that led to the privatization of land – a tenure system that increased the power of the landholding elites and further deprived the peasantry of resources. From an economic perspective, debate has been ongoing as to whether the lack of privatization in Ethiopia's land system has prevented a rise in inequality, instability, and economic decline. Many argue that smallholders would have been vulnerable to land speculation and inequitable land accumulation had they been entitled to sell their land (USAID 2016).

Years after the establishment of the 1995 constitution, the Ethiopian government also sought to introduce a land certification program in the aim of reducing tenure insecurity and its negative impact on smallholder private investment. Thus, beginning in 2003 and over the next five years, the Ethiopian government was able to register approximately 25 million rural parcels in four of its main regions: Amhara, Tigray, Oromia, and the less remote parts of the Southern Nations Nationalities and Peoples Region (SNNPR). According to the World Bank, this participatory, pro-poor, and gender-sensitive certification program was "one of the largest, fastest, and most low-cost processes globally" (Deininger, Selod, and Burns 2011, 6).

Meanwhile, the new government also pursued complementary agricultural development policies, which were highly supportive of smallholder producers. Its Agricultural Development Led Industrialization (ADLI) strategy stated that since Ethiopia was a labour-rich and capital-poor country, the government should cater to and support smallholders (Lavers 2012a). By strengthening its most labour-intensive industry – through inputs such as irrigation, fertilizer, improved seed, credit services, and capacity development programs – the government posited that it could generate sustainable economic growth while improving national food security and stimulating downstream and upstream agricultural linkages. One of the key pillars of this strategy was the aforementioned continued guarantee of usufruct land rights for smallholders. As previously mentioned, this strategy has arguably prevented distressed land sales and the re-establishment of a land-governing elite (Lavers 2013).

Ethiopia is home to more than eighty ethnic groups, some of which are unrecognized or do not live within their designated ethnic territories, and many of the smaller among these groups were marginalized under the new ethno-regional framework. For example, although the government accorded Tigrayans, Amharas, Oromos, Afars, Somalis, and Hararis dominant ethnic status with their respective regional states, it denied such status to other groups with similar claims, such the Gurage, Sidama, and Woleyta. The territorialization of ethnicity was also illogical and detrimental for most towns and cities, which often contained a mix of ethnicities. Further, many ethnic minorities were marginalized because they did not speak the language of the new regional administration, or were discriminated against by the dominant group. Ethnic tensions also increased in many areas as various groups vied for exclusive rights over a territory's administration, which provided access to central government resources (Keller 2002).

The 2005 elections signalled to the EPRDF that if they hoped to stay in power, significant changes had to be made. From an economic perspective, given that significant growth in the agricultural sector had yet to be realized but remained essential to the country's poverty reduction strategy and overall economic growth, the central government expanded its focus from smallholder production to large-scale commercial agriculture, trade, and foreign investment – encouraging to foreign-owned enterprises looking to invest in Ethiopia's agriculture and other natural resource sectors. The ADLI strategy previously hailed by the government thus became subsumed within this new strategy and the significant economic growth it was expected to produce (interview with Mr Getachew Regassa, Secretary General, Addis Ababa Chamber of Commerce, 16 April 2014). The result was that the EPRDF's new focus on sustained high economic growth as a basis for retaining power, with its emphasis on FDI-driven commercial farming, came at the expense of household-based, smallholder-led agriculture.

Ethiopia has been assessed against the FAO's Voluntary Guidelines on the Responsible Governance of Tenure of Land, Fisheries and Forests (VGGT), with limited results. In terms of eligibility for compensation for expropriation, a lack of clear definition as to what constitutes public purpose limits greatly the positive impact of the country's policies, which were adopted for formally registered and recognized customary rights but fail to provide adequate protection to other tenure systems. Similarly, the limited scope of transparency and participation in the expropriation process is quite concerning and lacks critical indicators, including identification of affected landowners, requirements for a feasibility study, a social impact assessment, and even a basic cost-benefit assessment. These limitations are extensive and do not provide an adequate system of protection that would allow for long-term, broad-based development. The very limited role of the government – in the case of the VGGT, government is under no obligation to minimize or prevent involuntary resettlement – and the absence of a legal framework suitable to allow for robust resettlement and rehabilitation procedures is also a major risk for the stability of use of land-based extractive development (Land Portal, n.d.).

The Growing Threat of Ethnic-Based Conflict and State Fragility

The run-up to Ethiopia's 2005 elections demonstrated promise in terms of democratic process; the opposition parties at the time had gained significant popularity and were allowed to campaign and appear in state-televised debates (Abbink 2011). However, critics claim that after the realization dawned on the ruling party that the opposition would be able to form a coalition government, votes began disappearing during a non-transparent vote count (Abbink 2011). This, they argue, permitted a drastic turnaround and a narrow win for the EPRDF. Subsequent attempts to challenge the election's outcome in the courts offered little hope for a recount, as the "partisanship, lack of independence and integrity, and subservience of the electoral body and the judicial system to the EPRDF" (Berhanu 2012, 11) were clearly apparent.

Given that "foreign" NGOs are prohibited from conducting any form of awareness-raising or advocacy initiatives with regard to agricultural and land policies, the Ethiopian government entertains very few suggestions for alternative governance models in its natural resource sector. Yet, it is in this political context that the Ethiopian government has implemented significant changes to the country's agricultural policy framework – changes embodied by its new strategy prioritizing large-scale commercial agriculture.

In pursuing the objective of facilitating economic growth and stability through large-scale commercial agriculture by foreign-owned enterprises, the government has been accused of denying pastoralists and shifting cultivators "their right not to be displaced from their own land" under Article 40 (5) of the constitution (Ethiopia 1995). This creates an interesting scenario whereby efforts to "govern" foreign-owned private-sector actors contributes to, rather than reduces, the tension and instability that the country faces. Many critics have pointed to the central government's indiscriminate expropriation of land under the pretext that it is "unused," even as it ignores the land's crucial uses for pastoralism and shifting cultivation by nomadic Ethiopian peoples (interview with Dr Meheret Ayenew, Executive Director, Forum for Social Studies, 17 April 2014). Though foreign investment has the potential to offer much in the way of knowledge and technology transfer, there is also evidence to suggest that land acquisitions

178 GOVERNANCE, CONFLICT, AND NATURAL RESOURCES IN AFRICA

in Ethiopia have displaced smallholder agriculturalists and prohibited pastoralists from accessing their ancestral lands without providing them with compensatory employment opportunities (Moreda 2015). If persons displaced by large-scale land leases are offered employment, it is typically on a casual basis with little in the way of job security (Rahmato 2011). Moreover, despite receiving the legally mandated financial compensation from the Ethiopian government, Lavers (2012b) and Shepherd (2013) note that displaced smallholders must struggle to preserve their prosperity following appropriation of their lands, as the compensation they receive is often deemed insufficient.

While these changes were made without consultation at the local level, they were undeniably influenced by foreign stakeholders, as the changes became an important part of retaining state legitimacy in the eyes of international donors – a situation that alludes to private sector–driven governance. The repressive tactics which the Ethiopian government had been accused of using during the 2005 elections – including torture, arbitrary imprisonment, and sustained harassment of critics (HRW 2006) – triggered a backlash from donors and activists alike, and soured Ethiopia's relationship with the international community.[3] Many human rights groups called on donors to revisit and reduce their aid flows to Ethiopia as they felt they would be used to uphold an increasingly authoritarian regime (Albin-Lackey 2005). Thus, in the years following the 2005 elections, the Ethiopian government actively sought to rebuild its reputation in order to re-establish its legitimacy as a worthy destination for development aid and foreign investment.

The government has allowed for an increased share of foreign investment (from both public- and private-sector actors) in Ethiopian land since 2005, with foreign investments accounting for 74.4 per cent of the total land requested for large-scale agricultural production as of 2012 (Baumgartner 2012). The largest investors in Ethiopia today are companies from the Middle East (21.5 per cent), Western Europe (22.4 per cent), South Asia (13.2 per cent), and North America (8.4 per cent) (Baumgartner 2012), with investment dollars flowing mostly to Ethiopia's floriculture, food, meat, vegetable, and biofuel sectors.[4] The result has been drastic changes in Ethiopia's land market. According to the Ethiopian Investment Agency (interview with Mr Aklilu Mariam, Director for Information and Invest-

Ethiopia: Land Distribution

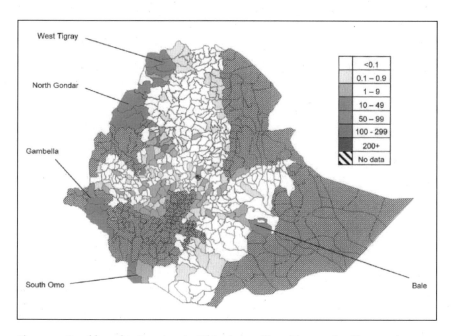

Figure 5.1 Land leased to investors in Ethiopia by village (thousands of hectares). *Source*: Lavers 2012a.

ment, EIA, 17 April 2014), three and a half million hectares of land had been allocated for large-scale lease investments between 1996 and 2008, with much of this land made available in the remote, lowland areas in the west and south of the country, and an increasing portion allocated specifically in the Benishangul-Gumuz, Gambella, and SNNPR regions (see Figure 5.1).

Lack of Positive Change in Ethiopia's Agricultural Sector

In view of the government's argument that a shift to commercial agriculture would ultimately benefit small landholders, it is important to consider the nuanced weaknesses of the commercial agriculture model in the development context, a subject often glossed over in the literature. For instance, contrary to employment creation expectations, commercial agriculture tends to replace labour-intensive smallholder farming techniques with capital-intensive technologies. It has been claimed that large-scale commercial farming is also likely to degrade the surrounding environment and decrease the sustainability of nearby smallholder production, due to its more intensive use of fresh waterways, fertilizers, pesticides, and fossil fuels for machinery (Vermeulen and Cotula 2010; Anseeuw 2013). The United Nations Special Rapporteur on the Right to Food also noted that a significant loss of agrobiodiversity is typically associated with large-scale monocultures (Ozden 2013), which weaken the stability, sustainability, and resilience of agricultural systems in the face of weather- and pest-related shocks. According to Altieri and Nicholls (2008, 474), polycultural agriculture techniques yield advantages of 20 to 60 per cent as they "reduce losses due to weeds, insects and diseases and make a more efficient use of the available resources of water, light and nutrients." There is therefore a growing recognition that more balance is needed within the Western, "modernized" approach to agriculture, as it may be worsening the potential for ecological shocks, damaging the environment, and further marginalizing the majority of the world's agricultural population (Weis 2010).

In contrast, smallholder farming in Ethiopia emphasizes ecological diversity, systems integration and synergies, and the inclusion and development of poor smallholders. This type of farming, in fact, generates more jobs than large-scale farming due to its low level of mechanization (Herren et al. 2012) and allows for higher aggregate production levels per unit of land due to crop diversification. Furthermore, it delivers greater returns, thanks to associated agricultural techniques that produce higher yields with fewer inputs. Similarly, nomadic livestock or shifting agricultural production offers the spatial flexibility needed for the arid and semi-arid climates typical of the Ethiopian highlands. In allowing herds of livestock to move over great distances, or cultivation activities to rotate over time through different plots of land, pastoralism and shifting cultivation offer important benefits to populations in areas where rainfall, and hence the availability of water and fodder, is variable (van den Brink 2006).

Governments must do more to create effective monitoring and review processes for large-scale foreign-owned investments, and put structures in place to establish impactful scopes of action for foreign-owned private-sector actors. In the case of Ethiopia, a failure to closely review contracts in favour of quick financial returns exacerbates these challenges. Ethiopians are regularly faced with national agreements that fail to address issues of accountability among all parties, ensure the protection of traditional and subsistence-based livelihoods, defend against the displacement of farmers and pastoralists, and encourage environmental sustainability and the like. In addition, reports and interviews indicate that agriculture agreements between the Ethiopian government and multinational corporations have largely failed to include robust frameworks that define responsibilities and outline adequate corporate social responsibility measures, with the government placing emphasis instead on rapid industrialization and attracting FDI (Besada 2017).

There are also concerns regarding the potential impacts of foreign investments that are initiated with little understanding of, or concern for, the socioeconomic and political context of the host community, especially if the expectation exists that those foreign-owned enterprises should contribute more broadly to peace, stability, and sustainable growth. Many of these negative impacts are already occurring in Ethiopia, undermining the government's argument that encouraging and properly governing large-scale foreign investments will ultimately benefit smallholder producers (Taffesse, Brown, and Minten 2018). For example, in the case of knowledge spillovers, foreign investors are often expected to provide appropriate market services and the technical knowledge to help producers upgrade their standards in order to meet market requirements. Yet, "when related to the total number of smallholders, only a minority has actually been able to participate in such schemes" (Bosc et al. 2013, 13). Instead, the most common opportunities are unskilled jobs, and even these are not necessarily offered to local communities.[5] Furthermore, such unskilled positions do little to teach smallholders about the operational requirements of large-scale farming. Meanwhile, many of the mechanized and energy-intensive farming techniques used by large-scale investors are unlikely to be viable for smallholder use, given that small-scale farmers often lack the necessary resources to develop and maintain such infrastructure (Lavers 2012a).

There has been anecdotal evidence to suggest a casual disregard, at times, for enforcing regulations requiring foreign investors to hire local labour, thereby inhibiting the former's contribution to this aspect of sustainable economic growth (interview with Mr Aklilu Mariam, Director for Information and Investment, EIA, 17 April 2014). As such, not all projects provide employment opportunities, and many of those who are employed are offered casual contracts, meaning they have little employment security and thus contribute little to local economic growth (Rahmato 2011). According to data collected by the Embassy of India in Ethiopia, for example, more than 90 per cent of the 110,000 Ethiopian workers employed in 2008 by Indian companies were seasonal workers (Shepherd 2013). One project in the lowlands also demonstrated the tension between Indigenous lowland labour and that of a growing group of highland seasonal migrant farmers willing to move for agricultural work (Moreda 2015). In this case, the Indigenous community was displaced from its ancestral lands for the benefit of a foreign investor and then marginalized in the subsequent hiring of local labour.[6]

This was confirmed separately by an EU delegation to Ethiopia, which noted that most commercial farms hired foreign workers or workers from outside the local community, causing tensions between local and migrant groups (interview with Mr David Mogollon, Head for Rural Development and Food Security, EU Delegation to Ethiopia, 11 April 2014). That said, the decision made by commercial farms to hire foreign workers or workers outside the local community was not necessarily related to cost-effectiveness or productivity. Often, foreign investors that transplant expatriates to investment sites do so out of ignorance of the local context and needs; being new to Ethiopia, they may be acting on experience gained elsewhere. Moreover, on some occasions, workers were hired based on recommendations by national or local government officials.

Looking beyond skills and knowledge transfer and employment opportunities, the construction of rural infrastructure such as new roads and irrigation networks (a transactional obligation in many land deals) often caters to the company's needs rather than the local population's – or it remains privatized. The lack of expected returns for affected communities can have serious consequences, as many farmers sell their land or relocate to make way for large-scale agricultural investments on the promise that they will experience direct benefits. When this promise is only partially met, or even ignored, smallholders and pastoralists typically find themselves without land or are left to till less arable land. In these

Ethiopia: Land Distribution

cases, they often have no recourse for securing the compensatory investments promised to them.

This creates a situation in which foreign-owned enterprises are contributing to conflict and instability. This can spell trouble for a conflict-threatened country like Ethiopia, which performs well economically and operates solid institutions, but in which ethnic tensions due to land access and other developmental resource issues may threaten political and social stability. Indeed, such tensions were seen in 2016, when protestors attacked foreign-owned businesses in the Oromia and Amhara regions, with opposition political parties citing the absence of broad-based development for the country's poorest populations, despite large-scale foreign agriculture investment, as the source of discontent (Al Jazeera 2016). Many in the Oromia region argue that the government has repeatedly tried to forcibly evict them from fertile farmland, and used the expansion of regional capital to take control of arable fields for multinationals (Al Jazeera 2016; Dixon 2016). Rural farmers point to the decades-long process of villagization and land grabbing as having caused the forcible relocation of tens of thousands of individuals to make space for agriculture investments by foreign-owned companies (Smith 2015).

In contrast to many other countries, Ethiopia's infrastructure requirements for investors are minimal. According to a private investor in one case study, the Ethiopian government had acknowledged responsibility for all public infrastructure – roads, telecommunications, and electricity – while the investing company was to provide private infrastructure, including roads and irrigation systems internal to the investment area, and accommodations for employees (Shepherd 2013). Another study reported that the foreign investing company's only obligations were to repair and widen a dirt track leading to the project site and provide some plastic sheeting to a community school (Rahmato 2011). In any case, there were few benefits to the community: the investor cut down fruit trees to widen the road – eliminating an essential source of food security and income – and refused to compensate affected smallholders. In sum, a lack of investment regulations regarding contribution requirements to Ethiopia's infrastructure has significantly diminished the potential returns from these investments for affected smallholders, constituting a failure to leverage foreign-owned enterprises to contribute to conflict-containment strategies by ensuring participation and returns for smallholders as elements of land transactions and investments.

It also appears that the Government of Ethiopia has been using its own security sector (hard and soft power) resources to support a push toward large-scale commercialization of the agriculture and natural resource sectors. In 2012, Human Rights Watch reported that at least 3.6 million hectares in the Gambella region had been leased to multinational and local firms since 2008, much of the transfer orchestrated with the help of armed security forces driving people from their land (Horne and Bader 2012). According to this report, tens of thousands of Indigenous people have been forcibly removed from their homes in Gambella and placed in new villages with no meaningful consultation and without free, prior, and informed consent (Horne and Bader 2012). Although the stated goals of what should be a voluntary villagization program are to provide better access to basic infrastructure and agricultural assistance, the program has mostly taken place in areas where significant land investments have already been made or will be made in the future (Horne and Bader 2012). After interviewing more than 100 Gambella residents affected by the villagization program, HRW stated that it had found "widespread human rights violations at all stages" (Horne and Bader 2012). Rather than support a governance and regulatory system that fundamentally works to benefit local populations, situations like this one merely create animosity between those populations and foreign-owned enterprises. The Ethiopian population would benefit from broad-based, inclusive development based on the creation of strong governance frameworks in the agribusiness and land industries. The Political Economy of Natural Resource Governance concept provides major avenues for advancing such a governance framework.

The Ethiopian government's preference for and encouragement of large-scale foreign agricultural investments has had a negative effect on smallholder producers. Limitations on the freedom of Ethiopian civil society and academics to speak out have diminished awareness regarding the negative impacts of large-scale land leases on Ethiopian smallholders and pastoralists (Shepherd 2013; interview with Dr Zerihun Mohammed, socio-economic researcher, Forum for Social Studies, 17 April 2014).[7] Moreover, foreign investments in large-scale agricultural projects have yet to provide any significant benefits to smallholder producers, as existing governance systems do not require private-sector actors to contribute to sustainable development in any meaningful way. Alternative governance models can offer more inclusive and politically decentralized growth, which is necessary to regain smallholders' support, decrease ethnic tensions and, ultimately, achieve sustainable economic growth, stability, and peace.

Results

This case study broadly demonstrates that governance models that prioritize the production of labour-intensive smallholder crops, meaningful consultations with local communities, and due respect for local knowledge of agricultural production processes could facilitate inclusive and sustainable growth in Ethiopia. However, instead of being allies in achieving stability and sustainable growth, foreign-owned enterprises have become vehicles for deepening ethnic polarization, as the current policy framework in which they operate reinforces distrust in the state's ability or willingness to overcome the oppressive and ethnically repressive behaviour of previous regimes. Ultimately, the role of foreign investors in natural resource governance in a fragile state like Ethiopia is to support sustainable economic development efforts and contribute to conflict containment strategies through positive and fair involvement in land transactions and investment. The success of foreign investments in supporting such goals hinges on effective governance structures.

Regulation and Governance

Despite expectations, five to ten years after the enactment of the 1995 constitution and its related policies, agricultural growth, poverty, and food security had not improved significantly. Forward and backward production linkages were limited, in part due to extra income in Ethiopian households being directed to food rather than agricultural inputs. On the supply side, a lack of both public funds and capital accumulation in the private sector limited the larger investments needed to facilitate these linkages. Consequently, doubts concerning the economic arguments outlined in the government's ADLI strategy, which focused solely on smallholder agriculture as the engine for growth, subsequently convinced senior Ethiopian policy makers that an expanded agricultural approach was required (interview with Mr Getachew Regassa, Secretary General, Addis Ababa Chamber of Commerce, 16 April 2014).

In addition to limited economic impacts, earlier land and agriculture polices had also failed to protect vulnerable groups. For instance, despite the legal recognition of ethnic equality through federalism, the lowland regions and the ethnic groups dwelling there remained politically marginalized. Although a limited degree of autonomy was conferred upon them (Lavers 2012a) following a long history of inequality under imperial rule, during which the "lowland periphery was characterized by inequality, exploitation and extraction of resources through collection of tribute and taxes, and the slave and ivory trades" (Lavers 2012a, 125), the ethnic groups native to these regions, including the Anuak, Afar, and Somali peoples, were left with few skills and scant experience to administer their territories under the new ethno-federalist model. As a result, the central government continued to act on their behalf in governing their territories, thereby undermining the idea of ethnic equality and empowerment in these areas.

It can be argued that Ethiopia's previous policy framework for agricultural growth delivered poor economic outcomes. However, the current focus on encouraging large-scale commercial agriculture by foreign-owned enterprises – created in a vacuum of political opposition due to increasingly oppressive and authoritarian measures on the government's part (Alemu, Gabre-Madhin, and Dejene 2006; Lavers 2012a) – means that domestic stakeholders were unable to contribute to the policy framework, which was developed and tightly controlled by the Tigray People's Liberation Front under the influence of foreign stakeholders (e.g., development banks). The current agricultural strategy has effectively recentralized the ruling party's power over agricultural land. This policy change has created a complex link between the agricultural foreign-owned private sector and the growing fragility and instability of the Ethiopian state (Berhanu and Poulton 2014).

In an effort to expand the number of large-scale, commercial agricultural projects across the country, the Ethiopian government produced a

Ethiopia: Land Distribution

number of development plans. In light of a lack of public funds and capital accumulation in the domestic private sector, these plans have favoured the foreign private sector at the expense of smallholders. For example, Ethiopia's Plan for Accelerated and Sustained Development to End Poverty (PASDEP) for the 2005 to 2010 period emphasized the importance of commercial agriculture. This emphasis was then expanded to highlight foreign investment in Ethiopia's Growth and Transformation Plan (GTP) for the 2010–15 period. Specifically, the GTP noted the crucial role of large-scale investors in transforming the agricultural sector and the need to "attract and support strong foreign investments that play [an] important role in the country's economic development, for those sectors given special attention by the government" (MFED 2010, 29). Although foreign investors are prohibited from leasing land for more than fifty years, in light of the new plans and legislation, foreign land investors are now largely exempt from paying taxes on imports of capital goods and repatriated profits (Bossio et al. 2012).

Additionally, Ethiopian land is leased for very low rents, with the lowest of these available in the remote, sparsely populated lowland regions – which does act as an incentive for investments in more disadvantaged areas. As the Ministry of Agriculture (formerly the Ministry of Agriculture and Rural Development) stated in 2009, Ethiopia offers negligible lease rates compared to the surrounding region (Makki 2012). By shifting its focus toward foreign investments in large-scale commercial agricultural projects, the Ethiopian government also re-established central government authority over land transfers of 5,000 hectares or more through the enactment of the Council of Ministers Regulations of 2008 (Baumgartner et al. 2015). This shift in land governance was significant, as it ran contrary to both the 1995 constitution and the central government's reassurances that it would allow for ethnic self-determination through the empowerment of regional governments. This regulation has added to tension and instability (interview with Dr Meheret Ayenew, Executive Director, Forum for Social Studies, 17 April 2014).

Mainstream Western and African regional development institutions, such as the World Bank and the Alliance for a Green Revolution in Africa (AGRA), hailed the shift in focus from small- to large-scale agriculture as an essential step in improving agricultural productivity (Sharp, Ludi, and Gebreselassie 2007, 46), as well as a crucial pillar to increasing food production and economic growth. From the perspective of these institutions, the stagnation of the agricultural sector is attributable to the persistence of smallholder farms, with the only solutions being increased mechanization of agricultural operations and the economies of scale offered by large-scale farming – known as agriculture development-led industrialization (Lavers 2011). Given the lack of public funds and capital in Ethiopia's private sector, foreign investment presented itself as an apparent avenue for agricultural modernization, food security, and economic growth.

Ethiopia's most recent economic policies in the agricultural sector, which have focused increasingly on external, foreign-owned enterprises, has coincided with diminished internal political legitimacy due to a complete lack of space for opposition and the recentralization of significant decisions regarding agricultural land. This diminished legitimacy is demonstrated by the fact that Ethiopia has ranked consistently in the top 20 fragile states since 2007 (Fund for Peace 2018). Confronted with significant popular opposition to policy and legislative changes, the EPRDF has typically responded by becoming more insular and making agricultural policy changes in a political environment devoid of opposition or critical opinion, using the justification of a statist approach for economic governance (van Veen 2016). The most significant policy change, brought about at the behest of mainstream Western and African development institutions, was a shift in government support toward large-scale commercial agriculture, which effectively placed an entirely new emphasis on the role of foreign-owned enterprises in delivering growth. It also recentralized control within the country's land management structure, thereby undermining previous claims that the government supported ethnic equality. As a result, the private sector, which now consists mainly of foreign investors, is reinforcing the EPRDF's repressive tactics and thereby contributing to the country's growing fragility (Aalen 2009). As such, this case study provides unique insights into how lacklustre regulation of foreign-owned enterprises can contribute to a country's instability at the expense of economic growth and peace.

Beneficiation and Value Addition

In shifting its focus to large-scale, commercial agricultural projects, the Ethiopian government argued – as did various mainstream international and African development institutions – that this new agricultural model would ultimately benefit smallholder producers. Purported benefits were to include the creation of employment opportunities, development and improvement of rural infrastructure, new sources of knowledge transfer, and lucrative sale opportunities for African farmers looking to invest capital in other industries (Vermeulen and Cotula 2010).

Measures that would facilitate genuinely inclusive and sustainable growth in Ethiopia include: labour-intensive agricultural crops and labour-intensive investment models; meaningful consultations and renewed value placed on local agricultural knowledge; an inclusive and participatory biofuel and industrial crop production allocation framework; and broader support for developing the growth of domestic companies involved in agriculture. Consultation with central and local governments, as well as individual smallholders, that encourages large-scale farming companies to position projects in ways that have less of an impact on smallholder and pastoral populations or vulnerable ecologies is also necessary. Local farmers and herders typically have an excellent understanding of how livelihoods and food security may be achieved in their communities, as well as extensive expertise regarding local and regional soil, climate, and ecological issues. Integrating traditional agricultural knowledge offers a means to mitigate a large-scale project's social and environmental impacts, while opening up better-paid jobs for local experts and increasing production within a specific agricultural context.

Local consultation and free, prior, and informed consent (FPIC) are also essential to the security of investments, as discontent and unrest within communities surrounding new large-scale land acquisitions can jeopardize the sustainability of these kinds of projects (Baumgartner et al. 2015). Using FPIC as a basis for investment projects is not only essential from a human rights perspective, but is also beneficial in terms of local community support. Peasant forms of resistance, although more covert and disorganized in nature, can severely undermine large-scale agricultural land investments, as demonstrated by land encroachments by surrounding smallholders or intentional crop damage by local agricultural labourers. Since foreign-owned enterprises typically enter local arenas where land relations are dynamic or contested, consultation is crucial to understanding the local context and ensuring there is local support for incoming investments.

Violence in Oromia

Violence erupted in the Oromia region in 2015 in response to the government's intention to expand the boundaries of Addis Ababa, the national capital. One act of protest was the burning of the warehouses of a Dutch agricultural company, Solagrow PLC, which had taken over communal grazing lands in the region. Protesters had become increasingly concerned that the government was trying to take away their land (Schemm 2016).

Large-scale land acquisitions exacerbate food insecurity when smallholders' and pastoralists' access to land is revoked without adequate provision for alternative sources of food and water. Despite this, the Ethiopian government's incentives for foreign investors are extremely liberal, perhaps counterproductively so, with regard to the country's food security. For example, investments are given higher priority through additional tax exemptions for investors whose crops are destined for the export market (Lavers 2012b). According to Article 4 of the Council of Ministers Regulation no. 84/2003, which stipulated new investment incentives, investors engaged in manufacturing or agro-industrial activities or the production of agricultural products are exempt from income tax for at least five years if they export more than half their production or provide 75 per cent to exporters. In contrast, those exporting less than 75 per cent of their production are exempt only for a minimum of two years.

In addition to generous tax incentives, there has been a massive shift of land and water rights from customary to foreign users, a process that often occurs informally as a result of ambiguous land rights and water regulations.[8] In one case study in Oromia, for example, newly arrived foreign investors from the Netherlands, Russia, Israel, Palestine, and China caused changes to the community's previously informal communal rights to canal

Ethiopia: Land Distribution

infrastructure (Bues and Theesfeld 2012). Smallholder needs were neglected in favour of these more powerful investors, unfettered by the Ethiopian government, as they were able to divert water from traditionally communal sources. In another project, in which the agricultural firm Saudi Star was given land and water rights to develop a large-scale project on Anuak land in the Gambella region, communal land was again expropriated due to the perception that it was unused (Rahmato 2011). In fact, the land was far from being unused, as the Anuak people supplement their smallholder farming incomes with fishing and hunting activities, and honey production, thereby relying on their surrounding ecosystem for wild food sources in times of hardship. As a result, Saudi Star's deforestation of this previously communal land has worsened the local community's food security (Rahmato 2011). As well, rates of pay for Ethiopians working on land that has been acquired by private investors have fallen below the level required to replace the value of the smallholders' lost farmland. With US$0.80 per day as the norm for unskilled agricultural labour in Ethiopia in 2008 – one press report quoted a female worker earning just $0.47 per day (Shepherd 2013) – agricultural wage labour opportunities have offered a poor livelihood alternative given the rising cost of food.

Saudi Star

Saudi Star Agricultural Development PLC is the agricultural arm of MIDROC Africa Ltd, a Saudi company that is investing heavily in Ethiopia (Al Amoudi, n.d.). Currently managing 140,000 hectares of land in the Gambella region, the company plans to increase its investments to cover 500,000 hectares (ICTA 2014) as part of the King Abdullah Food Security Program (KAFSP). Saudi Star owner Sheikh Mohammed Hussein Al Amoudi intends to invest an additional $5 billion in Ethiopia's land between 2016 and 2021, which will have a significant impact on traditional land systems (farmlandgrab.org 2018).

Looking at the impact of large-scale land investments from a political perspective, many national laws overlook the need for FPIC or compensation for local populations in these types of transactions. Consequently, there is typically a lack of engagement or support from community stakeholders who have been displaced from their land. Ethiopia is no exception, and smallholders and pastoralists alike have exhibited overt resistance through peasant protests in several parts of the country.[9] They have also exhibited covert forms of resistance, such as slow encroachments on land parcelled out to investment projects and the quiet destruction of field crops and machinery (Rahmato 2011). The people of the Godere woreda in the Gambella region, for example, organized a series of meetings when they heard that an Indian agricultural company called Lucky Exports had acquired a lease of 5,000 hectares of forest to establish a tea plantation near their community (Rahmato 2011). People in the Godere woreda (a district of the Gambella region) prepared an alternative land use plan that would preserve the forest and provide youth employment, and presented it to the federal government – an example of a successful lobbying effort that halted a planned plantation project. However, resistance has become the exception to the rule in the Gambella region (Horne and Bader 2012).

With regard to the Ethiopian government's provision of compensation for expropriated land, Lavers (2012b, 907) noted that, on the whole, displaced smallholders "seem to receive the legally required compensation of ten times the average annual income over the previous five years." However, he also noted that it is questionable whether this amount is sufficient. Some farmers do not have the financial capacity to handle a significant amount of money, having never done so before. According to one Ethiopian farmer interviewed in 2011, "the birr [Ethiopia's currency] lasted a few months, but the land has been lost for generations" (Shepherd 2013, 9). In addition, multiple projects have demonstrated the potential divisive effects of compensation when given without adequate consideration of the local context. For example, one largely Amharic village in the predominantly Oromo town of Bishoftu did not receive the intended compensation from an investor because local Oromo authorities denied the payment (Shepherd 2013). In cases like this, large-scale land leases were used by dominant ethnic groups to exert power over other groups through disproportionate allocations of land or imbalanced distributions of compensation payments.

Future Opportunities

Considerations in Developing an Effective Governance Framework

Although Ethiopia remains heavily reliant on agriculture for export revenue and GDP growth, the share of manufacturing in the country's GDP has been trending upward over the past decade, with some of this manufacturing output attributed to exports. This is a transformation that should not be overlooked. Ethiopia has increasingly been creating manufacturing jobs, moving labour from the smallholder agriculture sector to processing and manufacturing (UNDP 2017). The World Bank and other observers identify Ethiopia as the African country with the greatest prospect for attracting the lower end of global manufacturing that China is currently "exporting" to low-wage developing economies. Should the country explore alternative foreign-owned enterprise investment models for this sector, particularly those that include collaborative governance institutions and components, manufacturing could be the sector that drives sustainable development, peace, and stability.

Although growth in smallholder agriculture and pastoralism can positively affect food security due to the linkage between production, household consumption, and domestic markets, it can be equally detrimental if negatively affected by climate change and other risks such as price shocks, which are becoming more prevalent. Farmers and herders currently have no mechanisms with which to deal with impacts from climate change patterns. Equally, smallholder producers are vulnerable to the growing prevalence of economic shocks in the international agricultural sector, as demonstrated by the devastating effects of multiple food price spikes over the past ten years.

The Government of Ethiopia implemented the Productive Safety Net Programme (PSNP), a social protection scheme, in 2005. One of the largest social safety net programs in the world, the PSNP aims to improve Ethiopia's food security by providing direct support to the country's most vulnerable populations and through income diversification via small public work projects for other citizens. The PSNP is complemented by the country's larger Food Security Programme, which seeks to raise household incomes through resettlement grants, household income–generating packages, and water harvesting.

Although social safety net programs offer an avenue for addressing food insecurity, income diversification through private-sector opportunities offers a path for mitigating agricultural risks. In other countries, this diversification has typically occurred through the creation of non-agricultural income sources (FAO et al. 2015). However, given the lack of secure job opportunities in most industrial and service sectors in Africa, it is worth exploring the agricultural sector for potential alternatives. Given Ethiopia's existing agricultural expertise, large-scale commercial agricultural projects should be explored at greater length as a potential means for creating alternative sources of secured income for smallholder farmers and pastoralists. Various investment models could be employed to counteract the negative impacts of large-scale commercial farms – e.g., diminishing returns on labour, compromised land and water quality, and decreasing biodiversity – and thus to answer both the immediate needs of smallholder populations as well as longer-term benefits such as income diversification opportunities and sustainable land use.

It is also important to consider Ethiopia's macroeconomic environment. As of 2015, roughly 90 per cent of Ethiopia's export portfolio consisted of agricultural commodities – typically sold at declining global prices – while manufactured goods constituted 71 per cent of its import portfolio (Terfassa 2009; World Bank, n.d.[i]). The same sources show that although crop prices have increased in recent years, Ethiopia's net trade in goods and services has been caught in a downward spiral since 2003, largely due to rising inflation. This has negatively affected the country's foreign exchange currency reserves, which are required for the import of capital goods. At the request of the IMF, the Ethiopian government devalued the birr by close to 20 per cent in 2010 in an attempt to spur export growth and import substitution development (Lavers 2012a).

Following this move, the Ethiopian government must now strike a balance between the competing interests of its new export-oriented strategy and the food security needs of its smallholder farmers. This balance is particularly crucial given that Ethiopia's main commodity exports are mostly agricultural in nature. More specifically, coffee, sesame seeds, and edible vegetables (see Figure 5.2) constitute a large proportion of exports;

Ethiopia: Land Distribution

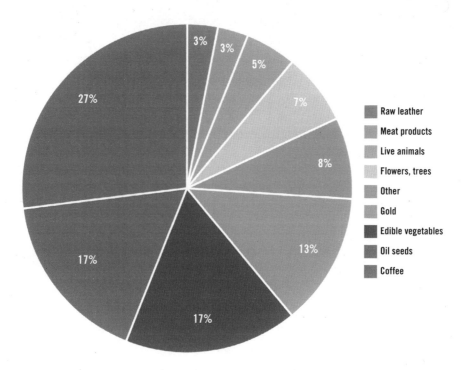

Figure 5.2 Composition of merchandise exports for 2014–15.
Source: IMF 2015, 15.

cereal crops have largely remained within the domestic market despite dominating Ethiopia's crop production (Spielman et al. 2010). This lack of cereal exports is attributable to a 2006 directive that banned exports of cereal crops when food shortages were imminent (Lavers 2012a).[10] While the government hopes to export cereals eventually, Ethiopia's major cereal crops, which include teff, wheat, maize, sorghum, and barley, currently afford few surpluses as they continue to constitute the core of Ethiopia's food economy – accounting for 64 per cent of the population's calorie consumption.

In light of the difficulties in exporting food crops, the Ethiopian government has instead demonstrated increased interest in agricultural investments destined for biofuel crop production. In 2007, the government created a Biofuel Development and Utilization Strategy (BDUS), followed by a Biofuel Unit within the Ministry of Water and Energy when the latter was established in 2010. The BDUS states that as of 2007, 23.3 million hectares of suitable land were available in Ethiopia for biofuel production. Today, one-third of poor farmers allocate approximately 15 per cent of their land to production under contract with biofuel companies (Negash and Swinnen 2013). According to the manager of the Biofuel Unit, the government aims to have the country's biodiesel production reach 450 million litres per year by 2020, despite a lack of any substantive evidence of production to date (Ratcliffe 2015).

Despite the possible economic benefits, the rise of biofuel crops has put pressure on the land sector, as well as food and water security, with farmland being increasingly converted from production of food crops to biofuel crops. According to a 2010 World Bank inventory of large-scale land acquisitions, 35 per cent of projects in Ethiopia were intended to produce biofuel crops, in comparison to 37 per cent set aside for food (De Schutter 2010).[11] As of 2012, biofuel crop production represented up to 50 per cent of FDI (Bossio et al. 2012). Although some biofuel crops, such as certain oilseeds, offer the flexibility of being equally useful for food consumption – which accords smallholders some flexibility in negotiating between different markets – the increased emphasis on biofuel crops can even threaten food prices on a global scale. When biofuel production increases at an exponential rate, as it did just before the 2007–08 global food price crisis, the impact on food-insecure populations can be detrimental.[12]

The jatropha crop, which can grow in relatively infertile soil and arid climates, offers an important biofuel crop alternative, as it is grown in areas where food crops are less likely to be sustained (Wendimu 2016). In Ethiopia, however, the livelihoods of many pastoralists and cultivators depend on such ecological environments. Although Ethiopia's national biofuel strategy has relegated biofuel production to "marginal" land,[13] the issue remains problematic. As discussed earlier, the government's determination as to what constitutes marginal land has been highly contentious, mainly as a result of ongoing official disregard for the livelihoods of lowland nomadic producers.

While it is important to ensure growth in Ethiopia's export revenue, the country's current trade and exchange rates suggest that it is equally crucial

Ethiopia: Land Distribution

to alleviate the cost of imported agricultural inputs (seeds and fertilizer) through the creation of domestic input markets. Since the late 1990s, a number of donors have encouraged the Ethiopian government to work with the private sector to develop more competitive agricultural input markets (Berhanu 2012). Thus far, however, the government has only supported private-sector engagement for EPRDF member organizations. Government control over pricing and distribution of agricultural inputs, with little meaningful engagement with the private sector, has resulted in a "high cost of inputs, insufficient credit services and rationing, and a lack of varieties that are appropriate to farmers' needs" (Berhanu 2012, 15). Additional studies and informants have revealed that state-run input markets, coupled with a credit-based supply framework for these inputs, has compelled farmers to become overly dependent on the ruling party, and thus vulnerable to political pressure. Berhanu (2012) therefore argues that a state monopoly in Ethiopia's agricultural input markets not only inflates costs for producers, but also allows for their political control through the threat of sanctions in the case of credit defaults.

In developing an inclusive, participatory, and food-secure private-sector governance framework and scope of action for the agricultural sector, it is important to consider Ethiopia's need for additional employment opportunities generated by foreign-owned enterprises, sustainable and biodiverse land use, foreign currency earnings, and competitive domestic input markets. There are indeed opportunities to leverage the macroeconomic environment in Ethiopia to drive sustainable growth in a conflict-fragile environment through the involvement of private-sector actors. Improved economic outcomes, including tangential economic growth derived from subsidiary and adjacent sectors such as manufacturing, offers Ethiopians a formidable opportunity for a sustainable, peaceful, and stable future. Foreign-owned enterprises are critical in this regard, especially as the country continues to push further toward the industrialization of subsistence and smallholder farming. Other needs may equally be addressed through this process: sustainable and biodiverse land use; foreign currency earnings; competitive domestic market inputs; beneficiation and value addition for communities, and others.

Possible Approaches to an Effective Governance Framework

As per the Political Economy of Natural Resource Governance framework posited in this book, possible private-sector changes that would facilitate inclusive and sustainable growth in Ethiopia include: investment models that focus on labour-intensive agricultural crops; promoting meaningful consultations and the use of local agricultural knowledge; an inclusive and participatory biofuel and industrial crop production allocation framework; and broader support for domestic companies producing agricultural inputs. Given that harvesting certain crops, such as cotton, rice, and vegetables, is more labour-intensive than it is for others, focusing production on these crops would help large-scale farms soak up the excess in agricultural labour. Additionally, certain investment models, such as contract farming,[14] enable the labour-intensive smallholder farming model to continue unhindered, while expanding smallholder access to relevant markets. Floriculture, contract farming, and coffee cooperatives offer important lessons in this regard. One of Ethiopia's more successful crops, fresh-cut flowers[15] are highly labour-intensive, meaning that in most cases this crop creates enough additional demand for labour to overcome the income lost from other types of smallholder production (Lavers 2012b). Flower projects also take up less land, which in turn displaces fewer smallholder farmers. Although the short lifespan of fresh flowers requires that these large-scale farms be located near the Addis Ababa airport for quick export, and the advanced production technologies and controlled conditions required for flower farming make it difficult to contract out to smallholders, this type of production does offer a unique advantage in terms of its off-farm employment creation potential for smallholders living close to the country's capital (Mano et al. 2011; Melese and Helmsing 2010).[16]

With that said, peasant-organized cooperatives, and the negotiating power they typically provide, have also allowed for a more successful investment model in Ethiopia's coffee sector. According to multiple respondents in Becker and Wittmeyer's study, these new cooperatives allow Ethiopian farmers to "intervene in the markets to increase the price of coffee by approximately 50%" (2013, 770). Given the important role of coffee in Ethiopia's export market, such bottom-up adaptations underscore another way of promoting smallholder-supportive investments.

In terms of boosting Ethiopia's exports, if biofuel and industrial crop production were to be carefully considered in an inclusive, participatory, and food-secure allocation framework, biofuel crops combined with the technology to convert them to energy could offer greater energy security and accelerate the development of rural areas (Escobar et al. 2009). They could also offer another lucrative non-food export crop, as demonstrated by the increasing demand for airline biofuels and the European Union's goal to draw ten per cent of the region's transport fuel from renewable sources, such as biodiesel, by 2020 (European Commission, n.d.). Some of the most crucial issues in creating this allocation framework nevertheless extend beyond agricultural policies and would require the Ethiopian government to re-evaluate its attitudes toward traditionally nomadic ethnic groups, as well as its modes of engagement with ethno-regional governments. In the interest of mitigating the detrimental impacts of disadvantaging certain ethnic groups over others, the Ethiopian government should seriously re-evaluate the Council of Ministers Regulations of 2008, which recentralized land administration functions from the regions to the government, as well as its general approach to pastoral and shifting cultivator groups (Hodbod 2013).

Similarly, given the overwhelming demand for agricultural inputs from farmers and exporters, and the public's historical sensitivity to authoritarian approaches, the Ethiopian government needs to reconsider how it engages with and supports its domestic input market. In light of the current monopoly of EPRDF-aligned companies in these sectors, there is a need to actively encourage and incentivize private-sector actors to enter these markets.[17] Increased competition should drive down prices, make smallholder producers less vulnerable to exploitative relationships with input companies, and offer a better impression with regard to equal support for all ethnic groups on the part of the government. Expansion of these backward linkages to a point where prices elicit stronger smallholder demand offers not only the potential for greater agricultural yields, but also the possibility for additional employment opportunities in other sectors. Likewise, forward linkages should be encouraged within the domestic private sector given its potential to spur industrialization. Adding value to agricultural projects through agro-processing and other businesses would allow Ethiopian smallholders to create and expand export industries that are not beholden to commodity prices, and create jobs in the process (Mulatu and Grando 2011).

A variety of options, as well as innovative combinations of these options, would enable a greater and more positive contribution by foreign-owned enterprises in Ethiopia's natural resource sectors, specifically agriculture. Although some foreign investment would be helpful in providing employment through larger, labour-intensive production models, the Ethiopian government should, wherever possible, provide similar, if not better, incentives for domestic actors through international-domestic partnerships or standalone domestic enterprises. This is not to say that the government should curtail large-scale foreign investments altogether, but that it should instead frame such partnerships both legally, in terms of oversight, and normatively, so as to produce better economic outcomes that positively impact a broader section of Ethiopia's population. Incentives such as income tax exemptions and duty-free capital goods imports could support this objective. Given the government's ultimate goal of state legitimacy, these considerations and suggestions should offer some insight into how to build an inclusive, empowering, and sustainable agricultural policy framework that caters to Ethiopia's macroeconomic needs.

Conclusion

The role and contribution of foreign-owned enterprises operating in natural resource sectors in sub-Saharan Africa as agents of development largely depends on the type of governance structure in place at the national level and the approach to governance adopted by the state. For the purposes of this study, three types of state governance structures were identified and analyzed: politically stable, post-conflict, and conflict-threatened. A proposed new theoretical approach – the Political Economy of Natural Resource Governance – was used to investigate how governance structures influence the nature and involvement of foreign-owned companies and investors operating in the extractive and land resource sectors, both in the wider development process and specifically in terms of their contribution to economic growth, peace and political stability, and sustainable development.

Analysis of three sub-Saharan countries exemplified by these three political/economic states – Ghana, Sierra Leone, and Ethiopia – indicates that foreign actors impact governance structures in ways that either strengthen or weaken those structures through their activities. These findings form the basis for certain policy conclusions concerning the role and ideal involvement of foreign-owned enterprises in the enhancement of natural resource governance.

As impactful actors, foreign-owned enterprises involved in natural resource extraction in the three country case studies are bound to impact governance structures profoundly and, in the process, it is hoped, create mutually beneficial frameworks that enhance broad-based development and promote a business-prone environment. In this sense, foreign actors and states alike are involved in a strategy to transform the socioeconomic landscapes in these countries – a strategy that takes into consideration communities' needs for stable and sufficient income sources and access to opportunity, and the investors' need to generate profits. Consequently, the notion of transformation – at the core of the PENRG model – entails a mutually beneficial impact of governance systems upon the host state and population, and upon the business actors, particularly foreign-owned ones.

Conclusions from the case study findings are grouped as follows: relevance to the main research questions; the notion of "collaborative governance" as the ideal governance approach; good governance and management of natural resources in stable, post-conflict, and conflict-threatened countries; recommendations for an appropriate analytical framework for investigating natural resource governance; a way forward and future research considerations; and the contribution of this research project to current knowledge.

The ideal role of the private sector in natural resource governance in a stable country such as Ghana, a post-conflict country like Sierra Leone, and a fragile, conflict-threatened Ethiopia is to support efforts to establish sustainable long-term economic development and political stability. In the context of each country's situation, the Political Economy of Natural Resources Governance framework provides evidence-based tools for tackling Africa's "resource curse" and moving each country forward and toward long-term, broad-based economic and social development.

In the case of Ghana, the absence of a regulatory framework coupled with a heavy bureaucratic system impedes value addition and beneficiation processes, while promoting corruption at every level of the system. Both Sierra Leone and Ethiopia are profoundly impacted by mismanagement or simply a general lack of governance systems in the realm of natural resources. In the case of Ethiopia, the PENRG framework provides tools to tackle the widespread mismanagement of land resources in situations where knowledge of locally based practices is negated by the activities of large agribusiness-oriented farms. Such limitations in developing adequate measures to promote stable, sustainable, development-oriented systems of natural resource governance with respect to foreign-owned companies are tackled throughout this book.

Conclusion 203

Main Research Questions

In exploring the answers to the research questions posed in Chapters 1 and 2, it has been argued that appropriate systems of natural resource governance can influence the contribution of private-sector actors and foreign-owned enterprises to the socioeconomic and political development of host countries in politically stable, post-conflict, or conflict-threatened contexts. For each case study, considerable effort has been spent in identifying how governance systems in each context can be created, bolstered, supported, and ultimately repaired so as to achieve the best involvement possible.

Each chapter provides details on how local conditions may impact foreign-owned private-sector actors to contribute to positive economic, social, and development outcomes; how a scope of action can be embedded in governance and operationalized through policy and programming; and which entry points and junctures can be used in each case to effect change. In politically stable countries, the role of foreign-owned private-sector actors is to contribute to economic growth and sustainable development through additional revenues, to reliable corporate social responsibility programs, and to capacity building. In post-conflict countries, the ideal contribution is deemed to be aiding post-conflict reconstruction, economic transformation, and development while working to enhance natural resource governance frameworks, institutions, and regulations. Finally, in conflict-threatened countries, foreign-owned enterprises should contribute to a conflict containment strategy through judicious involvement in equitable and sustainable resource transactions and investment. Each case study assesed how governance structures enable or constrain foreign-owned private-sector actors in assuming these roles.

Case Study 1: Ghana

In Ghana, natural resource governance presents an opportunity for truly positive contributions to sustainable economic growth. The success of the private sector in achieving this ideal situation hinges on effective natural resource governance at both the national and local levels. Historically, the role of mining was to help catalyze economic growth, while the recent discovery of oil presents an opportunity to accelerate sustainable change and stability. Foreign-owned enterprises have contributed significantly to economic growth, but the benefits of such expanded output have not been shared with local communities in mining and oil-producing areas owing to weakness in existing governance structures. Moreover, the role of foreign-owned enterprises in contributing to overall stability has been largely supportive, with only a few – if any – initiatives having led to indirect or tangential impacts via CSR or capacity-building programs.

The private sector's positive record is not surprising in a country where stability has been established, something the Ghanaian government has largely been responsible for maintaining. Activities pursued by mining and oil companies were also investigated in the research; while creating some economic and employment opportunities for local communities in areas where they operate, there is still room for improvement and more needs to be done in terms of mandatory legislation and governance system requirements for local content, beneficiation, value addition, and CSR. The chapter recommended a collaborative governance approach to increase participation by all stakeholders in natural resource governance and to strengthen linkages between foreign, national, and local actors. This collaboration should be based on communication, consent, and consensus.

The relationship between the government, the private sector, and local communities remains a core concern for many oil and mining communities, which are intent on benefitting directly from economic growth that is directly linked to local resource development. The research found that the considerable efforts taken by the Ghanaian government, in concert with civil society, in improving natural resource governance (Debrah and Graham 2015) has led to much progress, especially in terms of policy making and scientific research on offshore drilling (Chalfin 2015). However, improvements remain to be made with regard to redistributing natural resource revenues, tackling corruption, and realizing sustainable development. Increasingly, workable partnerships appear to be evolving in the face of increased private investment, with the government, private sector, and oil and mining communities gaining a better knowledge of the issues related to natural resource governance.

Conclusion

Case Study 2: Sierra Leone

In Sierra Leone, natural resource governance presents an opportunity for significant positive growth in sustainable development, peace, and stability, as well as a means by which to encourage private-sector participation in achieving these goals. The role of foreign-owned enterprises in a post-conflict country such as Sierra Leone is to support peacebuilding and reconstruction efforts. The argument has also been made that the private sector's success hinges on efficient and resilient governance at both the national and local levels – as in Ghana – including an operationalized scope of action. It is alleged that illicit mining operations helped fuel the country's civil war between 1991 and 2002. Since the end of the war, the private sector – namely foreign investors, particularly mining companies – has contributed to the resumption of economic growth, but the benefits of such expanded output have not been shared with local communities in mining areas, nor have they necessarily translated into sustainable stability. Moreover, the contribution of foreign-owned enterprises to post-conflict stability has produced mixed results, with the prospect of violence looming in areas where some of these private-sector actors operate due to growing grievances on the part of local communities regarding the lack of benefits.

This state of affairs is inherently tied to misperceptions surrounding the roles to be played by various government bodies, including Mineral Advisory Boards, the Ministry of Mines and Mineral Resources (MMMR), and community groups and organizations, along with weak governance and corruption at the national and local levels. These misperceptions have hindered the opportunities created by progressive legislation, policy, and other arrangements such as community development agreements (CDAs). This lack of coordination is not confined to the Government of Sierra Leone's relationships with private companies, as the government is also said to suffer from insufficient internal coordination between the National Revenue Authority, the MMMR, other departments and agencies, and local councils (World Bank 2008; Fanthorpe and Gabelle 2013). As in the case of Ghana, the research found evidence to suggest that some companies are engaged in practices that pay little heed to the needs and interests of mining communities, fuelling animosity and thus also instability. An increase in

206   GOVERNANCE, CONFLICT, AND NATURAL RESOURCES IN AFRICA

financial and capacity-building support for natural resource governance is evidently a priority for the government, but a prerequisite to accessing these finances must entail better oversight of initiatives such as community development funds (CDFs) and scrutiny of mining companies' activities.

Interviews undertaken in the course of the fieldwork have shed light on the modus operandi that has prevailed since the end of the civil war. These observations outline the challenges relating to the political conditions that have shaped the environment for the private sector and influenced the country's natural resource governance. Sierra Leone appears to have moved beyond the legacies of armed conflict, though sociopolitical relations between government entities, the private sector, and community representatives remain a core concern for many mining communities (Reno 2003). Natural resource management by the government, paramount and local chiefs, and councils are characterized by corrupt practices and the misappropriation of mining revenues. Nevertheless, workable partnerships appear to be evolving in the face of increased private investment, with better knowledge of issues related to natural resource governance now evident among the government and private-sector actors, as well as in mining communities.

While the interviews conducted in Sierra Leone revealed conditions and examples that could be interpreted cynically, the recommendations for policy options to boost sustainable development through governance reform are innovative. Moreover, they reflect a persistent and resilient society that believes in the possibility of transformational change, despite unending poverty and missed opportunities. Interviewees' suggestions regarding CDAs and the proposal for a comprehensive study on backward linkages in Sierra Leone's mining sector, with the objective of developing a systemic approach framework, could be a new point of departure for all stakeholders in Sierra Leone's future.

Case Study 3: Ethiopia

In conflict-threatened Ethiopia, natural resource governance also presents an opportunity to leverage foreign-owned enterprises as engines of sustainable economic growth, peace, and stability. As such, Borras's approach

Conclusion

of land acquisitions by foreign-owned or -controlled economic actors, and his focus on capitalistic systems of wealth extraction, is particularly interesting (Borras et al. 2012). Although foreign investments have become a vehicle for ethnic polarization, the argument is made that such investment could instead be leveraged to support efforts to drive inclusive economic growth and reduce the country's fragility by repairing the broken system that currently facilitates inequitable land transactions. The findings also support the argument that the success of foreign-owned enterprises in this role hinges on efficient and resilient governance. Ethiopia's underlying fragility, driven by the threat of ethnic conflict, has worsened over the past decade due to factionalized elites, limited recognition of human rights and the rule of law, and group grievance pressures, among other issues. Indeed, inclusive national discourse has declined in favour of an economy-driven narrative that lacks broader consideration for democratic performance, human rights, and human development indicators. In addition to aggravating historical sensitivities and grievances among ethnic groups, the government's authoritarian approach has had negative effects on economic governance, as highlighted in the country's agricultural sector, since there are few avenues by which the government may receive input on the impact and effectiveness of regulatory frameworks.

Despite the lack of critical feedback from field investigations undertaken in Ethiopia, the recent and growing interest in existing and emerging international and African governance guidelines for land-based foreign investments does provide some indication that greater attention and better protections for smallholder producers are required in the face of growing transnational demand for agricultural land. For example, sub-Saharan African countries have placed a stronger emphasis on the need for land policies that adequately consider the land pressures created by an increasingly liberalized and globalized land market.

Land pressures include a disregard for smallholder protections in international law and mainstream development directives. Dell'Angelo et al. insist on these developments and what they describe as coercion and dispossession in the context of a global land rush in which Ethiopia is a critical provider (Dell'Angelo et al. 2017). Similar concerns raised by Borras and Franco in a 2010 article question the validity of what the authors describe as transnational commercial land transactions (Borras and Franco 2012). While international law has been effective in strengthening protection of foreign investment, it has offered little protection to small-holders. Donors and development institutions have also increased pressure on African countries, and particularly on Addis Ababa, to facilitate private investment in large-scale commercial agriculture. Consequently, there has been growing momentum to tackle this issue at the global level through governance frameworks that offer voluntary guidelines for countries where vulnerable landholders are at risk. The issue has also been broached at the continental level through the Land Policy Initiative (LPI) – a joint project of the African Union, the United Nations Economic Commission for Africa, and the African Development Bank – which works to strengthen land rights and secure livelihoods for African populations. In 2010, the LPI published *Land Policy in Africa* (AUC et al. 2010), which contains a framework and guidelines to encourage African countries to develop policies and legislation to protect vulnerable groups in the face of both foreign and domestic large-scale agricultural investments. In accordance with its African counterparts, it would be prudent for the Ethiopian government to reconsider and be open to further debate on how to incentivize and regulate both foreign and domestic private-sector actors – including smallholder producers – to leverage the latent opportunities for inclusive and sustainable growth that Ethiopia's agricultural sector has always offered.

Good Governance and Management of Natural Resources: Diverging Economic and Security Outcomes in Politically Stable, Post-Conflict, and Conflict-Threatened Countries

The differing political/economic situations of countries – stable, post-conflict, or conflict-threatened – continue to affect the roles and contributions of foreign-owned enterprises in bringing about sustainable development, stability, and peace. This is due to the nature of each type of governance system and the state institutions associated with it.

Conclusion

Category 1: Politically Stable

More than most African states, Ghana has achieved diverse results and tremendous progress in leveraging foreign-owned enterprises through the passage of legislation and implementation of governance structures. As an indication of Ghana's recent economic progress, driven primarily by the mining and hydrocarbon sectors, poverty levels have decreased over the last decade and the rate of unemployment is notably lower than the sub-Saharan African average.

Despite these successes, there is a pervasive sense that the Ghanaian government could do better. The country has not struck a mutually reinforcing and equitable balance between attracting investment and stimulating economic diversification and sustainable development. More importantly, although the national government in Accra has tried to use mining and energy tax revenues and royalties to promote development activities, only some of these efforts have produced the expected outcomes and few have contributed more broadly to general stability. Accordingly, governance of the country's natural resource sector does not function effectively, meaning that Ghana does not benefit as much as it should from its natural endowment.

Natural resources, especially gold, have been a bedrock of economic progress in Ghana for almost forty years. However, the mining sector could play a greater role in helping the country achieve sustainable economic growth, peace, and stability by facilitating poverty reduction, social development, economic transformation, and environmental protection. For this to happen, the country's "40-Year National Development Plan," published in 2017, must give the sector the attention it deserves, placing it at the core of Ghana's future and putting in place the regulatory systems necessary for its development. These would address corruption and infrastructure issues and facilitate integration with other sectors. The Ghanaian government is increasingly taking mining issues seriously and should be commended for its progress in terms of implementing certain good governance structures, particularly its local content requirements for the mining sector.

Yet, despite these positive steps, policies that translate natural resource revenues into poverty alleviation and sustainable development could be introduced. By passing legislation and imposing regulations, the government has already demonstrated that it can align benefits accrued by the natural resource sector with national social priorities. Policy implementation gaps do remain, stemming from the practices and philosophies of private-sector actors, which have realized only a fraction of their responsibility to uplift Ghanaian society and, more specifically, the communities directly affected by their operations. Together with the government, foreign-owned enterprises could be a key driver of transformational change if governance at the national and local levels were more effective.

Category 2: Post-Conflict

In practical terms, Sierra Leone's economic reconstruction efforts would need to be sustained and enforced via the export of natural resources, primarily diamonds and iron ore. While management of the mining sector remains a daunting task for the current government, other initiatives have begun to bear fruit. In recent years, the Government of Sierra Leone has taken further steps to attract FDI. These include introducing legislation such as the Investment Code (2005), the Business Registration Act (2007), the Investment Promotion Agency Act (2007), the Companies Act (2009), and the Bankruptcy Act (2009). Furthermore, a national Private Sector Development Plan came into effect in 2009 (US Embassy, Freetown 2011). These reforms are aimed at providing greater protection for companies investing in Sierra Leone, streamlining the process of business engagement, and opening up more opportunities for ownership and management of resources.

Despite these achievements, Sierra Leone's post-conflict environment continues to seriously hamper the level of investment in the country and the degree to which it can diversify its economy. Indeed, the country's long-term stability and the consolidation of its democracy requires that it move away from resource extraction as the dominant source of revenue. The aftereffects of the conflict include a severe shortage of skilled workers and managers, rampant corruption, a lack of infrastructure (roads and technology), cumbersome customs procedures, a weak judiciary, the absence of an effective land titles system, and an underdeveloped banking system. Each of these issues continues to deter investors. In addition to

Conclusion

these structural challenges, once companies arrive in Sierra Leone, they face both governance roadblocks and community pressures related to corporate social responsibility duties, which often entails contributions to post-conflict reconstruction (interview, Mr Molla Alemu March, Program Manager, Youth Employment and Empowerment Program, UNDP Sierra Leone, 28 March 2014).

Concerns have been raised that large mining corporations have not earned the social licences to operate in mining communities. The perception among interviewees was that these corporations need to do more with regard to addressing social issues – in particular: health, skills development, employment creation, and education – while refraining from using CSR activities as promotional mechanisms to win praise and support from the government and multilateral institutions. In stark contrast, representatives of mining companies noted that the corporations have done their best to provide for people living in communities affected by their operations.

While CDAS and diamond area community development funds (DACDFS) have been identified by some as potential remedies for the endemic difficulties involved in leveraging Sierra Leone's resource wealth for long-term economic growth and development, challenges and weaknesses pertaining to their implementation remain. The often chaotic, fragmented, and uncoordinated nature of policies is regarded as the biggest obstacle to doing business in Sierra Leone and an excuse, when implementing CSR initiatives, to avoid complying with recent legislation and policies such as CDAS, CDFS, and the DACDF (interview with Mr Yero Baldeh, Resident Representative, African Development Bank Sierra Leone, 3 March 2014).

Cuts in corporate contributions to the government, which have occurred due to differential investor treatment, uncoordinated government mineral policies, and ineffective implementation of legislation by various agencies and departments, have translated into a reduction in government revenues at both the national and local levels. This fundamentally limits the government's material ability to spearhead post-conflict reconstruction and enhanced governance. Weak regulatory mechanisms have resulted in irregular disbursement of CDFS, with resultant impacts on local development programs agreed upon with mining communities.

Such inefficiencies, coupled with allegations of theft and corruption by local councils and paramount chiefs, have resulted in mining companies opting not to participate in CDAs and instead establishing company-specific CSR programs.

Because of perceived political instability in the subregion, and given its existing infrastructure deficits and poor governance, Sierra Leone does not have the favourable image needed to attract international investment. While, on the one hand, low investment levels hinder democratic development and peacebuilding efforts, on the other, problems also may arise when corporations already operating and investing in Sierra Leone fall short of their potential to contribute to post-conflict reconstruction, sustainable economic growth, peace, and stability. That said, this case study concludes with the argument that foreign-owned enterprises have the transformational potential to play a crucial role in fostering post-conflict recovery and providing economic opportunities through job creation and the provision of social services such as schools and healthcare, thereby consolidating reconstruction and peacebuilding efforts currently underway.

Category 3: Conflict-Threatened

When one considers that Ethiopia and the East Africa region are disproportionately affected by hunger and other food security concerns, it is problematic to learn that although foreign investments in Ethiopia's agricultural sector have culminated in improved infrastructure, new roads and irrigation networks are frequently the result of the companies' needs being catered to rather than those of the local populations. The government's minimal requirements for social and economic contributions by mining companies toward the regions in which they operate are exacerbated by large-scale land acquisitions – particularly in instances where the land-access rights of smallholder agriculturalists or pastoralists are revoked without reasonable provision for other sources of livelihood, such as alternative land or employment opportunities. Over the long term, if current trends continue and Ethiopia should experience increasing temperatures and more sporadic precipitation, the country will be at greater

Conclusion

risk of drought and flood. This may culminate in a decline in agricultural productivity, which could have a substantial impact on the country's food and water security, as well as ecological systems.

Foreign investment incentives offered by the Ethiopian government appear to be relatively liberal, yet fail to promote and leverage private-sector contributions to conflict containment strategies and equitable distribution of revenues and returns from land transactions, an especially urgent consideration given the need to protect the country's food security. Additional tax exemptions are offered to foreign investors that export the crops they produce. Moreover, there has been a substantial shift in property rights over land and water from smallholder agriculturalists, pastoralists, and other customary users to foreign investors – a shift chiefly due to the ambiguity surrounding the property rights regime governing these resources. These developments, and the problems they cause, are exacerbated by the low wages paid to agricultural workers in the face of rising food prices, as well as the fact that many Ethiopian laws do not sufficiently account for free, prior, and informed consent (FPIC) in transactions involving the acquisition of large land holdings for agricultural purposes. Consequently, there is often limited engagement and support for foreign investment on the part of community stakeholders who have been displaced, which has led to peasant protests in several regions. In many instances, large-scale leases of agricultural land to foreign investors have had a negative impact on Ethiopia's smallholder agriculturalists and pastoralists, including displacement without compensation. The foregoing developments have given rise in recent years to tension, strife, and conflict. Nevertheless, the adoption of alternative governance models, including the referenced collaborative governance approach, may be a workable solution.

A re-evaluation of the legislation responsible for recentralizing land administration functions, as well as a reconsideration of the government's general approach to pastoral and shifting cultivator groups, could also prove to be broadly beneficial to the citizens. Despite the presence of highly factionalized elites, weak recognition of human rights, limited rule of law, and marginalized ethnic groups, Ethiopia's agricultural sector offers development opportunities for well-regulated foreign-owned enterprises

214 GOVERNANCE, CONFLICT, AND NATURAL RESOURCES IN AFRICA

and constitutes a complex linkage between foreign investment and the country's fragile interethnic situation.

The Way Forward: Policy Issues, Development Implications, and Directions for Future Research

The Responsibility of Resource Companies

Governments have a commitment to their citizens to hold foreign-owned enterprises accountable to good corporate practices. As natural resource industries have the potential to promote sustainable development, peace, and stability for broad segments of the population, and can bring about or bolster political stability if resources are shared in a transparent and sustainable manner, meaningful collaboration on resource governance in this regard is critical. The "resource curse" does not need to be the norm. Rather, as the Ghanaian case study shows, resource extraction can lead to economic growth and contribute to realizing a country's economic priorities – there are *resource blessings*. Of course, Ghana is not a perfect example, as corruption, mismanagement, and poor practices hinder further positive contributions linked to natural resource exploitation. Whether it is land (in Ethiopia's case), mining (in the cases of Sierra Leone and Ghana), or hydrocarbons (Ghana), natural resource exploitation has the ability to transform economies. When operating under a functional and effective natural resource governance system, foreign-owned enterprises can generate a sense of obligation to promote sustainable economic development and growth that is relevant to their specific contexts.

This is insufficient, however, to completely transform economies and pull people out of poverty. This can only happen when there is a critical effort to promote secondary industries that rely on or feed into the mining and hydrocarbon sectors, which generate local employment opportunities and revenues for communities and government. These foreign-owned enterprises have the responsibility to contribute to the national well-being of resource-rich countries. Indeed, emergent literature argues that private-sector actors, especially mining companies, are becoming key partners and leaders in promoting and facilitating development, often

Conclusion

taking on greater responsibility from ill-equipped government and traditional donors (Black and O'Bright 2016; Ite 2005).

Promoting Accountable Business Practices through Stronger Structures

A number of important steps may be taken to promote broad-based sustainable development, peace, and stability in local communities in the areas of local content, beneficiation, and value addition, and some of these have been explored in the three case studies. First, to promote accountable business practices at the national and local levels, and to maintain stable relations between community members and the private sector, government must begin to devise better contracts and take stronger negotiating positions to ensure social and human security, and compliance with progressive environmental laws that protect communities from unforeseen circumstances. Government must also demonstrate to communities that it will stand for them when corporations, foreign or local, break laws, and promote a long-term vision in which extraction is not an end in itself but a tool for broad-based development.

The private sector has the potential to be the primary engine of growth in stable, resource-rich democracies in Africa. However, this possibility can only be realized by imposing strong, coherent, and strategic governance structures, at both the national and local levels, that clearly define the role of foreign-owned enterprises in facilitating sustainable economic growth, peace, and stability. Not surprisingly, one ongoing issue is how best to remedy gaps in policy implementation: in this regard, there are many ideas, institutions, laws, and regulations, but implementation of these overlapping frameworks is sometimes quite difficult and often remains incomplete. Much more time should be spent to determine whether necessary policies have been implemented and, where they have not, to identify the reasons for this failure and locate solutions. Lack of capacity is likely one reason, but lack of political will is an even greater problem (interview with Dr Kwesi Aning, Director for Academic Affairs and Research, Kofi Annan International Peacekeeping Centre, 24 February 2014; interview with Dr Elias Ayuk, Director, UN University Institute for Natural Resources in Africa, 24 February 2014).

Local Consultation and Bottom-Up Ideas

It is critical that effective local consultation take place, allowing new ideas to emerge from the bottom up. Ideas from on-the-ground experts deserve attention, specifically in regard to advocacy, community participation in decision making, and design of monitoring frameworks (Owusu-Koranteng 2013). Importantly, community service organizations (CSOs) lack adequate support, specifically in terms of resources and technical knowledge, to participate effectively in natural resource governance. One promising avenue is that donors identify credible local NGOs and CSOs, design working documents together, discuss their concepts, and then implement them together. Such collaboration could be scaled up easily, beginning as a pilot program but open to extension for additional years (interview with Dr Allan Lassey, Senior Advisor, Extractive Resource Governance, GIZ, 27 August 2015). Within civil society, top-down and bottom-up strategies could be proposed and developed by community groups and research institutions. CSOs and NGOs should have a larger voice in governance so that such strategies may receive greater attention.

Consultation with central and local governments, as well as individual smallholders, enables large-scale companies to position projects in ways that have less of a negative impact on smallholder, artisanal, and pastoral populations and on vulnerable ecologies. Local farmers, miners, and herders typically have an excellent understanding of how livelihoods and food security are derived in their communities, as well as extensive expertise regarding the soil, climate, and ecological issues in their region. Integrating traditional agricultural and extractives knowledge offers a means to mitigate a large-scale project's social and environmental impacts, while opening up better-paid jobs for local experts and increasing production within a specific agricultural context.[1]

Local consultation and FPIC are also essential to investor security, as discontent and unrest within communities in regard to new, large-scale land acquisitions can jeopardize the sustainability of such projects (Baumgartner et al. 2015). Using FPIC as a basis for investment projects is not only essential from a human rights perspective but also beneficial in terms of local community support. Populace-led forms of resistance, although

Conclusion 217

often covert and seemingly disorganized, can severely undermine large-scale investments, as demonstrated by land encroachments by neighbouring smallholders and intentional crop damage by local agricultural labourers in Ethiopia. Since foreign-owned enterprises often enter local arenas where land relations are dynamic or contested, consultation is crucial to understanding local context and establishing local support for incoming investments.

Summary

In every case, to attain the appropriate level and type of private-sector involvement in natural resource governance systems and thereby facilitate inclusive and sustainable growth, the possible transformative measures include: shifts toward labour-intensive agricultural crops and labour-intensive investment models; meaningful consultations, with renewed value being placed on local agricultural knowledge; an inclusive and participatory biofuel and industrial crop production allocation framework; and broader support for the growth of domestic companies producing agricultural inputs.

Beyond labour-intensive approaches, it is important that governments in each country emphasize and take steps to integrate local content, beneficiation, and value addition into business practices and operations. These changes would result primarily in a move away from reliance on natural resources and toward economies that are more dependent on human resources and technological innovation. Such changes would also be more conducive to the markets where they operate. For foreign mining corporations, engaging in efforts to grow local businesses and technological innovation by promoting local content, beneficiation, and value addition will inevitably result in better relationships with local communities as well as increased revenues, as companies will spend less money on security, cash payouts, and court cases arising from disputes. In the long term, increased goodwill between local communities and foreign investors will promote political stability, social cohesion, and peace in resource-rich countries. As such, governments must strengthen the implementation of laws and regulations within a broad governance framework, under which investors are required to support and contribute to local content, beneficiation, and value addition through the use of revenues gleaned from local minerals, agriculture, and hydrocarbon resources.

Development outcomes depend primarily on how national and local government actors in resource-rich countries manage their relations with the private sector, especially foreign-owned enterprises. They also depend on the degree of integration of these private-sector actors within, and their understanding of, the governance structures created by these countries to manage resource revenues and investments.

Concluding Observations

An important distinguishing feature of this research, from an academic perspective, lies in the use of in-depth interviews, in each case study country, to analyze governance concepts and practices, arrive at theory-guided conclusions that may be applied in various contexts, and develop an improved analytical framework: the Political Economy of Natural Resource Governance (PENRG). Together, these methods contribute to knowledge of the role and impact of foreign actors in the management and governance of natural resources in Africa, as well as how to undertake such critical analysis. Clearly, foreign-owned enterprises are affected by existing governance structures and interactions with governments, which establish roles and responsibilities for these actors and enable outcomes that may subsequently influence changes in the governance structures themselves. This mutually enforcing relationship is captured in the analytical framework of this book. The merits of this knowledge contribution rest in being better able to construct detailed systemic explanations of natural resource management and governance in Africa; in more progressive perceptions regarding the role, impact, and responsibility of foreign-owned and private-sector actors in diverse developing contexts; and in understanding, in greater depth, how such actors' relations with governments in the region evolve over time.

The extent to which foreign-owned enterprises in resource-rich countries such as Ghana, Sierra Leone, and Ethiopia are viewed either with hope and praise, or continued suspicion and widespread discontent, will

Conclusion 219

depend greatly on how local and national government actors manage their relations with the private sector. It will also depend on the degree of collaboration, cooperation, consultation, and engagement with foreign private-sector actors within governance structures created to manage resource rents and investments within the broader framework and commitments agreed to under the Africa Mining Vision. The private sector has the potential to bring about transformation and change for the better in the economic and social fabrics of conflict-threatened and post-conflict countries, and to serve as the engine of growth in stable, resource-rich democracies in Africa. However, this can only be possible with strong, coherent, and strategic national and local governance structures that define clearly the role and responsibilities of the private sector to all stakeholders, including mining communities.

Notes

INTRODUCTION

1 On 25 September 2015, world governments meeting at the United Nations adopted seventeen Sustainable Development Goals (SDGs) aimed at ending extreme poverty, ensuring prosperity for all, and protecting the environment. The SDGs replace the Millennium Development Goals (MDGs) adopted in 2000. Each SDG outlines specific measurable targets to be achieved by 2030.

CHAPTER ONE

1 The Africa Mining Vision was adopted by heads of state at a 2009 African Union summit, and is linked to the Mining Policy Framework tabled at the United Nations Commission on Sustainable Development (UNCSD) in 2011 by the forty-eight-member Intergovernmental Forum on Mining, Minerals, Metals and Sustainable Development (IGF) (Janneh and Ping 2011). The AMV and its associated Action Plan form the most complete framework for collaborative governance on a continent with fifty-four national governments and abundant natural resources (Besada and Shaw 2014).

2 As dependent variables, these concepts are translated as "peace" and "stability" for the purposes of this book. State stability, in this context, refers to political and social stability, and economic growth.

3 For a seminal application of the agent-structure problem in the field of political science, see Wendt (1987).

CHAPTER TWO

1 For a discussion of the dimensions of state fragility, see Hannan and Besada (2007).

2 The present research was inspired by a volume edited by Mahoney and Rueschemeyer (2003). The study describes the research accomplishments and future agendas of comparative historical research and its explanatory power in regard to to large-scale development outcomes, including state formation and restructuring in Africa.

3 According to the World Bank, national poverty headcount ratio is the percentage of the population living below the national poverty line. National estimates are based on population-weighted subgroup estimates from household surveys. Poverty headcount ratio in the population is measured based on national (i.e., country-specific) poverty lines.

CHAPTER THREE

1 All these GDP figures, despite their different sources, are calculated using data from the Ghana Statistical Service.

2 For a recent analysis of how money is spent by gold-mining companies and split between stakeholders (specifically employees, suppliers, communities, investors, and the government), see World Gold Council (2013).

3 For an overview of Ghana's oil discoveries, see Asamoah (2012).

4 For more information, see GNPC (n.d.).

5 For the history of Ghana's National Energy Board, established in the mid-1980s to undertake energy planning and policy development, and disbanded by the government in 1991; and for a discussion on the importance of developing comprehensive national energy plans and institutionalizing the formulation and coordination of energy sector strategies, see Turkson (1990).

6 An account set up by the government, which receives allocations from oil-and-gas revenues in support of government budgets.

7 Ghana's petroleum revenues are first held in an intermediary Petroleum Holding Fund from which they are then allocated to the Ghana National Petroleum Corporation, the Annual Budget Funding Amount, and Ghana's two sovereign wealth funds, the Ghana Heritage Fund and the Ghana Stabilization Fund. The purpose of the Ghana Heritage Fund is to accumulate revenues for future generations of Ghanaians. The Ghana Stabilization Fund's purpose is to mitigate the negative effects of oil revenue volatility on the national budget and sustain public expenditure capacity in the unanticipated event of a revenue shortfall. Together, the two funds are known as the Ghana Petroleum Funds.

NOTES TO PAGES 108–78

8 All information related to pedagogical, academic, and technical training activities involving Tullow Oil is available on the Tullow Group Scholarship Scheme webpage: https://www.tullowgroupscholarshipscheme.org/index. php. The program operated in various African and South American countries.

9 An exceptional starting point is Polus (2013).

CHAPTER FOUR

1 The National Recovery Strategy's four priority areas were: transforming and promoting community development; rebuilding state authority and state organizations; initiating economic reconstruction; and peacebuilding and restoration of human rights. For more information, see Relief Web (2002).

2 The English-language designation for the highest-level political leader in a regional or local polity or country administered politically with a chief-based system.

3 Councils in districts containing or yielding diamonds for mining.

4 For more information, see: http://sierraleone.revenuesystems.org.

5 See the criticisms around Section 1502 of the Dodd-Frank Act and the smuggling of gold from the Democratic Republic of the Congo, Uganda, Rwanda, and Burundi.

6 The Mines and Minerals Act expresses this as "one percent of one percent of gross revenue earned by the mining operations in the previous year," but this been repeatedly reported to be a mistake by the director of mines, who is chiefly responsible for managing and implementing the act.

CHAPTER FIVE

1 Smallholder agriculture is practised by families using only or mostly family labour. It includes the raising of crops, animal husbandry, forestry, and artisanal fisheries.

2 The decision to maintain Ethiopian land as public property meant that Ethiopians retained usufruct rights to their land, with the sale, transfer, and mortgage of land remaining strictly prohibited. With that said, Ethiopians may now inherit and rent land (Rahmato 2009).

3 These included Amnesty International and Human Rights Watch, as well as the American, British, and EU governments.

4 According to Lavers (2012b), the largest investors in Ethiopia to date have been companies from India, Germany, Israel, and Saudi Arabia.

5 In some cases, labour is imported entirely from the foreign investor's country of origin, thereby undermining any employment benefit to local populations. Alternatively, if sourced from the country of investment, jobs are not necessarily offered to affected populations in the communities where the investment is based, as more skilled workers from other parts of the country are willing to relocate.

6 According to one local resident, "they [private investors] don't want to employ our people" (Moreda 2015, 530). The resident noted that their community was perceived as unskilled and lazy in comparison to the highland farmers. This perception is supported by an interview in a separate case study in which it was discovered that pastoralists were viewed by investors as poor labourers (Becker and Wittmeyer 2013).

7 Although the research team for this report attempted to conduct field research on this issue in Gambella and the SNNPR with the help of Ethiopian researchers, delays in securing government approvals prevented the research from moving forward.

8 Although the Ethiopian government enacted the 2005 Water Resources Management Proclamation, which states that "domestic [municipal] use shall have priority over and above any other water uses," implementation of these laws is very limited (Bossio et al. 2012). Furthermore, large-scale lease agreements permit the development and use of surface and subsurface water without any preconditions.

9 Local populations have also taken part in outright conflicts with investors in villages far from main towns, where government forces could not easily intervene (Rahmato 2011).

10 The export ban on teff, the Ethiopian staple grain, was lifted in 2015 due to its potential to become the next big grain in health and upscale markets. The Ethiopian government is closely monitoring its production, however, to ensure that high international prices do not drive low domestic prices upward as well.

11 With the more recent downward trend in oil and gas prices, however, investors unmotivated by environmental concerns have likely stepped back from biofuel projects and thus slowed the race for biofuel production.

NOTES TO PAGES 196–216

12 As the demand for biofuel crops increases, so too do the prices for these crops. If they increase beyond the prices paid by the food industry, then food prices for these crops rise to the point of inaccessibility.

13 Previous jatropha projects years earlier have failed in this environment.

14 Contract farming is the sourcing of agricultural production from smallholders.

15 This sector was introduced to Ethiopia through foreign investments due to growing demand in European markets.

16 Although concern has been expressed over the environmental impacts of the flower industry due to the widespread use of chemical fertilizers and pesticides (Getu 2009), Ethiopian regulations, international partnerships, and market certification and labelling programs have the potential to improve the economic, social, and environmental sustainability of this sector.

17 It is important to consider the potential role of pastoralists in this regard, as organic fertilizers are more environmentally sustainable and also offer potential value addition for pastoralist outputs.

CONCLUSION

1 The ways in which local knowledge might reduce negative environmental effects include resource conservation technologies, improved techniques for organic and low-input systems, reducing water pollution, biological substitutes for agrochemicals, and reducing the agricultural sector's dependence on fossil fuels (Kiers et al. 2008).

References

Aalen, L. 2006. "Ethnic Federalism and Self-Determination for Nationalities in a Semi-Authoritarian State: The Case of Ethiopia." *International Journal on Minority and Group Rights* 13 (2/3): 243–61.

– 2009. "The End of Democracy? Curtailing Political and Civil Rights in Ethiopia." *Review of African Political Economy* 36 (120): 193–207.

Aaronson, S.A. 2011. "Limited Partnership: Business, Government, Civil Society, and the Public in the Extractive Industries Transparency Initiative (EITI)." *Public Administration and Development* 31 (1): 50–63.

Abbink, J. 2011. "Ethnic-Based Federalism and Ethnicity in Ethiopia: Reassessing the Experiment after 20 Years." *Journal of Eastern African Studies* 5 (4): 596–618.

Abdulai, A.G. 2017. "Competitive Clientelism and the Political Economy of Mining in Ghana." ESID Working Paper 78. Manchester: Effective States and Inclusive Development Research Centre. http://dx.doi.org/10.2139/ssrn.2986754. Also available at: https://ssrn.com/abstract=2986754.

Ablo, A. 2015. "Local Content and Participation in Ghana's Oil and Gas Industry: Can Enterprise Development Make a Difference?" *Extractive Industries and Society* 2 (2).

Abor, J., and P. Quartey. 2010. "Issues in SME Development in Ghana and South Africa." *International Research Journal of Finance and Economics* 39: 218–28.

Abubakari, M., P.K.B. Asamoah, and F.O. Agyemang. 2018. "Ghana and Sustainable Development: The 40-Year National Development Plan in Retrospective." *Journal of Human Resource and Sustainability Studies* 6: 24–36.

Acosta, A.M. 2013. "The Impact and Effectiveness of Accountability and Transparency Initiatives: The Governance of Natural Resources." *Development Policy Review* 31 (1): 89–105.

Acemoglu, D., J.A. Robinson, and S. Johnson. 2002. "Reversal of Fortune: Geography and Institutions in the Making of the Modern World Income Distribution." *Quarterly Journal of Economics* 117 (4): 1231–94.

ACEP (Africa Centre for Energy Policy). 2015a. *Illicit Financial Flows and the Extractives Industry in Ghana.* Accra: ACEP. http://www.osiwa.org/publication/view/illicit-financial-flows-and-the-extractive-industry-in-ghana.

– 2015b. *The Role of Extractive Resource Revenues in Bridging the Financing Gap in Pro-Poor Sectors in Ghana. The Cases of Education, Health and Agriculture.* Accra: African Centre for Energy Policy. Accra: ACEP. http://www.osiwa.org/publication/view/the-role-of-extractive-resource-revenues-in-bridging-the-financing-gap-in-pro-poor-sectors-in-ghana.

ACET (African Center for Economic Transformation). 2014. *The Public-Private Sector Dialogue on Mining Governance in Ghana Series.* https://acetforafrica.org/publications/working-papers/the-public-private-sector-dialogue-on-mining-governance-in-ghana-series/.

ACHPR and IWGIA (African Commission on Human and Peoples' Rights and International Work Group for Indigenous Affairs). 2006. *Indigenous Peoples in Africa: The Forgotten Peoples? The African Commission's Work on Indigenous Peoples in Africa.* Copenhagen: ACHPR and IWGIA. https://www.iwgia.org/en/resources/publications/305-books/2545-indigenous-peoples-in-africa-the-forgotten-peoples-the-african-commissions-work-on-indigenous-peoples-in-africa.html.

Adam, M.A. 2016. "Ghana's New Petroleum Act Shows the Common Resolve of Ghanaians to Good Governance in Oil and Gas Management – ACEP." Press release, 5 August. https://storage.googleapis.com/stateless-acep-africa/2020/06/88169244-5th-august-2016-ghana%E2%80%99s-new-petroleum-act-shows-the-common-resolve-of-ghanaians-to-good-governance-in-oil-and-gas-management-%E2%80%93-acep.pdf.

Adam Smith International. 2013. "Local Content Assessment Report: Sierra Leone." https://assessments.hpc.tools/sites/default/files/assessments/sl_final_local_content_assessment_report_11mar2013.pdf.

Adams, D., D. Ullah, P. Akhtar, K. Adams, and S. Saidi. 2019. "The Role of Country-Level Institutional Factors in Escaping the Natural Resource Curse: Insights from Ghana." *Resources Policy* 61: 433–40.

Adenew, B. 2004. "The Food Security Role of Agriculture in Ethiopia." *Journal of Agricultural and Development Economics* 1 (1): 138–53.

REFERENCES

AfCOP (African Community of Practice on Managing for Development Results). 2016. *Local Content in Ghana's Petroleum Industry: Solid Policy Undermined by Capacity Gaps*. Case study 17. Harare: African Capacity Building Foundation.

AfDB (African Development Bank). 2007. "Africa's Natural Resources: The Paradox of Plenty." Ch. 4 in *African Development Report 2007: Natural Resources for Sustainable Development in Africa*. Oxford, UK: AfDB and Oxford University Press. https://www.afdb.org/fileadmin/uploads/afdb/Documents/Publications/%28E%29%20AfricanBank%202007%20Ch4.pdf.

– 2012. "Mining Industry Prospects in Africa." 20 December. https://blogs.afdb.org/afdb-championing-inclusive-growth-across-africa/post/mining-industry-prospects-in-africa-10177.

– 2013. *Green Growth Sierra Leone: Transitioning Towards Green Growth: Stocktaking and the Way Forward*. Tunis: African Development Bank Group.

AfDB et al. 2014. *Sierra Leone 2014. Abidjan: African Economic Outlook*. African Development Bank, Organisation for Economic Co-operation and Development, and United Nations Development Programme. https://www.africaneconomicoutlook.org/sierra-leone/.

Afful-Koomson, T., and K.O. Asubonteng. 2013. *Collaborative Governance in Extractive Industries in Africa*. Accra: United Nations University Institute for Natural Resources in Africa.

Afful-Koomson, T. 2013a. "Collaborative Governance and Its Relevance for Extractive Industries in Africa." In *Collaborative Governance in Extractive Industries in Africa*, edited by T. Afful-Koomson and K.O. Asubonteng, 1–26. Accra: United Nations University Institute for Natural Resources in Africa.

– 2013b. "Enhancing Collaborative Governance of Extractive Industries in Africa." In *Collaborative Governance in Extractive Industries in Africa*, edited by T. Afful-Koomson and K.O. Asubonteng, 200–19. Accra: United Nations University Institute for Natural Resources in Africa.

African Elections Database. 2012. *Elections in Sierra Leone*. Accessed 2 August 2016. http://africanelections.tripod.com/sl.html#2002.

africanews.com. 2017. "Ethiopia Needs Policy on 'Sustainable Peace and Conflict Resolution' – Govt Body." 7 October 2017. https://www.africanews.com/2017/10/07/ethiopia-needs-policy-on-sustainable-peace-and-conflict-resolution-govt-body/.

africanews.com. 2019. "OLF Rebels in Ethiopia Give Up Arms: Oromo Officials."

16 February. https://www.africanews.com/2019/02/16/olf-rebels-in-ethiopia-have-given-up-arms-oromo-officials/.

Agola, N. 2016. *Technology Transfer and Economic Growth in Sub-Sahara African Countries: Lessons from East Asia.* Berlin: Springer.

Ahlenius, H. 2006. "Current and Potential Arable Land Use in Africa." Accessed 30 November 2020. https://www.grida.no/resources/7868.

Akabzaa, T., and A. Darimani. 2001. *Impact of Mining Sector Investment in Ghana: A Study of the Tarkwa Mining Region.* Draft report for SAPRI. http://www.saprin.org/ghana/research/gha_mining.pdf.

Akabzaa, T.M., J.S. Seyire, and K. Afriyie. 2007. *The Glittering Façade: Effects of Mining Activities on Obuasi and Its Surrounding Communities.* Accra: Third World Network – Africa.

Ake, C. 1975. "A Definition of Political Stability." *Comparative Politics* 7 (2): 271–83.

Akiwumi, F.A. 2012. "Global Incorporation and Local Conflict: Sierra Leonean Mining Regions." *Antipodes* 44 (3): 581–600.

Al Amoudi, M.H. n.d. Sheikh Mohammed Hussein Al Amoudi Official Website. Accessed 25 August 2018. https://www.sheikhmohammedalamoudi.info/.

Al Jazeera. 2016. "'Foreign Firms Attacked' as Ethiopia Protests Continue." 2 September. http://www.aljazeera.com/news/2016/09/firms-attacked-ethiopia-protests-continue-160902064459286.html.

Alao, A. 2007. *Natural Resources and Conflict in Africa: The Tragedy of Endowment.* New York: University of Rochester Press.

Albin-Lackey, C. 2005. "Suppressing Dissent: Human Rights Abuses and Political Repression in Ethiopia's Oromia Region." Human Rights Watch. https://www.hrw.org/report/2005/05/09/suppressing-dissent/human-rights-abuses-and-political-repression-ethiopias-oromia.

Alemu, D., E. Gabre-Madhin, and S. Dejene. 2006. "From Farmer to Market and Market to Farmer: Characterizing Smallholder Commercialization in Ethiopia." Paper submitted at "Bridging, Balancing, and Scaling Up: Advancing the Rural Growth Agenda in Ethiopia," Ethiopia Strategy Support Program (ESSP) Policy Conference, 6–8 June, Addis Ababa. https://www.research gate.net/publication/272565190_From_farmer_to_market_and_market_to_farmer_Characterizing_smallholder_commercialization_in_Ethiopia/link/5838314808ae3a74b49cce20/download.

Ali, D.A., S. Dercon, and M. Gautam. 2007. "Property Rights in a Very Poor

REFERENCES

Country: Tenure Insecurity and Investment in Ethiopia." Policy Research Working Paper 4363. Washington, DC: World Bank.

Ali, S., K. Sturman, and N. Collins. 2018. *Africa's Mineral Fortune: The Science and Politics of Mining and Sustainable Development*. London: Routledge.

Altieri, M.A., and C.I. Nicholls. 2008. "Scaling Up Agroecological Approaches for Food Sovereignty in Latin America." *Development* 51 (4): 472–80.

Ambaye, D.W. 2015. *Land Rights and Expropriation in Ethiopia*. New York: Springer.

Amighini, A.A., R. Rabellotti, and M. Sanfilippo. 2013. "Do Chinese State-Owned and Private Enterprises Differ in Their Internationalization Strategies?" *China Economic Review* 27 (C): 312–25.

Amoako-Tuffour, J., T. Aubynn, and A. Atta-Quayson. 2015. *Local Content and Value Addition in Ghana's Mineral, Oil, and Gas Sectors: Is Ghana Getting It Right?* Accra: African Center for Economic Transformation.

Amponsah-Tawiah, K., and K. Dartey-Baah. 2011. "Corporate Social Responsibility in Ghana." *International Journal of Business and Social Science* 2 (27): 107–12.

Amunwa, B., and M. Minio. 2011. *Counting the Cost: Corporations and Human Rights Abuses in the Niger Delta*. London: Platform.

Andersen, L. 2011. "Security Sector Reform and the Dilemmas of Liberal Peace-building." Working Paper 31. Copenhagen: Danish Institute for International Studies.

Andersen, T., and C. Dalgaard. 2013. "Power Outages and Economic Growth in Africa." *Energy Economics* 38 (C): 19–23.

Andrews, N. 2016. "Challenges of Corporate Social Responsibility (CSR) in Domestic Settings: An Exploration of Mining Regulation Vis-à-vis CSR in Ghana." *Resources Policy* 47: 9–17.

AngloAmerican. "Integrated Annual Report 2017: Re-Imagining Mining to Improve People's Lives." http://www.angloamerican.com/investors/annual-reporting.

AngloGold Ashanti. 2017. "Integrated Report 2017." https://www.anglogold ashanti.com/investors/annual-reports/.

Anne, I. 2012. *Water Governance – Challenges in Africa: Hydro-optimism or Hydro-pessimism?* Berne: Peter Lang.

Anseeuw, W. 2013. "The Rush for Land in Africa: Resource Grabbing or Green Revolution?" *South African Journal of International Affairs* 20 (1): 159–77.

Anwar, M.A. 2016. "India, the Biggest Land Investor in Ethiopia." *African Exponent*, 9 January. https://www.africanexponent.com/post/india-the-biggest-land-investor-in-ethiopia-1327.

Appel, H.C. 2012. "Walls and White Elephants: Oil Extraction, Responsibility, and Infrastructural Violence in Equatorial Guinea." *Ethnography* 13 (4): 439–65.

Arai, Y., A. Cissé, and M. Sock. 2010. *Promoting Job Creation for Young People in Multinational Enterprises and Their Supply Chains: Sierra Leone*. Geneva: International Labour Organization.

Arthur, P. 2012. "Avoiding the Resource Curse in Ghana: Assessing the Options." In *Natural Resources and Social Conflict: Towards Critical Environmental Security*, edited by M.A. Schnurr and L.A. Swatuk, 108–27. Basingstoke: Palgrave Macmillan.

Arthur, P., and E. Arthur. 2014. "Local Content and Private Sector participation in Ghana's Oil Industry: An Economic and Strategic Imperative." *Africa Today* 61 (2) 57–77.

Arthur, R., M.F. Baidoo, and E. Antwi. 2011. "Biogas as a Potential Renewable Energy Source: A Ghanaian Case Study." *Renewable Energy* 36 (5): 1510–16.

Aryee, N.A.B. 2001. "Ghana's Mining Sector: Its Contribution to the National Economy." *Resources Policy* 27 (2): 61–75.

Aryeetey, E., R.D. Osei, and P. Quartey. 2014. "Managing Ghana's Oil Boom: Summary of Key Findings and Policy Lessons." In *Managing Ghana's Oil Boom for Structural Transformation*, edited by E. Aryeetey, R.D. Osei, and P. Quartey, 1–7. Legon, Ghana: Sub-Saharan Publishers.

Asamoah, J. 2012. *The Global Oil and Gas Bonanza: Africa's Share*. Accra: Joasa Publications.

– 2013a. *Making the Oil and Gas Find in Ghana a Blessing*. 4th edition. Accra: Joasa Publications.

– 2013b. "The Management of Strategic Resources: The Oil and Gas Find in Ghana." In *Collaborative Governance in Extractive Industries in Africa*, edited by T. Afful-Koomson and K.O. Asubonteng, 181–99. Accra: United Nations University Institute for Natural Resources in Africa.

Asante, F.A., and P. Owasa. 2014. "Oil and Ghana's Development: Some Global Lessons in Governance and Institution Building." In *Managing Ghana's Oil Boom for Structural Transformation*, edited by E. Aryeetey, R.D. Osei, and P. Quartey, 144–66. Legon, Ghana: Sub-Saharan Publishers.

REFERENCES

Asmeri, R., T. Alvionita, and A. Gunardi. 2017. "CSR Disclosures in the Mining Industry: Empirical Evidence from Listed Mining Firms in Indonesia." *Indonesian Journal of Sustainability Accounting and Management* 1 (1): 16–22.

Aton, Adam. 2017. "Once Again, Climate Change Cited as Trigger for Conflict." *Scientific American*. 9 June. https://www.scientificamerican.com/article/once-again-climate-change-cited-as-trigger-for-war/.

Aubynn, T. n.d. "Mining and Sustainable Development: The Case of Ghana." PowerPoint presentation. Ghana Chamber of Mines. Accessed 17 August 2016. http://im4dc.org/wp-content/uploads/2013/07/Mining-and-Sustainable-Development-Ghana.pdf.

AUC et al. 2010. *Land Policy in Africa: Eastern Africa Regional Assessment*. Addis Ababa: African Union Commission, African Development Bank, and United Nations Economic Commission for Africa. http://www.uneca.org/sites/default/files/PublicationFiles/regional_assesment_eastafrica.pdf.

Auty, R.M. 1993. *Sustaining Development in Mineral Economies: The Resource Curse*. London: Routledge.

Ayee, J., T. Soreide, G.P. Shukla, and M. Le Tuan. 2011. *Political Economy of the Mining Sector in Ghana*. Washington, DC: World Bank.

Ayensu, F. 2013. "Managing Ghana's Oil Revenue: Ghana Petroleum Funds (Gpfs)." *Asian Journal of Humanities and Social Sciences* 1 (2): 148–61.

Ayling, R., and K. Kelly. 1999. "Dealing with Conflict: Natural Resources and Dispute Resolution." *Commonwealth Forestry Review* 76: 182–5.

B&FT. 2014. "Gas Won't Flow in April – Energy Minister." GhanaWeb. 3 February. http://www.ghanaweb.com/GhanaHomePage/economy/artikel.php?ID=299601.

Bache, I., and M. Flinders. 2004. *Multi-level Governance*. Oxford: Oxford Scholarship Online.

Bacon, R. 2001. *Petroleum Taxes: Trends in Fuel Taxes (and Subsidies) and the Implications*, Washington, DC: World Bank.

Baliamoune-Lutz, M., and L. Ndikumana. 2009. "Corruption and Growth in African Countries: Exploring the Investment Channel." African Development Bank Group. https://www.afdb.org/fileadmin/uploads/afdb/Documents/Knowledge/Conference_2007_anglais_16-part-III-4.pdf.

Ballentine, K. 2006. "Promoting Conflict-Sensitive Business in Fragile States: Redressing Skewed Incentives." In *Trade, Aid, and Security: An Agenda for Peace and Development*, ed. O. Brown, M. Halle, S.P. Moreno, and S. Winkler, 126–56. London: Earthscan.

Bank of Ghana. 2003. "Report on the Mining Sector November 2003."

Bannon, I., and P. Collier. 2003. *Natural Resources and Violent Conflict: Options and Actions*. Washington, DC: World Bank.

Basedau, M., and W. Lacher. 2006. "A Paradox of Plenty? Rent Distribution and Political Stability in Oil States." GIGA Working Papers 21. Hamburg: German Institute of Global and Area Studies.

Baumgartner, P. 2012. "Change in Trend and New Types of Large-Scale Investments in Ethiopia." In *Handbook of Land and Water Grabs in Africa: Foreign Direct Investment and Food and Water Security*, ed. T. Allan, M. Keulertz, S. Sojamo, and J. Warner, 176–90. Abingdon: Routledge.

Baumgartner, P., J. von Braun, D. Abebaw, and M. Muller. 2015. "Impacts of Large-Scale Land Investments on Income, Prices, and Employment: Empirical Analyses in Ethiopia." *World Development* 72: 175–90.

Bazilian, M., I. Onyeji, P. Aqrawi, B. Sovacool, E. Ofori, D.M. Kammen, and T. Van de Graaf. 2013. "Oil, Energy Poverty and Resource Dependence in West Africa." *Journal of Energy and Natural Resources Law* 31 (1): 33–52.

BBC. 2016. "What Do Oromo Protests Mean for Ethiopian Unity?" *BBC News*. 9 March. http://www.bbc.com/news/world-africa-35749065.

– 2017. "What Is behind Clashes in Ethiopia's Oromia and Somali Regions?" *BBC News*. 18 September. http://www.bbc.com/news/world-africa-41278618.

Becker, D.A., and H. Wittmeyer. 2013. "Africa's Land Rush and the Embedded Neoliberal State: Foreign Agricultural Investment in Ethiopia and Mozambique." *Comparative Sociology* 12 (6): 753–84.

Beevers, M.D. 2015. "Governing Natural Resources for Peace: Lessons from Liberia and Sierra Leone." *Global Governance: A Review of Multilateralism and International Organizations* 21 (2): 227–46.

Behzadan, Nazanin, Richard Chisik, Harun Onder, and Bill Battaile. 2017. "Does Inequality Drive the Dutch Disease? Theory and Evidence." *Journal of International Economics* 106 (May): 104–18. https://doi.org/10.1016/j.jinteco.2017.02.003.

Belete, A., J.L. Dillon, and F.M. Anderson. 1991. "Development of Agriculture in Ethiopia since the 1975 Land Reform." *Agricultural Economics* 6 (2): 159–75.

Ben Aïssa, M.S., M. Ben Jebli, and S. Ben Youssef. 2014. "Output, Renewable Energy Consumption and Trade in Africa." *Energy Policy* 66: 11–18.

Benin, S., and J. Pender. 2001. "Impacts of Land Redistribution on Land Man-

REFERENCES

agement and Productivity in the Ethiopian Highlands." *Land Degradation & Development* 12 (6): 555–68.

Bennett, A., and C. Elman. 2006a. "Complex Causal Relations and Case Study Methods: The Example of Path Dependence." *Political Analysis* 14 (3): 250–67.

– 2006b. "Qualitative Research: Recent Developments in Case Study Methods." *Annual Review of Political Science* 9: 455–76.

Berger, P.L., and T. Luckmann. 1966. *The Social Construction of Reality: A Treatise in the Sociology of Knowledge*. New York: Doubleday.

Berghs, M. 2012. *War and Embodied Memory: Becoming Disabled in Sierra Leone*. London: Routledge.

Berhanu, K. 2012. "The Political Economy of Agricultural Extension Policy in Ethiopia: Economic Growth and Political Control." Future Agricultures Consortium Working Paper 042. Accessed 06 September 2016. http://agris.fao.org/agris-search/search.do?recordID=GB2013201465.

Berhanu, K., and C. Poulton. 2014. "The Political Economy of Agricultural Extension Policy in Ethiopia: Economic Growth and Political Control." *Development Policy Review* 32 (s2): s197–s213. https://doi.org/10.1111/dpr.12082.

Berry, L., ed. 1994. "Gold." In *Ghana: A Country Study*. Washington, DC: Library of Congress. Accessed 23 August 2016. http://countrystudies.us/ghana/84.htm.

Bertelsmann Stiftung. 2014. *BTI 2014 – Sierra Leone Country Report*. Gütersloh, Germany: Bertelsmann Stiftung.

– 2016. *Sierra Leone Country Report*. Transformation Index. Gütersloh, Germany: Bertelsmann Stiftung. https://bti-project.org/content/en/downloads/reports/country_report_2016_SLE.pdf.

– 2018. *BTI 2018 – Sierra Leone Country Report*. Gütersloh, Germany: Bertelsmann Stiftung. https://www.bti-project.org/content/en/downloads/reports/country_report_2018_SLE.pdf.

Bertone, M.P., M. Samai, J. Edem-Hotah, and S. Witter. 2014. "A Window of Opportunity for Reform in Post-Conflict Settings? The Case of Human Resources for Health Policies in Sierra Leone, 2002–2012." *Conflict and Health* 8 (1): 11.

Besada, H. 2006. "Case Studies on the Impact of South African Mining Investment in Africa." Brenthurst Discussion Paper 10/2006.

– 2013. "Doing Business in Fragile States: The Private Sector, Natural Resources, and Conflict in Africa." Paper submitted to the High-level Panel on the Post-2015 Development Agenda. Accessed 23 August 2016. http://www.post2015hlp.org/wp-content/uploads/2013/06/Doing-Business-in-Fragile-States-The-Private-Sector-Natural-Resources-and-Conflict-in-Africa-FINAL-May-25-2013.pdf.

– 2016. *Policy Impacts on Africa's Extractive Sector: Ghana, the Dominance of Gold, and the Future of Oil*. Addis Ababa: United Nations Economic Commission for Africa.

– 2017. "Ethiopia: Natural Resource Exploitation and Emerging Investors." *Revue Gouvernance* 14 (1): 66–87.

Besada, H., V. Ermakov, and M. Ternamian. 2009. "Peacebuilding and the Role of the Private Sector in Post-Conflict West Africa: A Conceptual Framework." In *From Civil Strife to Peace Building: Examining Private Sector Involvement in West African Reconstruction*, ed. H. Besada, 1–14. Waterloo, ON: Wilfrid Laurier University Press.

Besada, H., and A. Goetz. 2012. "The Land Crisis in Southern Africa: Challenges for Good Governance." In *Southern African Development Community Land Issues: Towards a New Sustainable Land Relations Policy*, ed. B. Chigara, 169–94. Routledge: New York.

Besada, H., and P. Martin. 2013. *Research Report: Mining Codes in Africa: Emergence of a "Fourth" Generation?* Ottawa: North-South Institute.

Besada, H., and T. Shaw. 2014. *Governing Natural Resources for Africa's Development: Preface*. Ottawa: North-South Institute.

Besada, H., M.E. Tok, and L.M. Polonenko. 2019. *Innovating South-South Cooperation: Policies, Challenges and Prospects*. Ottawa: University of Ottawa Press.

Biney, A. 2009. "Land Grabs – Another Scramble for Africa. Walden Bello: Structural Adjustment destroyed African agriculture." TNI. 28 September. https://www.tni.org/es/node/4598.

Black, D., and B. O'Bright. 2016. "International Development and the Private Sector: The Ambiguities of 'Partnership.'" *International Journal* 71 (1):144–66. https://doi.org/10.1177/0020702015619566.

Blattman, C., and E. Miguel. 2010. "Civil War." *Journal of Economic Literature* 48 (1): 3–57.

Bloch, R., and G. Owusu. 2012. "Linkages in Ghana's Gold Mining Industry: Challenging the Enclave Book." *Resources Policy* 37 (4): 434–42.

Bloomberg. 2018. "Shandong Iron & Steel Group Co Ltd." Accessed 17 August

2018. https://www.bloomberg.com/research/stocks/private/snapshot.asp?
privcapId=42751952.

BMI Research. 2015. *Ghana Operational Risk Report: Q1 2016*. London: Business Monitor International.

Boakye, D., S. Dessus, Y. Foday, and F. Oppong. 2012. "Investing Mineral Wealth in Development Assets: Ghana, Liberia and Sierra Leone." Policy Research Working Paper Series 6089. Washington, DC: World Bank.

Boatemah, H.B., and G. Owusa. 2014. "Oil and the Western Region: Implications for Regional and Local Development." In *Managing Ghana's Oil Boom for Structural Transformation*, ed. E. Aryeetey, R.D. Osei, and P. Quartey, 196–224. Legon, Ghana: Sub-Saharan Publishers.

Bokpin, G.A., L. Mensah, and M.E. Asamoah. 2015. "Foreign Direct Investment and Natural Resources in Africa." *Journal of Economic Studies* 42 (4): 608–21.

Bond, P. 2008. "The Looting of Africa." In *Globalization and the Washington Consensus: Its Influence on Democracy and Development in the South*, ed. G. Lechini. Buenos Aires: Consejo Latinoamericano de Ciencias Sociales (CLASCO). http://biblioteca.clacso.edu.ar/ar/libros/sursur/lech/07bond.pdf.

Boon, E.K., and F. Ababio. 2009. "Corporate Social Responsibility in Ghana: Lessons from the Mining Sector." *IAIA09 Conference Proceedings: Impact Assessment and Human Well-Being*. 29th Annual Conference of the International Association for Impact Assessment, Accra International Conference Centre, Accra, 16–22 May 2009.

Borras, S.M., Jr, C. Kay, S. Gómez, and J. Wilkinson. 2012. "Land Grabbing and Global Capitalistic Accumulation: Key Features in Latin America." *Canadian Journal of Development Studies* 33 (4): 402–16.

Borras, S.M., Jr, and J.C. Franco. 2012. "Global Land Grabbing and Trajectories of Agrarian Change: A Preliminary Analysis." *Journal of Agrarian Change* 12 (1): 34–59.

Bosc, P., J. Berdegué, M. Goita, J.D. van der Ploeg, K. Sekine, and L. Zhang. 2013. *Investing in Smallholder Agriculture for Food Security. A Report by the High-Level Panel of Experts on Food Security and Nutrition*. Rome: Committee on World Food Security. http://www.fao.org/3/a-i2953e.pdf.

Bossio, D., T. Erkossa, Y. Dile, M. McCartney, F. Killiches, and H. Hoff. 2012. "Water Implications of Foreign Direct Investment in Ethiopia's Agricultural Sector." *Water Alternatives* 5 (2): 223–42.

Bracco, S. 2018. *The Economics of Biofuels: The Impact of EU Bioenergy Policy on Agricultural Markets and Land Grabbing in Africa*. London: Routledge.

Brauer, J., and J. Tepper Marlin. 2009. "Defining Peace Industries and Calculating the Potential Size of a Peace Gross World Product by Country and by Economic Sector." Annandale-upon-Hudson, NY: Economists for Peace and Security. https://www.files.ethz.ch/isn/126268/definingpeaceindustrieand calculatingapeacewgp.pdf.

Brock, L., H. Holm, G. Sørenson, and M. Stohl. 2012. *Fragile States*. Cambridge: Polity.

Brown, G., A. Langer, and F. Stewart. 2011. "A Typology of Post-Conflict Environments." CRPD Working Paper 1. Leuven: Centre for Research on Peace and Development, University of Leuven. https://soc.kuleuven.be/crpd/files/working-papers/wp01.pdf.

Buckles, D. 1999. *Cultivating Peace: Conflict and Collaboration in Natural Resource Management*. Ottawa: International Development Research Centre.

Bues, A., and I. Theesfeld. 2012. "Water Grabbing and the Role of Power: Shifting Water Governance in the Light of Agricultural Foreign Direct Investment." *Water Alternatives* 5 (2): 266–83.

Burnside, C., and D. Dollar. 2000. "Aid, Policies and Growth." *American Economic Review* 90: 847–68.

Bush, K.D., and R.J. Opp. 1999. "Peace and Conflict Impact Assessment." In *Cultivating Peace: Conflict and Collaboration in Natural Resource Management*, ed. D. Buckles, 185–202. Ottawa: International Development Research Centre; Washington, DC: World Bank Institute.

Bush, R. 2009. "'Soon There Will Be No-One Left to Take the Corpses to the Morgue': Accumulation and Abjection in Ghana's Mining Communities." *Resources Policy* 34 (1–2): 57–63.

Cabrales, A., and Hauk, E. 2011. "The Quality of Political Institutions and the Curse of Natural Resources." *Economic Journal* 121: 58–88.

Campbell, B. 2003. "Factoring in Governance Is Not Enough: Mining Codes in Africa, Policy Reform and Corporate Responsibility." *Minerals & Energy – Raw Materials Report* 18 (3): 2–13.

– 2012. "Corporate Social Responsibility and Development in Africa: Redefining the Roles and Responsibilities of Public and Private Actors in the Mining Sector." *Resources Policy* 37 (2): 137–43.

CAO (Compliance Advisor Ombudsman). 2010. "Ghana/Tullow Oil, Kosmos Energy & Jubilee FPSO-01/CAO Vice President Request." Washington, DC: World Bank. http://www.cao-ombudsman.org/cases/case_detail.aspx?id=166.

REFERENCES

Carbonnier, G. 2011. "The Global and Local Governance of Extractive Resources." *Global Governance* 17 (2): 135–47.

Cash, D.W., and S.C. Moser. 2000. "Linking Global and Local Scales: Designing Dynamic Assessment and Management Processes." *Global Environmental Change* 10 (2): 109–20.

Chalfin, B. 2015. "Governing Offshore Oil: Mapping Maritime Political Space in Ghana and the Western Gulf of Guinea." *South Atlantic Quarterly* 114 (1): 101–18.

Chamlee-Wright, E. 1997. *The Cultural Foundations of Economic Development: Urban Female Entrepreneurship in Ghana.* London: Routledge.

Chandran, R., and T. Gardner. 2017. "Calls to End Africa's 'Horrific' Land Deals after Indian Firm's Fallout." *Reuters*, 28 November 2017. https://www.reuters.com/article/us-ethiopia-landrights-india/calls-to-end-africas-horrific-land-deals-after-indian-firms-fallout-idUSKBN1DS1FK.

Chege, M. 2002. "Sierra Leone: The State That Came Back from the Dead." *Washington Quarterly* 25 (3): 147–60.

Chitor, B. 2012. *Ghana's Transitional Oil and Gas Industry: Legal, Corporate and Environmental Aspects.* Accra: Binditi Chitor.

Christensen, M.M., and M. Utas. 2008. "Mercenaries of Democracy: The 'Politricks' of Remobilized Combatants in the 2007 General Elections, Sierra Leone." *African Affairs* 107 (429): 515–39.

Chuhan-Pole, P., A.L. Dabalen, and B.C. Land. 2017. *Mining in Africa: Are Local Communities Better Off?* Washington, DC: World Bank Publications.

CIA (Central Intelligence Agency). 2015. "Ghana." *The World Factbook.* Washington, DC: CIA. https://www.cia.gov/library/publications/the-world-factbook/geos/gh.html.

– 2017. "Sierra Leone." *The World Factbook.* Washington, DC: CIA. https://www.cia.gov/library/publications/the-world-factbook/geos/sl.html.

CIVICUS. 2006. *Civil Society Index Report for the Republic of Sierra Leone: A Critical Time for Civil Society in Sierra Leone.* New York: CIVICUS.

Cleveland, T. 2015. *Diamonds in the Rough: Corporate Paternalism and African Professionalism on the Mines of Colonial Angola, 1917–1975.* Akron: Ohio University Press.

Collier, D., and J. Gerring, eds. 2009. *Concepts and Method in Social Science: The Tradition of Giovanni Sartori.* London: Routledge.

Collier, P. 2000. *Economic Causes of Civil Conflict and Their Implications for*

Policy. Washington, DC: World Bank. http://www.globalsecurity.org/military/library/news/2000/06/civilconflict.pdf.

– 2007. *The Bottom Billion: Why the Poorest Countries Are Failing and What Can Be Done About It*. New York: Oxford University Press.

Collier, P., and M. Duponchel. 2013. "The Economic Legacy of Civil War: Firm-Level Evidence from Sierra Leone." *Journal of Conflict Resolution* 47 (1): 65–88.

Collier, P., and A. Hoeffler. 2004. "Greed and Grievance in Civil War." *Oxford Economic Papers* 54: 563–95.

Commonwealth. 2017. "Sierra Leone: Economy." London: Commonwealth Secretariat. http://thecommonwealth.org/our-member-countries/sierra-leone/economy.

Cooke, E., S. Hague, and A. McCay. 2016. *The Ghana Poverty and Inequality Report: Using the 6th Ghana Living Standards Survey*. UNICEF. https://www.unicef.org/ghana/media/531/file/The%20Ghana%20Poverty%20and%20Inequality%20Report.pdf.

Cooper, I. 2018. "Sierra Leone President to Push Review of Mining Law, Contracts." Reuters, 25 May. https://af.reuters.com/article/topNews/id AFKCN1IQ1SJ-OZATP.

Corden, W., and J. Neary. 1982. "Booming Sector and De-Industrialization in a Small Open Economy." *Economic Journal* 92: 825–48.

Cornish, L. 2013. "Tonkolili – Sierra Leone – Three Projects in One: Prestigious Projects in Africa." *Inside Mining* 6 (8): 14–16.

Cotula, L. 2013. *The Great African Grab? Agricultural Investments and the Global Food System*. London: Zed Books.

Cotula, L., S. Vermeulen, R. Leonard, and J. Keeley. 2009. *Land Grab or Development Opportunity? Agricultural Investment and International Land Deals in Africa*. London: IIED, FAO, and IFAD. http://pubs.iied.org/pdfs/12561IIED.pdf.

Courson, E. 2009. *Movement for the Emancipation of the Niger Delta (MEND): Political Marginalization, Repression and Petro-Insurgency in the Niger Delta*. Discussion Paper 47. Uppsala: Nordiska Afrikainstitutet.

Cox, R.W. 1981. "Social Forces, States and World Orders: Beyond International Relations." *Millennium: Journal of International Studies* 10 (2): 126–55.

– 1983. "Gramsci, Hegemony and International Relations: An Essay in Method." *Millennium: Journal of International Studies* 12 (2): 162–75.

REFERENCES 241

Cubitt, C. 2014. "An Introduction to Governance in Africa." *Governance in Africa* 1 (1): 1–9.

Dafflon, B., and T. Madiès, eds. 2013. *The Political Economy of Decentralization in Sub-Saharan Africa: A New Implementation Model in Burkina Faso, Ghana, Kenya, and Senegal.* Washington, DC: World Bank.

DAG (Development Assistance Group Ethiopia). 2016. "Welcome." Accessed 11 August 2016. http://dagethiopia.org/new/.

Darimani, A. 2013. "Analysis of Governance in the Ghanaian Mining Sector." In *Collaborative Governance in Extractive Industries in Africa*, ed. T. Afful-Koomson and K.O. Asubonteng, 77–101. Accra: United Nations University Institute for Natural Resources in Africa.

Dasnois, N. 2012. "Uranium Mining in Africa: A Continent at the Centre of a Global Nuclear Renaissance." SAIIA Occasional Paper 122. Pretoria: South African Institute of International Affairs. https://saiia.org.za/research/uranium-mining-in-africa-a-continent-at-the-centre-of-a-global-nuclear-renaissance/.

Davis, G.A. 2009. "Extractive Economies, Growth, and the Poor." In *Mining, Society, and a Sustainable World*, ed. J.P. Richards, 37–60. Berlin: Springer-Verlag.

Davies, V.A.B. 2003. "War, Poverty and Growth in Africa: Lessons from Sierra Leone." Paper prepared for "Understanding Poverty and Growth in Africa," fifth annual conference of the Centre for the Study of African Economies (CSAE), St Catherine's College, Oxford University, 18–19 March 2003.

De Schutter, O. 2010. "The Emerging Human Right to Land." *International Community Law Review* 12 (3): 303–34.

De Soysa, I. 2001. "Paradise Is a Bazaar? Greed, Creed, Grievance and Governance." Discussion Paper 2001/42. United Nations World Institute for Development Economic Research.

Debrah, E., and E. Graham. 2015. "Preventing the Oil Curse Situation in Ghana: The Role of Civil Society Organisations." *Africa Insights* 7 (1): 21–41.

Deichmann, U., C. Meisner, S. Murray, and D. Wheeler. 2011. "The Economics of Renewable Energy Expansion in Rural Sub-Saharan Africa." *Energy Policy* 39 (1): 215–27.

Deininger, K., H. Selod, and A. Burns. 2011. *The Land Governance Assessment Framework: Identifying and Monitoring Good Practice in the Land Sector.* Washington, DC: World Bank Group.

Del Castillo, G. 2008. *Rebuilding War-Torn States: The Challenge of Post-Conflict Economic Reconstruction.* New York: Oxford University Press.

Dell'Angelo, J., P. D'Odorico, M.C. Rulli, and P. Marchand. 2017. "The Tragedy of the Grabbed Commons: Coercion and Dispossession in the Global Land Rush." *World Development* 92: 1–12.

Deloitte. n.d. "Invest in Ghana: A Stable Springboard into West Africa." Deloitte Southern Africa. Accessed 28 November 2017. https://www2.deloitte.com/za/en/pages/deloitte-africa/articles/invest-in-ghana-a-stable-spring board-into-west-africa.html.

Demissie, F. 2017. *Land Grabbing in Africa: The Race for Africa's Rich Farmland.* London: Routledge.

DFID (Department for International Development, UK). 2012. "Business Case and Intervention Summary: Local Content Study, Sierra Leone." https://study lib.net/doc/7030819/title—local-content-study—sierra-leone.

Dixon, R. 2016. "Foreign Businesses Are Torched in Protests, and Ethiopia Is in a State of Emergency." *Los Angeles Times,* 11 October. https://www.latimes.com/world/africa/la-fg-ethiopia-killings-oromo-protesters-20161011-snap-story.html.

Donham, D.L. 1999. *Marxist Modern: An Ethnographic History of the Ethiopian Revolution.* Berkeley: University of California Press.

Dontoh, E., and A. Janse Van Vuuren. 2017. "Ghana Consumer Prices Rise 9.3% in March From a Year Earlier." *Bloomberg News.* 10 April 2019. https://www.bnnbloomberg.ca/ghana-consumer-prices-rise-9-3-in-march-from-a-year-earlier-1.1242191.

DRC (Democratic Republic of the Congo). 2018. Mining Code of the Democratic Republic of the Congo. Available at: https://eiti.org/document/mining-code-of-democratic-republic-of-congo.

Dreher, A., V.F. Lang, and K. Richert. 2019. "The Political Economic of International Finance Corporation Lending." *Journal of Development Economics* 140: 242–54.

Dumett, R. 1999. *El Dorado in West Africa: The Gold Mining Frontier, African Labor, and Colonial Capitalism.* Akron: Ohio University Press.

Dupuy, K.E. 2014. "Community Development Requirements in Mining Laws." *Extractive Industries and Society* 1 (2): 200–15.

– 2017. "Corruption and Elite Capture of Mining Community Development Funds in Ghana and Sierra Leone." In *Corruption, Natural Resources and*

REFERENCES

Development: From Resource Curse to Political Ecology, ed. A. Williams and P. Le Billon, 69–79. Cheltenham, UK: Edward Elgar Publishing.

Easterly, W., R. Levine, and D. Roodman. 2004. "Aid, Policies and Growth: Comment." *American Economic Review* 94 (3): 774–80.

Edwards, D.P., S. Sloan, L. Weng, P. Dirks, J. Sayer, and W.F. Laurance. 2014. "Mining and the African Environment." *Conservation Letters* 7 (3): 302–11.

EITI (Extractive Industry Transparency Initiative). 2016a. "EITI Standard Requirements 2016." Oslo: EITI International Secretariat. https://eiti.org/document/eiti-standard-requirements-2016.

– 2016b. "Revenue collection." Freetown: Sierra Leone Extractive Industries Transparency Initiative. https://eiti.org/sierra-leone#revenue-collection.

Enria, L. 2018. *The Politics of Work in a Post-Conflict State: Youth, Labour and Violence in Sierra Leone.* Oxford: James Currey.

Ensene, K.A. 2018. *The Political Economy of Land and Agrarian Development in Ethiopia: The Arssi Region since 1941.* London: Routledge.

Erk, J. 2017. *The Ethnopolitics of Ethnofederalism in Ethiopia.* London: Routledge.

Escobar, J.C., E. Lora, O. Venturini, E. Yanez, E. Castillo, and O. Almazan. 2009. "Biofuels: Environment, Technology and Food Security." *Renewable and Sustainable Energy Reviews* 13 (6): 1275–87.

Essah, M., and N. Andrews. 2016. "Linking or De-linking Sustainable Mining Practices and Corporate Social Responsibility? Insights from Ghana." *Resources Policy* 50 (supp. C): 75–85. https://doi.org/10.1016/j.resourpol.2016.08.008.

Esteves, A.M., B. Coyne, and A. Moreno. 2013. *Local Content Initiatives: Enhancing the Subnational Benefits of the Oil, Gas and Mining Sectors.* New York: Natural Resource Governance Institute.

Ethiopia. 1975. Proclamation No. 31 of 1975: A proclamation to provide for the public ownership of rural lands. http://faolex.fao.org/cgi-bin/faolex.exe?rec_id=001828&database=faolex&search_type=link&table=result&lang=eng&format_name=@ERALL.

– 1995. Constitution of the Federal Democratic Republic of Ethiopia. http://www.wipo.int/edocs/lexdocs/laws/en/et/et007en.pdf.

Ethiopian Herald. 2018a. "Ethiopia: UAE Reveals U.S. $3 Billion Aid, Investment Package." 18 June. https://www.africapulse.com/2018/06/18/ethiopiauae-reveals-u-s-3-billion-aid-investment-package/.

– 2018b. "Ethiopia Tops Turkish Investment Destinations of Africa: EIC."

31 January. http://www.ethpress.gov.et/herald/index.php/news/national-news/item/10748-ethiopia-tops-turkish-investment-destinations-of-africa-eic.

European Commission. n.d. "Biofuels Overview." Accessed 25 July 2016. https://ec.europa.eu/energy/en/topics/renewable-energy/biofuels.

Evans, R. 2015. "Skills and Education: The Key to Unlocking Development from Mining." *AusIMM Bulletin*. 3 February. https://www.ausimmbulletin.com/feature/skills-and-education-the-key-to-unlocking-development-from-mining/.

Fabricius, C. et al. 2013. *Rights, Resources and Rural Development*. London: Routledge.

Fanthorpe, R., and C. Gabelle. 2013. *Political Economy of Extractives Governance in Sierra Leone*. Washington, DC: International Bank for Reconstruction and Development/World Bank.

FAO (Food and Agricultural Organization). 2012. "Voluntary Guidelines on the Responsible Governance of Tenure of Land, Fisheries and Forests in the Context of National Food Security." Rome: FAO Committee on World Food Security. http://www.fao.org/cfs/home/activities/vggt/en/.

– 2015. "Ghana – Country Fact Sheet on Food and Agriculture Policy Trends: Ghana." Rome: FAO. http://www.fao.org/3/a-i4490e.pdf.

FAO et al. (Food and Agriculture Organization, International Fund for Agricultural Development, and World Food Programme). 2015. *The State of Food Insecurity in the World 2015. Meeting the 2015 International Hunger Targets: Taking Stock of Uneven Progress*. Rome: FAO.

farmlandgrab.org. 2018. "Saudi Star." Accessed 30 November 2020. https://www.farmlandgrab.org/cat/show/431.

Fastmarkets MB. 2015. "African Minerals, London Mining and the Fall of Sierra Leone's Iron Ore Sector." *Metal Bulletin*, 10 March. https://www.metalbulletin.com/Article/3434921/African-Minerals-London-Mining-and-the-fall-of-Sierra-Leones-iron-ore-sector.html.

Ferme, M. 2001. *The Underneath of Things: Violence, History, and the Everyday in Sierra Leone*. Berkeley: University of California Press.

Fonjong, L.N., and V.Y. Fokum. 2015. "Rethinking the Water Dimension of Large-Scale Land Acquisitions in Sub-Saharan Africa." *Journal of African Studies and Development* 7 (4): 112–20.

Frankel, J. 2010. "The Natural Resource Curse: A Survey." Faculty Research

REFERENCES 245

Working Paper RWP10-005. Cambridge, MA: Harvard Kennedy School, Harvard University.

Frynas, J.G. 2000. *Oil in Nigeria: Conflict and Litigation between Oil Companies and Village Communities*. Munich: LIT Verlag.

Frynas, J.G., G. Wood, and T. Hinks. 2017. "The Resource Curse without Natural Resources: Expectations of Resource Booms and Their Impact." *African Affairs* 116 (463): 233–60. https://doi.org/10.1093/afraf/adx001.

Fund for Peace. 2017. "Fragile States Index 2017: Factionalization and Group Grievance Fuel Rise in Instability." http://fragilestatesindex.org/fsi/2017/05/14/fsi-2017-factionalization-and-group-grievance-fuel-rise-in-instability/.

– 2018. "Fragile States Index." https://fragilestatesindex.org/.

Gaffey, C. 2017. "Ethiopia Is Banning Armed Police from a Religious Festival in a Bid to Avoid a Stampede." *Newsweek*, 25 September. http://www.newsweek.com/ethiopia-conflict-oromo-irreecha-festival-670258.

Galant, A., and S. Cadez. 2017. "Corporate Social Responsibility and Financial Performance Relationship: A Review of Measurement Approaches." *Economic Research/Ekonomska Istraživanja* 30 (1): 676–93.

Garvin, T., T.K. McGee, K.E. Smoyer-Tomic, and E.A. Aubynn. 2009. "Community-Company Relations in Gold Mining in Ghana." *Journal of Environmental Management* 90 (1): 571–86.

Gberie, L. 2005. *A Dirty War in West Africa: The RUF and the Destruction of Sierra Leone*. Bloomington: Indiana University Press.

Gebreselassie, S. 2006. "Intensification of Smallholder Agriculture in Ethiopia: Options and Scenarios." Discussion Paper 007. Brighton: Future Agricultures Consortium, University of Sussex. http://citeseerx.ist.psu.edu/viewdoc/download?doi=10.1.1.411.1357&rep=rep1&type=pdf.

Gelb, A., ed. 1988. *Oil Windfalls: Blessing or Curse?* Oxford: Oxford University Press.

George, A.L., and A. Bennett. 2005. *Case Studies and Theory Development in the Social Sciences*. Cambridge, MA: MIT Press.

George, A.M. 2015. "The Power of Mining to Transform Development in Africa." Text of speech delivered at Investing in African Mining Indaba conference, Cape Town, 11 February 2015. World Bank. http://www.worldbank.org/en/news/speech/2015/02/11/the-power-of-mining-to-transform-development-in-africa.

Gepper, M., and K. Williams. 2007. "Global, National and Local Practices in

Multinational Corporations: Towards a Sociopolitical Framework." *International Journal of Human Resources Management* 17 (1): 49–69.

Getu, M. 2009. "Ethiopian Floriculture and Its Impact on the Environment: Regulation, Supervision and Compliance." *Mizan Law Review* 3 (2): 240–70.

Ghana. 2010. Draft National Mining Policy of Ghana. Accra: Minerals Commission. http://213.154.74.164/invenio/record/18584/files/mining%20policy%20of%20Ghana.pdf.

– 2011. Petroleum Revenue Management Act, 2011. https://www.mofep.gov.gh/sites/default/files/acts/Petroleum-Revenue-Management-ACT-815.pdf.

– 2013. Ghana Investment Promotion Centre Act (Act 865). *Ghana Gazette.* Accra: Government Printing Office.

Ghana Justice. 2016. "Petroleum (Exploration and Production) Act, 2016 to Provide Enabling Environment for Increased Private Participation and Investment in Ghana's Petroleum Sector." *Ghana Justice*, 15 August. http://ghanajustice.com/petroleum-exploration-and-production-act-2016-to-provide-enabling-environment-for-increased-private-participation-and-investment-in-ghanas-petroleum-sector.

Ghana News Agency. 2017. "Geo Professional Services Debunks Galamsey Allegation." *GH Headlines*, 11 June. http://ghheadlines.com/agency/ghana-news-agency/20170611/45541806/geo-professional-services-debunks-galam sey-allegation.

Ghana Petroleum Register. n.d. "Contract Areas." Accessed 27 July 2018. https://www.ghanapetroleumregister.com/contract-areas.

GHEITI (Ghana Extractive Industry Transparency Initiative). 2012. "2012 Annual Report." Accra: GHEITI Secretariat. https://eiti.org/sites/default/files/documents/Ghana_2012_ANNUAL_Activity_REPORT.pdf.

Giddens, A. 1979. *Central Problems in Social Theory: Action, Structure, and Contradiction in Social Analysis.* London: Macmillan.

GIPC (Ghana Investment Promotion Centre). n.d. "Investing in This Sector – Ghana Investment Promotion Centre (GIPC)." Accra: GIPC. Accessed 13 November 2017. http://www.gipcghana.com/invest-in-ghana/sectors/oil-and-gas/investing-in-this-sector.html.

Glaeser, E., R. La Porta, F. Lopez-de-Silanes, and A. Shleifer. 2004. "Do Institutions Cause Growth?" *Journal of Economic Growth* 9: 271–303.

Gleditsch, N.P., P. Wallensteen, M. Eriksson, M. Sollenberg, and H. Strand.

REFERENCES

2002. "Armed Conflict 1946–2001: A New Dataset." *Journal of Peace Research* 39 (5): 615–37.

Global Finance (online magazine). 2017. "Ethiopia GDP and Economic Data." https://www.gfmag.com/global-data/country-data/ethiopia-gdp-country-report.

GNPC (Ghana National Petroleum Corporation). n.d. "About Us – Overview." Accessed 17 August 2016. http://www.gnpcghana.com/overview.html.

Graham, A., S. Aubry, R. Künnemann, and S.M. Suarez. 2010. "Land Grab Study." FIAN International. https://www.fian.org/en/publication/article/land-grab-study-2462.

GRAIN. 2008a. "Seized! The 2008 Land Grab for Food and Financial Security." https://www.grain.org/article/entries/93-seized-the-2008-landgrab-for-food-and-financial-security.

– 2008b. "The Food Crisis and the Hybrid Rice Surge." https://www.grain.org/es/article/entries/665-the-food-crisis-and-the-hybrid-rice-surge.

Grant, A. 2015. *New Approaches to the Governance of Natural Resources: Insights from Africa*. London: Palgrave Macmillan.

Guardian (UK). 2018. "Landmark Case against British Mining Firm Begins in Sierra Leone." 7 February. https://www.theguardian.com/global-development/2018/feb/07/landmark-case-against-british-mining-firm-sierra-leone-tonkolili-iron-ore-ltd-police-brutality.

Gugerty, M.K., and A. Prakash. 2010. *Voluntary Regulation of NGOs and Non-profits: An Accountability Club Framework*. Cambridge, UK: Cambridge University Press

Gupta, S., F. Bornhorst, and J. Thornton. 2009. "Natural Resource Endowments and the Domestic Revenue Effort." *European Journal of Political Economy* 25: 439–46.

Gyamfi, S., M. Modjinou, and S. Djordjevic. 2015. "Improving Electricity Supply Security in Ghana: The Potential of Renewable Energy." *Renewable and Sustainable Energy Reviews* 43: 1035–45.

Gyimah-Boadi, E., and H. Kwasi Prempeh. 2012. "Oil, Politics, and Ghana's Democracy." *Journal of Democracy* 23 (3): 94–108.

Hagmann, T., and A. Mulugeta. 2008. "Pastoralist Conflicts and State-Building in the Ethiopian Lowlands." *Africa Spectrum* 43 (1): 19–37.

Hameed, S., and K. Mixon. 2013. *Private Sector Development in Fragile, Conflict-*

Affected, and Violent Countries. Washington, DC: Center for Strategic and International Studies.

Hannan, U., H. Besada. 2007. "Dimensions of State Fragility: A Review of the Social Science Literature." CIGI Working Paper 33. Waterloo, ON: Centre for International Governance Innovation.

Hanson, K., C. D'Alessandro, and F. Owusu. 2014. *Managing Africa's Natural Resources: Capacities for Development*. London: Palgrave Macmillan.

Haroon Akram-Lodhi, A., S.M. Borras Jr, and C. Kay, eds. 2009. *Land, Poverty and Livelihoods in an Era of Globalization: Perspectives from Developing and Transition Countries*. New York, Routledge.

Harvey, R. 2014. "Mining and Development: Lessons Learnt from South Africa and Beyond." Johannesburg: South African Institute of International Affairs. http://www.saiia.org.za/policy-briefings/mining-and-development-lessons-learnt-from-south-africa-and-beyond.

Hayden, S. 2016. "Ethiopia's Battle for Land Reforms Could Lead to Civil War: Opposition Leader." *Reuters*, 11 August. https://www.reuters.com/article/us-ethiopia-landrights-violence/ethiopias-battle-for-land-reforms-could-lead-to-civil-war-opposition-leader-idUSKCN10M12X.

Herren, H.R., A.M. Bassi, Z. Tan, and W.P. Binns. 2012. *Green Jobs for a Revitalized Food and Agriculture Sector*. New York: Natural Resources Management and Environment Department, Food and Agriculture Organization, United Nations.

Herring, R.J. 2015. *The Oxford Handbook of Food, Politics, and Society*. Oxford: Oxford University Press.

Heymann, T. 2014. "Understanding Who Benefits from Gold Mining." Maastricht: ECDPM. http://ecdpm.org/great-insights/value-chains-industrialisa tion/understanding-benefits-gold-mining/.

Hickel, J. 2018. *The Divide: Global Inequality from Conquest to Free Markets*. New York: W.W. Norton.

Hilson, A., G. Hilson, and S. Dauda. 2019. "Corporate Social Responsibility at African Mines: Linking the Past to the Present." *Journal of Environmental Management* 241: 340–52.

Hilson, G. 2002. "Land Use Competition between Small- and Large-Scale Miners: A Case Study of Ghana." *Land Use Policy* 19 (2): 149–56.

– 2012. "Corporate Social Responsibility in the Extractive Industries: Experiences from Developing Countries." *Resources Policy* 37 (2): 131–7.

REFERENCES 249

– 2018. "Why Is There a Large-Scale Mining 'Bias' in Sub-Saharan Africa?" *Land Use Policy* 81: 852–61.

Hilson, G., and B. Murck. 2000. "Sustainable Development in the Mining Industry: Clarifying the Corporate Perspective." *Resources Policy* 26 (4): 227–38.

Hirsch, J.L. 2001. *Sierra Leone: Diamonds and the Struggle for Democracy.* Boulder, CO: Lynne Rienner.

Hodbod, J.E. 2013. "The Impacts of Biofuel Expansion on the Resilience of Social-Ecological Systems in Ethiopia." Doctoral thesis, University of East Anglia.

Hodge, A., S. Shankar, D.S. Prasada Rao, and A. Duhs. 2011. "Exploring the Links Between Corruption and Growth." *Review of Development Economics* 15 (3): 474–90. https://doi.org/10.1111/j.1467-9361.2011.00621.x.

Hoffer, V. 2010. "Disclosure as Governance: The Extractive Industries Transparency Initiative and Resource Management in the Developing World." *Global Environmental Politics* 10 (3): 53–73.

Hoffman, D. 2011. *The War Machines: Young Men and Violence in Sierra Leone and Liberia.* Chapel Hill: Duke University Press.

Holden, S., and H. Yohannes. 2002. "Land Redistribution, Tenure Insecurity, and Intensity of Production: A Study of Farm Households in Southern Ethiopia." *Land Economics* 78 (4): 573–90.

Hooghe, L., and G. Marks. 2002. "Types of Multi-Level Governance." *European Integration Online Papers*, 5 (11).

Horne, F., and L. Bader. 2012. "Waiting Here for Death: Forced Displacement and 'Villagization' in Ethiopia's Gambella Region." Human Rights Watch. https://www.hrw.org/sites/default/files/reports/ethiopia0112webwcover_0.pdf.

Hout, W. 2015. "Putting Political Economy to Use in Aid Policies." In *A Governance Practitioner's Notebook: Alternative Ideas and Approaches*, ed. A. Whaites et al., 83–97. Paris: Organisation for Economic Co-operation and Development. https://www.oecd.org/dac/accountable-effective-institutions/Governance%20Notebook%201.4%20Hout.pdf.

HRW (Human Rights Watch). 2006. "Ethiopia: Events of 2005." https://www.hrw.org/world-report/2006/country-chapters/ethiopia.

– 2009. "Ethiopia: New Law Ratchets up Repression." https://www.hrw.org/news/2009/01/08/ethiopia-new-law-ratchets-repression.

– 2017 "Ethiopia: Events of 2016." https://www.hrw.org/world-report/2017/country-chapters/ethiopia.

Humphreys, M. 2005. "Natural Resources, Conflict and Conflict Resolution." *Journal of Conflict Resolution* 49: 508–37.

ICMM (International Council on Mining and Metals). 2012. *Community Development Toolkit*. London: ICMM.

– 2015. *Mining in Ghana – What Future Can We Expect?* https://www.icmm.com/website/publications/pdfs/mining-parterships-for-development/mining-in-ghana_what-future-can-we-expect.

ICTA (Institute of Environmental Science and Technology). 2014. "Saudi Star Agriculture and Irrigation Project in Gambela, Ethiopia, 2018." *Environmental Justice Atlas*. Last updated 24 June 2014. Barcelona: ICTA, Universitat Autonoma de Barcelona. https://ejatlas.org/conflict/saudi-star-agriculture-and-irrigation-project-in-gambela-ethiopia.

IDEA (Institute for Democracy and Electoral Assistance). 2018. *Political Parties and Natural Resource Governance: A Practical Guide for Developing Resource Policy Positions*. https://www.idea.int/publications/catalogue/political-parties-and-natural-resource-governance.

IEA (International Energy Agency). 2014. *African Energy Outlook – Executive Summary: A Focus on Energy Prospects in Sub-Saharan Africa.*" World Energy Outlook Special Report. https://www.icafrica.org/fileadmin/documents/Knowledge/Energy/AfricaEnergyOutlook-IEA.pdf.

IFC (International Finance Corporation). 2015. *Update of the Needs and Opportunities Assessment (Gap Analysis)*. Washington, DC: International Finance Corporation.

IFPRI (International Food Policy Research Institute). 2009. "'Land Grabbing' by Foreign Investors in Developing Countries: Risks and Opportunities." Washington, DC: IFPRI. http://www.ifpri.org/blog/land-grabbing-foreign-investors-developing-countries.

IFS (Institute for Fiscal Studies). 2015. "Ghana: Impact of Falling Crude Oil Prices." Occasional Paper No. 5. Accra: Institute for Fiscal Studies.

Ikelegbe, A. 2005. "The Economy of Conflict in the Oil-Rich Niger Delta Region of Nigeria." *Nordic Journal of African Studies* 14 (2): 208–34.

– 2013. *Oil, Environment and Resource Conflicts in Nigeria*. Munich: LIT Verlag.

IMANI (IMANI Center for Policy & Education). 2010a. "IMANI Alert: Single Spine Salary Agitations: Signs of Things to Come." *Modern Ghana*, 17 September. https://www.modernghana.com/news/296656/imani-alert-single-spine-salary-agitations-signs-of-thing.html.

REFERENCES

– 2012b. "IMANI: GNPC Confuses Ghanaians about Abnormal Jubilee Costs." https://www.myjoyonline.com/business/imani-gnpc-confuses-ghanaians-about-abnormal-jubilee-costs/.

– 2013a. "Ghana Gas Project Is 33% Complete." https://www.ghanaweb.com/GhanaHomePage/business/Ghana-Gas-Project-is-33-complete-IMANI-270227.

– 2013b. "Budget 2014: Worrying Perspectives from IMANI Ghana." https://www.ghanaweb.com/GhanaHomePage/NewsArchive/Budget-2014-Worrying-Perspectives-from-IMANI-Ghana-294593.

IMANI Ghana. 2010. "IMANI Special Report: Ghana's 'Integrated Aluminum' Fever." *Modern* Ghana, 5 February. https://www.modernghana.com/news/262638/imani-special-report-ghanas-integrated-aluminum-fever.html.

– 2012. "Ghana: The Threat of Decay: An IMANI Pre-Election Report." *Modern Ghana*, 25 November. https://www.modernghana.com/news/432571/ghana-the-threat-of-decay.html.

IMC Worldwide. 2016. "Sierra Leone: Building the Capacity of the Government PPP Unit." Last updated 14 December 2016. http://www.imcworldwide.com/project/sierra-leone-building-the-capacity-of-the-government-ppp-unit/.

IMF (International Monetary Fund). 2011. *Sierra Leone: 2011 Second and Third Reviews under the Extended Credit Facility.* Washington DC: IMF.

– 2015. *The Federal Democratic Republic of Ethiopia: Staff Report for the 2015 Article IV Consultation.* Washington, DC: IMF. https://www.imf.org/external/pubs/ft/scr/2015/cr15300.pdf.

Issifu, A.K. 2016. "Corporate Responsibility in Peace Building, Conflict Prevention and Development: The Role of the Mining Sector in Ghana." *Journal of Interdisciplinary Conflict Science* 2 (2).

Ite, U.E. 2005. "Poverty Reduction in Resource Rich Developing Countries: What Have Multinational Corporations Got to Do with It?" *Journal of International Development* 17 (7): 913–29.

Jackson, D.R. 2017. *US Foreign Policy in the Horn of Africa: From Colonialism to Terrorism.* London: Routledge.

Jakobi, P.A., and K.D. Wolf. 2013. *The Transnational Governance of Violence and Crime.* London: Palgrave Macmillan.

Janneh, A., and J. Ping. 2011. *Minerals and Africa's Development: The International Study Group Report on Africa's Mineral Regimes.* Addis Ababa: United Nations Economic Commission for Africa (UNECA).

Jensen, N. 2006. "Democratic Institutions and Expropriation Risk for Multinational Investors." SSRN Paper. https://papers.ssrn.com/sol3/papers.cfm?abstract_id=869460.

– 2008. "Political Risk, Democratic Institutions and Foreign Direct Investment." *Journal of Politics* 70 (4): 1040–52.

Jerven, M. 2015. *Why Economists Get It Wrong*. London: Zed Books.

Jingushi, A.W. 2015. "Post-Conflict Security Sector Reform, and the Roles of the Military and the Police: The Case of Sierra Leone." *NIDS Journal of Defense and Security* 16: 37–59.

Johnson, J.C., C. Avenarius, and J. Weatherford. 2006. "The Active Participant-Observer: Applying Social Role Analysis to Participant Observation." *Field Methods* 18 (2): 111–34.

Johnson, O.E.G. 2011. "Financial Sector Reform and Development in Sierra Leone." Working Paper 11/0560. London: International Growth Centre, London School of Economics. https://www.theigc.org/wp-content/uploads/2014/09/Johnson-2011-Working-Paper.pdf.

Joskow, P. 1987. "Contract Duration and Relationship-Specific Investments: Empirical Evidence from Coal Markets." *American Economic Review* 77: 168–85.

Kaldor, M., and J. Vincent. 2006. *Evaluation of UNDP Assistance to Conflict-Affected Countries: Case Study Sierra Leone*. New York: United Nations Development Programme.

Kanu, J. 2010. *Mining Revenue Streams and Their Development Impact on Communities Affected by Mining*. Freetown: Network Movement for Justice and Development.

Kanyako, V. 2016. "Donor Policies in Post-War Sierra Leone." *Journal of Peacebuilding & Development* 11 (1): 26–39. https://doi.org/10.1080/15423166.2016.1146035.

Kapika, J., and A. Eberhard. 2013. *Power-Sector Reform and Regulation in Africa: Lessons from Kenya, Tanzania, Uganda, Zambia, Namibia and Ghana*. Pretoria: Human Sciences Research Council.

Karekezi, S., and W. Kithyoma. 2002. "Renewable Energy Strategies for Rural Africa: Is a PV-Led Renewable Energy Strategy the Right Approach for Providing Modern Energy to the Rural Poor of Sub-Saharan Africa?" *Energy Policy* 30 (11–12): 1071–86.

Kargbo, S.M., and P.A. Adamu. 2009. "Financial Development and Economic

REFERENCES

Growth in Sierra Leone." *West African Journal of Monetary and Economic Integration* 9 (2): 30–61.

Karl, T.L. 1997. *The Paradox of Plenty: Oil Booms and Petro-States.* Berkeley: University of California Press.

Kaufmann, D., A. Kraay, and M. Mastruzzi. 2007. "Governance Matters VI: Aggregate and Individual Governance Indicators for 1996–2006." World Bank Policy Research Working Paper 4280. Washington, DC: World Bank.

Kawamato, K. 2012. "Diamonds in War, Diamonds for Peace: Diamond Sector Management and Kimberlite Mining in Sierra Leone." In *High-Value Natural Resources and Peacebuilding*, ed. P. Lujala and S.A. Rustad. London: Earthscan.

Kayizzi-Mugerwa, S., and J.C. Anyanwu. 2015. *Creating Local Content for Human Development in Africa's New Natural Resource-Rich Countries.* Flagship Report Paper Series 6. Addis Ababa: African Development Bank and Bill & Melinda Gates Foundation.

Keeley, J., W.M. Seide, A. Eid, and A.L. Kidewa. 2014. *Large-Scale Land Deals in Ethiopia: Scale, Trends, Features and Outcomes to Date.* London: International Institute for Environment and Development. http://pubs.iied.org/pdfs/12575IIED.pdf.

Keen, D. 2005. *Conflict and Collusion in Sierra Leone.* London: James Currey.

Kefale, A. 2013. *Federalism and Ethnic Conflict in Ethiopia: A Comparative Regional Study.* London: Routledge.

Keller, E.J. 2002. "Ethnic Federalism, Fiscal Reform, Development and Democracy in Ethiopia. *African Journal of Political Science* 7 (1): 21–50.

Kessides, I.N. 2014. "Powering Africa's Sustainable Development: The Potential Role of Nuclear Energy." *Energy Policy* 74 (supp. 1): 57–70. https://doi.org/10.1016/j.enpol.2014.04.037.

Khairo, S.A., G. Battese, and J.D. Mullen. 2005. "Agriculture, Food Insecurity and Agricultural Policy in Ethiopia." *Outlook on Agriculture* 34 (2): 77–82.

Khan, S.A., and V. Ahmed. 2014. "Peaceful Economies: Assessing the Role of the Private Sector in Conflict Prevention in Pakistan." *International Journal of Security and Development* 3 (1): 1–9.

Kiers, E., R. Leakey, A. Izac, J. Heinemann, and E. Rosenthal. 2008. "Agriculture at a Crossroads." *Science* 320: 320–1.

Killick, T. 2010. *Development Economics in Action: A Study of Economic Policies in Ghana.* London: Routledge.

Kimberley Process. 2018. "Sierra Leone." https://www.kimberleyprocess.com/en/sierra-leone.

Klotz, A., and C. Lynch. 2007. *Strategies for Research in Constructivist International Relations*. New York: M.E. Sharpe.

Knoope, P., and G. Chauzal. (2016). *Beneath the Apparent State of Affairs: Stability in Ghana and Benin*. The Hague: Clingendael, Netherlands Institute of International Relations. https://www.clingendael.org/publication/beneath-apparent-state-affairs-stability-ghana-and-benin.

Kopf, Dan. 2017. "The Story of Ethiopia's Incredible Economic Rise." *Quartz Africa*, 26 October. https://qz.com/1109739/ethiopia-is-one-of-the-fastest-growing-economies-in-the-world/.

Kopinski, D., A. Polus, and W. Tycholiz. 2013. "Resource Curse or Resource Disease? Oil in Ghana." *African Affairs* 112 (449): 583–601.

KPMG. 2016. "The Impact of Corruption." Country Report. Pretoria: KPMG International.

Kraus, J. 2002. "Capital, Power and Business Associations in the African Political Economy: A Tale of Two Countries, Ghana and Nigeria." *Journal of Modern African Studies* 40 (3): 395–436.

Krauss, C. 2017. "Oil Prices: What to Make of the Volatility." *New York Times*, 15 May. https://www.nytimes.com/interactive/2017/business/energy-environment/oil-prices.html.

Kumah-Abiwu, F. 2017. "Democratic Institutions, Natural Resource Governance, and Ghana's Oil Wealth." *Social Sciences* 6 (1).

Kusi-Sarpong, S., J. Sarkis, X. Wang, and W.L. Filho. 2014. "Sustainable Supply Chain Management Practices in Ghana's Mining Industry." Working Paper WP2-2014. Worcester, MA: Center for Sustainability in Business, Foisie School of Business, Worcester Polytechnic Institute.

Kwawukume, S. 2012. *Ghana's Oil and Gas Discoveries: Towards Full Maximum Benefits*. Revised edition. Tema, Ghana: Solomon Kwawukume.

Lancaster, C. 2007. *"We fall down and get up": State Failure, Democracy and Development in Sierra Leone*. Washington, DC: Center for Global Development.

Land Portal. n.d. "Ethiopia – Context and Land Governance." Accessed 17 May 2019. https://landportal.org/book/narratives/2017/countries-ethiopia.

Langdon, J. 2009. *Indigenous Knowledge, Development and Education*. Rotterdam: Sense Publishers.

Laryea, A.D.A. 2014. "Oil and Structural Transformation in Ghana." In *Manag-*

ing Ghana's Oil Boom for Structural Transformation, ed. E. Aryeetey et al., 8–48. Legon, Ghana: Sub-Saharan Publishers.

Lavers, T. 2011. "The Role of Foreign Investment in Ethiopia's Smallholder-Focused Agricultural Development Strategy." Working Paper 2. Land Deals Politics Initiative. Brighton: University of Sussex.

– 2012a. "'Land Grab' as Development Strategy? The Political Economy of Agricultural Investment in Ethiopia." *Journal of Peasant Studies* 39 (1): 105–32.

– 2012b. "Patterns of Agrarian Transformation in Ethiopia: State-Mediated Commercialisation and the 'Land Grab.'" *Journal of Peasant Studies* 39 (3–4): 795–822.

– 2013. "Food Security and Social Protection in Highland Ethiopia: Linking the Productive Safety Net to the Land Question." *Journal of Modern African Studies* 51 (3): 459–85.

Le Billon, P. 2001. "The Political Ecology of War: Natural Resources and Armed Conflicts." *Political Geography* 20 (5), 561–84. https://doi.org/10.1016/S0962-6298(01)00015-4.

– 2008. "Corrupting Peace? Peacebuilding and Post-conflict Corruption." *International Peacekeeping* 15 (3): 344–61.

Leech, B.L. 2002. "Asking Questions: Techniques for Semi-Structured Interviews." *PS: Political Science and Politics* 35: 663–68.

Lisk, F. 2013. "'Land Grabbing' or Harnessing of Development Potential in Agriculture? East Asia's Land-Based Investments in Africa." *Pacific Review* 26 (5): 563–87.

Little, P.D., J. McPeak, G. Gebru, and S. Desta. 2010. "Policy Options for Pastoral Development in Ethiopia and Reaction from the Regions." Report Number 4: Pastoral Economic Growth and Development Policy Assessment, Ethiopia. Addis Ababa: Department for International Development, Government of Ethiopia. https://jomcpeak.expressions.syr.edu/wp-content/uploads/Pastoral_Growth_Study_POLICY_RECOMMENDATIONS_Paper_4_FINAL_P11.pdf.

Lučić, D., M. Radiši, and D. Dobromirov. 2016. "Causality between Corruption and the Level of GDP." *Economic Research/Ekonomska Istraživanja* 29 (1): 360–79. https://doi.org/10.1080/1331677X.2016.1169701.

Lujala, P., N.P. Gleditsch, and E. Gilmore. 2005. "A Diamond Curse? Civil War and a Lootable Resource." *Journal of Conflict Resolution* 49 (4): 538–62.

Luke, D.F., and S.P. Riley. 1989. "The Politics of Economic Decline in Sierra

Leone." *Journal of Modern African Studies* 27 (1): 133–41. www.jstor.org/stable/161359.

Maconachie, R. 2009. "Diamonds, Governance and 'Local' Development in Post-Conflict Sierra Leone: Lessons for Artisanal and Small-Scale Mining in Sub-Saharan Africa?" *Resources Policy* 34 (1): 71–9.

– 2011. "Harnessing Natural Resources for Community Development in Post-War Sierra Leone? The Case of the Diamond Area Community Development Fund." Discussion Paper, "ESF Workshop – Beyond the Resource Curse: New Dynamics in the Management of Natural Resources: New Actors and Concepts," Paris, 3–4 November. https://researchportal.bath.ac.uk/en/publications/harnessing-natural-resources-for-community-development-in-post-wa.

– 2012. "The Diamond Area Community Development Fund: Micro-Politics and Community-Led Development in Post-War Sierra Leone." In *High-Value Natural Resources and Post-Conflict Peacebuilding*, ed. P. Lujala and S.A. Rustad, 261–73. London: Earthscan.

Maconachie, R., and T. Binns. 2007. "Beyond the Resource Curse? Diamond Mining, Development and Post-Conflict Reconstruction in Sierra Leone." *Resources Policy* 32 (3): 104–15.

Maconachie, R., and G. Hilson. 2013. "Editorial Introduction: The Extractive Industries, Community Development and Livelihood Change in Developing Countries." *Community Development Journal* 48 (3): 347–59.

Mahamba, F., and B. Lewis. 2019. "Congo Miner SMB Leaves ITSCI Responsible Sourcing Scheme over Cost." *Reuters*, 8 January. https://www.reuters.com/article/us-itsci-congo/congo-miner-smb-leaves-itsci-responsible-sourcing-scheme-over-cost-idUSKCN1P20OV.

Mahoney, J. 2007. "Qualitative Methodology and Comparative Politics." *Comparative Political Studies* 40 (2): 122–44.

Mahoney, J., and D. Rueschemeyer, eds. 2003. *Comparative Historical Analysis in the Social Sciences*. New York: Cambridge University Press.

Makki, F. 2012. "Power and Property: Commercialization, Enclosures, and the Transformation of Agrarian Relations in Ethiopia." *Journal of Peasant Studies* 39 (1): 81–104.

Makki, F., and C. Geisler. 2011. "Development by Dispossession: Land Grabbing as New Enclosures in Contemporary Ethiopia." Paper presented at the International Conference on Global Land Grabbing, Institute of Development Studies, University of Sussex, Brighton, 6–8 April 2011. https://www.future-agricultures.org/wp-content/uploads/pdf-archive/Fouad%20Makki%20and %20Charles%20Geisler.pdf.

Manek, N. 2018. "As Crude Tests Begin, Ethiopia Touts Nascent Oil, Gas Industry." Bloomberg, 29 June. https://www.bloomberg.com/news/articles/2018-06-29/as-crude-tests-begin-ethiopia-touts-nascent-oil-gas-industry.

Mano, Y., T. Yamano, A. Suzuki, and T. Matsumoto. 2011. "Local and Personal Networks in Employment and the Development of Labor Markets: Evidence from the Cut Flower Industry in Ethiopia." *World Development* 39 (10): 1760–70.

Marando, E., and D. Kayo. 2004. *The Regulation of the Power Sector in Africa: Attracting Investment and Protecting the Poor.* London: Zed Books.

Marda, M., and J. Bangura. 2010. *Sierra Leone beyond the Lomé Peace Accord.* London: Palgrave Macmillan.

Margulis, M.E, N. McKeon, and S.M. Borras Jr., eds. 2014. *Land Grabbing and Global Governance.* London: Routledge.

Mark-Thiesen, C. 2018. *Mediators, Contract Men, and Colonial Capital: Mechanized Gold Mining in the Gold Coast Colony, 1879–1909.* Rochester, NY: Rochester University Press.

Matondi, P.B., K. Havnevik, and A. Beyene. 2011. *Biofuels, Land Grabbing and Food Security in Africa.* London: Zed Books.

McFerson, H.M. 2009. "Governance and Hyper-Corruption in Resource-Rich African Countries." *Third World Quarterly* 30 (8): 1529–47.

McKay, B., F.B. Rodriguez, and D. Fajardo. 2016. "The Voluntary Guidelines of the Responsible Governance on Tenure of Land, Fisheries and Forest in the Context of National Food Security in Colombia: Towards Democratic Land-Based Resource Control." Colloquium Paper 19, "Global Governance/Politics, Climate Justice and Agrarian/Social Justice: Linkages and Challenges – An International Colloquium," International Institute of Social Studies, The Hague, 4–5 February 2016.

McMahon, G., and CEMMATS Group. 2007. *Mining Sector Reform in Sierra Leone: A Strategic Environmental and Social Assessment.* Washington, DC: World Bank.

McSherry, B. 2006. "The Political Economy of Oil in Equatorial Guinea." *African Studies Quarterly* 8 (6): 23–45.

Melese, A.T., and A.H.J. Helmsing. 2010. "Endogenisation or Enclave Formation? The Development of the Ethiopian Cut Flower Industry." *Journal of Modern African Studies* 48 (1): 35–66.

MEP (Ministry of Energy and Petroleum, Ghana). 2013. Petroleum (local content and local participation in petroleum activities) regulations 2013 (LI 2204). Accra: Ministry of Energy and Petroleum.

MFED (Ministry of Finance and Economic Development, Ethiopia). 2010. *Growth and Transformation Plan (GTP) 2010/11–2014/15*. Addis Ababa: MFED.

Miguel, E., and J. Bellows. 2006. "War and Institutions: New Evidence from Sierra Leone." *American Economic Review* 96: 394–9.

MMMR (Ministry of Mines and Mineral Resources, Sierra Leone). n.d.(a). "About National Minerals Agency." http://slminerals.org/about-national-minerals-agency/.

– n.d.(b). "Key Minerals." Freetown: Government of Sierra Leone. https://slminerals.org/key-minerals/.

MMRPA and MLG (Ministry of Mineral Resources and Political Affairs and Ministry of Local Government). 2008. "Diamond Area Community Development Fund (DACDF) – Operational Procedures and Guidelines." Freetown: Government of Sierra Leone.

Mohan, G., and K.P. Asante. 2015. "Transnational Capital and the Political Settlement of Ghana's Oil Economy." ESID Working Paper 49. Manchester: Effective States and Inclusive Development Research Centre, University of Manchester.

Moreda, T. 2015. "Listening to Their Silence? The Political Reaction of Affected Communities to Large-Scale Land Acquisitions: Insights from Ethiopia." *Journal of Peasant Studies* 42 (3–4): 517–39.

Morgera, E. 2007. "Significant Trends in Corporate Environmental Accountability: The New Performance Standards of the International Finance Corporation." *Colorado Journal of International Environmental Law and Policy* 18 (1): 147–84.

Motherwell, J.T. 2010. *Final Report of First In-Country Visiting Independent Expert, Environmental and Social Monitoring Jubilee Field Development, Ghana.* Accra: Tullow Ghana.

MTI (Ministry of Trade and Industry, Ghana). 2014. National Corporate Social Responsibility (CSR) Policy (Draft One). Accra: Type Company Limited.

– 2016. Ghana National Export Strategy for the Non-Traditional Sector. Accra: Type Company Limited.

Mulatu, B., and S. Grando. 2011. "Barley Research and Development in Ethiopia." Proceedings of the 2nd National Barley Research and Development

REFERENCES 259

Review Workshop, Holetta Agricultural Research Center (HARC), Holetta, Ethiopia, 28–30 November 2006. Aleppo: ICARDA.

Murphy, K., A. Shleifer, and R. Vishny. 2000. "Industrialization and the Big Push." In *Readings in Development Economics*, vol. 1, ed. P. Bardhan and C. Udry. Cambridge, MA: MIT Press.

Muvunyi, F. 2016. "Factbox: Niger Delta's Unending Conflict." DW.com, 13 June. http://www.dw.com/en/factbox-niger-deltas-unending-conflict/a-19326956.

NACE (National Advocacy Coalition on Extractives). 2009. *Sierra Leone at the Crossroads: Seizing the Chance to Benefit from Mining.* https://curtisresearch.org/wp-content/uploads/sierra-leone-at-the-crossroads.2.pdf.

– 2011. *Still at the Crossroads: An Update on Sierra Leone's Chance to Benefit from Mining.* http://www.nacesl.org/newnace/docs/Sierra%20Leone%20Report%202011_follow%20up%20crossroad.pdf.

Neethling, T. 2007. "Pursuing Sustainable Peace through Post-Conflict Peace-building: The Case of Sierra Leone." *African Security Studies* 16 (3): 81–95.

Negash, M., and J.F.M. Swinnen. 2013. "Biofuels and Food Security: Micro-Evidence from Ethiopia." *Energy Policy* 61: 963–76.

Nest, M. 2011. *Coltan.* Cambridge: Polity.

Nhemachena, A., and T.V. Warikandwa. 2017. *Mining Africa: Law, Environment, Society and Politics in Historical and Multidisciplinary Perspectives.* Yaoundé: Langaa RPCIG.

Nkomo, J.C. 2006. "The Impact of Higher Oil Prices on Southern African Countries." *Journal of Energy in Southern Africa* 17 (1): 10–17.

NRGI (Natural Resource Governance Institute). n.d. "Ghana – Extractive Industries – Natural Resource Governance Institute."

Nyame, F.K., and J.A. Grant. 2014. "The Political Economy of Transitory Mining in Ghana: Understanding the Trajectories, Triumphs, and Tribulations of Artisanal and Small-Scale Operators." *Extractive Industries and Society* 1 (1): 75–85.

O'Faircheallaigh, C. 2013. "Community Development Agreements in the Mining Industry: An Emerging Global Phenomenon." *Community Development* 44 (2): 222–38.

– 2015. "Social Equity and Large Mining Projects: Voluntary Industry Initiatives, Public Regulation and Community Development Agreements." *Journal of Business Ethics* 132 (1): 91–103.

Obalola, M. 2008. "Beyond Philanthropy: Corporate Social Responsibility in the Nigerian Insurance Industry." *Social Responsibility Journal* 4 (4): 538–48.

OECD (Organisation for Economic Co-operation and Development). 2015. "States of Fragility 2015: Meeting Post-2015 Ambitions." Paris: OECD. https://www.oecd.org/dac/conflict-fragility-resilience/docs/FINAL%20States%20of%20Fragility%20Highlights%20document.pdf.

– 2016. *Corruption in the Extractive Value Chain: Typology of Risks, Mitigation Measures and Incentives*. Paris: OECD Development Centre. http://www.oecd.org/dev/Corruption-in-the-extractive-value-chain.pdf.

– n.d. "Policy Dialogue on Natural Resource-based Development (PD-NR)." Paris: OECD. https://www.oecd.org/dev/natural-resources.htm.

Okoh, G.A. 2014. "Grievance and Conflict in Ghana's Gold Mining Industry: The Case of Obuasi." *Futures* 62 (pt A): 51–7.

Okpanachi, E., and N. Andrews. 2012. "Preventing the Oil 'Resource Curse' in Ghana: Lessons from Nigeria." *World Futures: The Journal of New Paradigm Research* 68 (6): 430–50.

Okudzeto, E., W.A. Mariki, S.S. Senu, and R. Lal. 2015. "African Economic Outlook: Ghana." https://www.africaneconomicoutlook.org/ghana/.

Olsen, M. 2014. "Discourse, Complexity, Normativity: Tracing the Elaboration of Foucault's Materialist Concept of Discourse." *Open Review of Educational Research* 1 (1): 28–55.

Omeje, K. 2013. *Extractive Economies and Conflicts in the Global South: Multi-Regional Perspectives on Rentier Politics*. Burlington, VT: Ashgate.

– 2017. "Extractive Economies and Conflicts in the Global South: Re-Engaging Rentier Theory and Politics." In *Extractive Economies and Conflicts in the Global South: Multi-Regional Perspectives on Rentier Politics*, ed. K. Omeje, 19–44. London: Routledge.

OPEC (Organization of the Petroleum Exporting Countries). 2017. *World Oil Outlook 2040*. Vienne: OPEC Secretariat. http://www.opec.org/opec_web/flipbook/WOO2017/WOO2017/assets/common/downloads/WOO%202017.pdf.

Osei-Assibey, E. 2014. "Nature and Dynamics of Inequalities in Ghana." *Development* 57 (3–4): 521–30.

Osei-Tutu, J.A. 2012. *Managing Expectations and Tensions in Ghana's Oil-Rich Western Region*. Governance of Africa's Resources Programme Policy Briefing 55. Johannesburg: South African Institute of International Affairs.

REFERENCES

Oshionebo, E. 2018. "Sovereign Wealth Funds in Developing Countries: A Case Study of the Ghana Petroleum Funds." *Journal of Energy & Natural Resources Law* 36 (1): 33–59.

Otto, J.M. 2017. "How Do We Legislate for Improved Community Development?" WIDER Working Paper 2017/102. Helsinki: United Nations University World Institute for Development Economics Research. https://www.econstor.eu/bitstream/10419/163071/1/884888053.pdf.

Ovadia, J.S. 2014. "Local Content and Natural Resource Governance: The Cases of Nigeria and Angola." *Extractive Industries and Society* 1 (2): 137–46.

– 2016a. "Local Content Policies and Petro-Development in Sub-Saharan Africa: A Comparative Analysis." *Resources Policy* 49 (supp. C): 20–30. https://doi.org/10.1016/j.resourpol.2016.04.003.

– 2016b. "Local Content Policies, Natural Resource Governance and Development in the Global South." In *Governing Natural Resources for Africa's Development*, ed. H.G. Besada, 156–71. London: Routledge.

– 2017. *The Petro-Developmental State in Africa: Making Oil Work in Angola, Nigeria and the Gulf of Guinea*. New York: Cambridge University Press.

– 2018. "State-Led Industrial Development, Structural Transformation and Elite-Led Plunder: Angola (2002–2013) as a Developmental State." *Development Policy Review* 36: 587–606.

Ovadia, J.S., and C. Wolf. 2018. "Studying the Development State: Theory and Method in Research on Industrial Policy and State-Led Development in Africa." *Third World Quarterly* 39 (6): 1056–76.

Owusu-Andsah, F., and R.C. Smardon. 2015. "Mining and Agriculture in Ghana: A Contested Terrain." *International Journal of Environment and Sustainable Development* 14 (4): 371–97.

Owusu-Koranteng, H. 2005. "Presentation on the Social Impact of Gold Mining in Ghana: Unequal Distribution of Burdens and Benefits and Its Implications on Human Rights." Paper presented at the 11th EADI General Conference, Bonn, 22–24 September 2005.

– 2013. "Mining Investment and Participation of Community People in Decisions of Development Programs in Ghana." PowerPoint presentation delivered at the Wacam Ravi Festival.

Oxford Analytica. 2014. "Oil Firms May Need to Foster Local Capacity in Ghana." *Oxford Analytica Daily Brief*, 25 March. https://dailybrief.oxan.com/Analysis/DB189812.

Ozden, M. 2013. *The Right to Land*. Geneva: CETIM.

Pan, X., J. Sha, H. Zhang, and W. Ke. 2014. "Relationship between Corporate Social Responsibility and Financial Performance in the Mineral Industry: Evidence from Chinese Mineral Firms." *Sustainability* 6 (7): 4077–101.

Patey, L.A. 2007. "State Rules: Oil Companies and Armed Conflict in Sudan." *Third World Quarterly* 28 (5): 997–1016.

– 2012. "Lurking beneath the Surface: Oil, Environmental Degradation, and Armed Conflict in Sudan." In *High-Value Natural Resources and Peacebuilding*, ed. P. Lujala and S.A. Rustad. London: Earthscan.

Payne, J., and D. Zhdannikov. 2018 "Chinese Control of Cobalt Supply Is Risk for Car Industry: Glencore." *Reuters*, 20 March. https://www.reuters.com/article/us-glencore-cobalt-china-autos/chinese-control-of-cobalt-supply-is-risk-for-car-industry-glencore-idUSKBN1GW1XV.

Peligal, R.E. 2014. "Whose Development, Human Rights Abuses in Sierra Leone's Mining Boom." Human Rights Watch. https://www.hrw.org/report/2014/02/19/whose-development/human-rights-abuses-sierra-leones-mining-boom.

Peschka, M.P., and J.J. Emery. 2011. "The Role of the Private Sector in Fragile and Conflict-Affected States." World Development Report 2011 Background Papers. Washington, DC: World Bank.

Peters, K. 2011. *War and the Crisis of Youth in Sierra Leone*. Cambridge: Cambridge University Press.

Platform. 2012. "Tullow Oil's Foul Play in Ghana." 28 June. London: Platform. http://platformlondon.org/2012/06/28/tullow-oils-foul-play-in-ghana/.

Polus, A. 2013. "The Inevitability of the 'Resource Curse' in Sub-Saharan Africa? Relations between NGOs and Governments in Zambia, Botswana and Ghana." *Polish Quarterly of International Affairs* 4: 77–94.

Pottas, A. 2014. "Addressing Africa's Infrastructure Challenges." Deloitte. https://www2.deloitte.com/ye/en/pages/energy-and-resources/articles/africas-infrastructure.html.

Prandi, M., and J.M. Lozano. 2010. "CSR in Conflict and Post-Conflict Environments: From Risk Management to Value Creation." Barcelona: Escola de Cultura de Pau and Esade Institute for Social Innovation, Ramon Llull University.

PwC (PricewaterhouseCoopers). 2015a. *2015 Tax Facts and Figures: A Quick Guide to Taxation in Ghana*. Accra: PricewaterhouseCoopers (Ghana).

REFERENCES

https://www.pwc.com/gh/en/assets/pdf/ghana-tax-facts-and-figures-2015.pdf.

– 2015b. *Over Taxed? Does the Tax Regime Encourage New Mines?* Pricewater-houseCoopers Australia Africa Practice. https://www.pwc.com.au/industry/energy-utilities-mining/assets/australia-africa-practice-aug15.pdf (accessed 18 August 2016)?

– 2016. "Impact of Corruption on Nigeria's Economy." Lagos: Pricewaterhouse-Coopers (Nigeria).

– 2017. "Learning to Leapfrog: Africa Oil and Gas Review." Report on Current Developments in the Oil and Gas Industry in Africa. Pricewaterhouse-Coopers (South Africa).

Quinn, M., ed. 2016. *Governance and Health in Post-Conflict Countries: The Ebola Outbreak in Liberia and Sierra Leone*. New York: International Peace Institute. https://www.ipinst.org/wp-content/uploads/2016/06/1606_Governance-and-Health.pdf.

Rahmato, D. 2009. "Ethiopia: Agriculture Policy Review." In *Digest of Ethiopia's National Policies, Strategies and Programs*, ed. T. Assefa, 129–52. Addis Ababa: Forum for Social Studies.

– 2011. "Land to Investors: Large-Scale Land Transfers in Ethiopia." FSS Policy Debate Series 1. Addis Ababa: Forum for Social Studies.

Raji, R. 2016. "Is the Development Bias of Sub-Saharan Africa's SWFs Appropriate?" *macroafricaintel Daily Brief*, 6 January. Lagos: Macroafricaintel Investment LLC. https://macroafricaintel.com/2016/01/06/thematic-is-the-developmental-bias-of-sub-saharan-africas-swfs-appropriate/.

Ramdoo, I. 2016. "Local Content Policies in Mineral-Rich Countries. An Overview." Discussion Paper 193. Maastricht: European Centre for Development Policy Management.

Ratcliffe, V. 2015. "Ethiopia Plans to Revive Biodiesel Production." *Financial Times*, 24 February. http://blogs.ft.com/beyond-brics/2015/02/24/ethiopia-plans-to-revive-to-biodiesel-production/.

Relief Web. 2002. "National Recovery Strategy: Sierra Leone 2002–2003." http://reliefweb.int/report/sierra-leone/national-recovery-strategy-sierra-leone-2002-2003.

Reno, W. 1997. *Humanitarian Emergencies and Warlord Economies in Liberia and Sierra Leone*. UNU-WIDER Working Paper 140. Helsinki: World Institute for Development Economics Research, United Nations University.

– 2003. "Political Networks in a Failing State: The Roots and Future of Violent Conflict in Sierra Leone." *Internationale Politik und Gesellschaft* 10 (2): 45–6.

reportingoilandgas.org. 2016. "Oil Rakes in US \$3.3 bn in 5 Yrs." 16 August. http://www.reportingoilandgas.org/oil-rakes-in-us3-3bn-in-5yrs/.

Reuters. 2009. "Factbox – Foreign Forays into African Farming." 20 March. http://www.reuters.com/article/africa-land-ventures-idUSLK10422520 090320?sp=true.

Richard, P. 1996. *Fighting for the Rain Forest: War, Youth and Resources in Sierra Leone*. London: African Issues.

Roberts, D. 2008. "Post Conflict State Building and State Legitimacy: From Negative to Positive Peace?" *Development and Change* 39 (4): 537–55.

Rodríguez-Pose, A., and G. Cols. 2017. "The Determinants of Foreign Direct Investment in Sub Saharan Africa: What Role for Governance?" *Regional Science Policy & Practice* 9 (2): 63–81. https://doi.org/10.1111/rsp3.12093.

Rosenau, J.N. 1995. "Governance in the Twenty-First Century." *Global Governance* 1 (1): 13–43.

Rosendorff, B.P., and J.R. Vreeland. 2006. "Democracy and Transparency: Theory and the Missing Data." Yale University working paper.

Ross, M.L. 2004. "What Do We Know about Natural Resources and Civil War?" *Journal of Peace Research* 41: 337–56.

– 2012. *The Oil Curse: How Petroleum Wealth Shapes the Development of Nations*. Princeton University Press.

– 2015. "What Have We Learned about the Resource Curse?" *Annual Review of Political Science* 18 (1): 239–59. https://doi.org/10.1146/annurev-polisci-052213-040359.

Royce, A. 2004. "A Definition of Peace." *Peace and Conflict: Journal of Peace Psychology* 10 (2): 101–16.

Rush, S.J., and E.J. Rozell. 2017. "A Rough Diamond: The Perils of the Kimberley Process." *Archives of Business Research* 5 (11): 101–7.

Rustad, S.C.A., H. Buhaug, Å. Falch, and S. Gates. 2011. "All Conflict Is Local: Modeling Sub-National Variation in Civil Conflict Risk." *Conflict Management and Peace Science* 28 (1): 15–40.

RWI (Revenue Watch Institute). 2015. "It's Time for a Re-think on Natural Resource Management in Sierra Leone." https://resourcegovernance.org/blog/its-time-re-think-natural-resource-management-sierra-leone.

Sachs, J.D., and A.M. Warner. 1995. "Natural Resource Abundance and Econ-

REFERENCES

omic Growth." NBER Working Paper 5398. Cambridge, MA: National Bureau of Economic Research. http://www.nber.org/papers/w5398.pdf.

– 1997. "Sources of Slow Growth in African Economies." *Journal of African Economies* 6: 353–76.

– 1999. "The Big Push, Natural Resource Booms and Growth." *Journal of Development Economics* 59: 43–76.

Sakyi, P.A., J.K. Efavi, D. Atta-Peters, and R. Asare. 2012. "Ghana's Quest for Oil and Gas: Ecological Risks and Management Frameworks." *West African Journal of Applied Ecology* 20 (1): 57–72.

Sanderson, H. 2019. "Congolese Army Deployed to Glencore Copper Mine Following Deaths." *Financial Times*, 4 July. https://www.ft.com/content/5464d61a-9e3b-11e9-b8ce-8b459ed04726.

Santiago, A.P. 2014. "Guaranteeing Conflict Free Diamonds: From Compliance to Norm Expansion under the Kimberley Process Certification Scheme." *South African Journal of International Affairs* 21 (3): 413–29.

Sartori, G. 1970. "Concept Misformation in Comparative Politics." *American Political Science Review* 64 (4): 1033–53.

Schemm, P. 2016. "Ethiopia Confronts Its Worst Ethnic Violence in Years." *Washington Post*, 14 January. https://www.washingtonpost.com/world/ethiopia-is-facing-its-worst-ethnic-violence-in-years/2016/01/13/9dbf9448-b56f-11e5-8abc-d09392edc612_story.html.

Schiffman, R. 2013. "Multinationals Carving Up Africa for food." *Sydney Morning Herald*, 30 December. http://www.smh.com.au/world/multinationals-carving-up-africa-for-food-20131229-301jk.html.

Schubert, J., U. Engel, and E. Macamo. 2018. *Extractive Industries and Changing State Dynamics in Africa: Beyond the Resource Curse.* London: Routledge.

Seawright, J., and J. Gerring. 2008. "Case Selection Techniques in Case Study Research: A Menu of Qualitative and Quantitative Options." *Political Research Quarterly* 61 (2): 294–308.

Senoo, J. E., and S.E. Armah. 2015. "Assessing the Effectiveness of Ghana's Local Content Policy in the Oil and Gas Industry." *Journal of Energy and Economic Development* 1 (1): 22–61.

Shahnawaz, S., and J. Nugent. 2004. "Is Natural Resource Wealth Compatible with Good Governance?" *Review of Middle East Economics and Finance* 2: 159–91.

Sharp, K., E. Ludi, and S. Gebreselassie. 2007. "Commercialisation of Farming in Ethiopia: Which Pathways?" *Ethiopian Journal of Economics* 16 (1): 39–54. https://doi.org/10.4314/eje.v16i1.39823.

Shaw, T. et al. 2006. "A Decade of Human Security: What Prospects for Global Governance and New Multilateralisms?" *In a Decade of Human Security: Global Governance and New Multilateralism*, ed. S. MacLean, D. Black, and T. Shaw (Aldershot, UK: Ashgate Publishing), 3–18.

Shaw, T.M. 1982. "Beyond Neo-Colonialism: Varieties of Corporatism in Africa." *Journal of Modern African Studies* 20 (2): 239–61.

Shepherd, B. 2013. *GCC States' Land Investments Abroad: The Case of Ethiopia*. Doha: Center for International and Regional Studies, School of Foreign Service in Qatar, Georgetown University.

Shete, M., and M. Rutten. 2015. "Impacts of Large-Scale Farming on Local Communities' Food Security and Income Levels: Empirical Evidence from Oromia Region, Ethiopia." *Land Use Policy* 45: 282–92.

Sidi Bah, A., A. Mosioma, and D. McNair, eds. 2010. *Sierra Leone Report – Building a Fair, Transparent and Inclusive Tax System in Sierra Leone*. Tax Justice Country Report Series. Chesham Bucks, UK: Tax Justice Network, Budget Advocacy Network (BAN), and National Advocacy Coalistion on Extractives (NACE). http://www.bansl.org/Sierra%20Leone%20Tax%20report.pdf.

Sierra Leone. 2002. National Commission for Privatization Act, 2002. https://sierralii.org/sl/legislation/act/2002/12.

Sierra Leone. 2009a. *An Agenda for Change: Second Poverty Reduction Strategy (PRSP II) 2008–2012*. https://unipsil.unmissions.org/sites/default/files/agenda_for_change_0.pdf.

Sierra Leone. 2009b. Mines and Minerals Act, 2009. https://sierralii.org/sl/legislation/act/2009/12.

Sierra Leone. 2010a. *Government Budget and Statement of Economic and Financial Policies for the Financial Year, 2011*. http://www.sewa.news/2011/11/government-of-sierra-leone-budget-and.html.

Sierra Leone. 2010b. Public-Private Partnership Act, 2010. http://www.sierra-leone.org/Laws/The%20Public%20Private%20Partnership%20%20Act,%202010.pdf.

Sierra Leone. 2012. *The APC Manifesto 2012: Transformation for National Prosperity*. Freetown: All People's Congress.

Sierra Leone. 2013. "The Agenda for Prosperity: Road to Middle Income Status

REFERENCES

– Sierra Leone's Third Generation Poverty Reduction Strategy Plan 2013–2018." http://www.sierra-leone.org/Agenda%204%20Prosperity.pdf.

Sinopec Group. 2018. "2017Annual Report and Accounts." http://www.sinopec.com/listco/en/Resource/Pdf/20180325036.pdf.

SLEITI (Sierra Leone Extractive Industries Transparency Initiative). 2010. *First Sierra Leone EITI Reconciliation Report*. Vienna, VA: Verdi Consulting and Grant Thornton.

SMBC Mineral Resources. 2011. "Africa – Mineral Wealth Spurs Growth."

Smillie, I. 2013. "Blood Diamonds and Non-State Actors." *Vanderbilt Journal of Transnational Law* 46 (4): 1003–24.

Smillie, I., L. Gberie, and R. Hazleton. 2000. "The Heart of the Matter: Sierra Leone, Diamonds and Human Security (Complete Report)." Ottawa: Partnership Africa Canada. https://cryptome.org/kimberly/kimberly-016.pdf.

Smith, D. 2011. "Shell Accused of Fuelling Violence in Nigeria by Paying Rival Militant Gangs." *Guardian* (UK), 2 October. http://www.theguardian.com/world/2011/oct/03/shell-accused-of-fuelling-nigeria-conflict.

– 2015. "Ethiopians Talk of Violent Intimidation as Their Land Is Earmarked for Foreign Investors." *Guardian* (UK), 14 April. https://www.theguardian.com/world/2015/apr/14/ethiopia-villagisation-violence-land-grab.

Snapir, B., D.M. Simms, and T.W. Waine. 2017. "Mapping the Expansion of Galamsey Gold Mines in the Cocoa Growing Area of Ghana Using Optical Remote Sensing." *International Journal of Applied Earth Information and Geoinformation* 58: 225–33.

Soule, A.H. 2016. *Les Afar, la révolution éthiopienne et le régime du Derg (1974–1991)*. Paris: Centre français des études éthiopiennes.

Spielman, D.J., D. Byerlee, D. Alemu, and D. Kelemework. 2010. "Policies to Promote Cereal Intensification in Ethiopia: The Search for Appropriate Public and Private Roles." *Food Policy* 35 (3): 185–94.

Sreedharan, E. 2007. *A Manual of Historical Research Methodology*. Trivandrum, India: Centre for South Indian Studies.

Standing A., and G. Hilson. 2013. *Distributing Mining Wealth to Communities in Ghana: Addressing Problems of Elite Capture and Political Corruption*. U4 Issue 5. Bergen: U4 Anti-Corruption Center, Chr Michelsen Institute. https://www.cmi.no/publications/4791-distributing-mining-wealth-to-communities-in-ghana.

Stanley, L. 2012. "The Difference between an Analytical Framework and a Theoretical Claim: A Reply to Martin Carstensen." *Political Studies* 60 (2): 474–82.

Steinweg, T., and I. Römgens. 2015. *African Minerals in Sierra Leone – How a Controversial Iron Ore Company Went Bankrupt and What That Means for Local Communities.* Amsterdam: Centre for Research on Multinational Corporations.

Stevens, P., G. Lahn, and J. Kooroshy. 2015. *The Resource Curse Revisited.* London: Chatham House, Royal Institute of International Affairs.

Suffragio. 2012. "Final Sierra Leone Election Results Confirm Koroma's Reelection, APC Parliamentary Win." 27 November. http://suffragio.org/2012/11/27/.

Svensson, M. 2019. "Ethnic Federalism and Political Transition: A Study of Private Media Opinions on Ethnic Politics, Human Rights and Democracy in a Changing Ethiopia." Master's thesis, University of Uppsala.

Taffesse, A.S., P. Brown, and B. Minten. 2018. *The Economics of Teff: Exploring Ethiopia's Biggest Cash Crop.* Washington, DC: International Food Policy Research Institute.

Takoradi Technical University. 2016. "Strategic Plan 2016–2020." http://www.ttu.edu.gh/ttu/downloads/1/file2017711_20027.pdf.

Temkin, S. 2017. "2017 – Africa's Oil & Gas Sector Continues to Show Growth." PricewaterhouseCoopers (South Africa). https://www.pwc.co.za/en/pressroom/oil-gas-africa-continent.html.

Temple, P. 2008. "Diamond Sector Reform in Sierra Leone: A Program Perspective." In *Artisanal Diamond Mining: Perspectives and Challenges*, ed. K. Vlassenroot and S. Van Bockstael, 234–52. Brussels: Egmont.

Tenenbaum, B., C. Greacen, T. Siyambalapitiya, and J. Knuckles. 2014. *From the Bottom Up: How Small Power Producers and Mini-Grids Can Deliver Electrification and Renewable Energy in Africa.* Washington, DC: World Bank.

Tenkorang, E.Y., and P. Osei-Kufuor. 2013. "The Impact of Gold Mining on Local Farming Communities in Ghana." *Journal of Global Initiatives: Policy, Pedagogy, Perspective* 8 (1): 25–44.

Terfassa, B. 2009. "Ethiopia's Trade and Investment Policy." In *Digest of Ethiopia's National Policies, Strategies and Programs*, ed. T. Assefa, 283–312. Addis Ababa: Forum for Social Studies.

Teschner, B.A. 2012. "Small-Scale Mining in Ghana: The Government and the Galamsey." *Resources Policy* 37 (3): 308–14.

Themnér, A., and R. Sjöstedt. 2020. "Buying Them Off or Scaring Them Straight: Explaining Warlord Democrats' Electoral Rhetoric." *Security Studies* 29 (1): 1–33.

REFERENCES 269

Thomson, F. 2014. "Why We Need the Concept of Land-Grab-Induced Displacement." *Journal of Internal Displacement* 4 (2): 43–65.

Tilly, C., ed. 1975. *The Formation of National States in Western Europe*. Princeton, NJ: Princeton University Press.

Toigo, P. 2015. "From Extractive Resources to Human Development: Opportunities For Health And Education in West Africa." 23 November. Abidjan: African Development Bank. https://blogs.afdb.org/fr/measuring-the-pulse-of-economic-transformation-in-west-africa/post/from-extractive-resources-to-human-development-opportunities-for-health-and-education-in-west-africa-15042.

Torvik, R. 2009. "Why Do Some Resource-Abundant Countries Succeed While Others Do Not?" *Oxford Review of Economic Policy* 25 (2): 241–56.

Toulmin, C. 2009. "Securing Land and Property Rights in Sub-Saharan Africa: The Role of Local Institutions." *Land Use Policy* 26 (1): 10–19.

Trading Economics. n.d. "Ghana GDP Annual Growth Rate." Accessed 23 November 2017. https://tradingeconomics.com/ghana/gdp-growth-annual.

Tsebelis, G. 2002. *Veto Players: How Political Institutions Work*. Cambridge, MA: MIT Press.

Tullow Oil. 2012. "Corporate Responsibility Report: Creating Shared Prosperity." Accra: Tullow Oil. file:///Users/hanybesada/Downloads/2013-tullow-cr-report.pdf.

– 2015. "Report of the External Independent Monitoring Group: Jubilee Project." Accra: Tullow Oil. https://www.tullowoil.com/application/files/4415/8491/7805/jubilee-field_2015-environmental-and-social-audit-report.pdf.

Turkson, J.K. 1990. "Planning for the Energy Sector in Ghana: Emerging Trends and Experiences." *Energy Policy* 18 (8): 702–10.

Turok, B. 2013. "Problems in the Mining Industry in South Africa." Maastricht: ECDPM. http://ecdpm.org/great-insights/growth-to-transformation-role-extractive-sector/problems-mining-industry-south-africa/.

Tutu, K. 2011. "Trade for Sustainable Development: The Story of Cocoa, Gold and Timber Exports in Ghana." Roundtable discussion organized by the Institute of Economic Affairs (IEA), Accra, 2011." *Business and Financial Times* (Ghana) 12 (9): 1–3.

Twerefou, D.K. 2014. "Experiences in Managing Oil Issues: The Norwegian Experience and Its Implications for Ghana." In *Managing Ghana's Oil Boom for Structural Transformation*, ed. E. Aryeetey et al., 49–74. Legon, Ghana: Sub-Saharan Publishers.

Ukiwo, U. 2009. *Causes and Cures of Oil-Related Niger Delta Conflicts.* NAI Policy Notes. Uppsala: Nordiska Afrikainstitutet. http://www.diva-portal.org/smash/record.jsf?pid=diva2:235296.

UN (United Nations). 2015. "Concept Note – High-level Expert Group Meeting – Towards the Post-2015 Development Agenda and the African Agenda 2063: Enhancing the management of Africa's Extractive Industries to promote inclusive and sustainable industrial development, structural economic transformation and inclusive and resilient economic growth." New York: UN. 24 February. https://www.un.org/en/africa/osaa/pdf/events/20150224/concept note.pdf.

– 2016. "Secretary-General, in Secretary Council, Stresses Promotion of Water-resource Management as Tool to Foster Cooperation, Prevent Conflict." https://www.un.org/press/en/2016/sc12598.doc.htm.

– 2018. Letter from United Nations Group of Experts on the Democratic Republic of the Congo to the President of the United Nations Security Council, 20 May 2018.

UNCTAD (United Nations Conference on Trade and Development). 2011. "Trade and Development Report, 2011." Geneva. https://unctad.org/system/files/official-document/tdr2011_en.pdf.

UNDP (United Nations Development Programme). 2011. "Managing Natural Resources for Human Development in Low-Income Countries." Working Paper 2011-002. New York: UNDP. http://www.undp.org/content/dam/rba/docs/Working%20Papers/Natural%20Resources%20Low-Income%20Countries.pdf.

– 2012. "Strategy Note: UNDP's Strategy for Supporting Sustainable and Equitable Management of the Extractive Sector for Human Development." New York: UNDP. https://www.undp.org/content/undp/en/home/library page/poverty-reduction/inclusive_development/strategy-note—undps-strategy-for-supporting-sustainable-and-equ.html.

– 2014. "Human Development Report 2014: Explanatory Note on 2014 HDR Composite Indices: Sierra Leone." New York: UNDP. http://www.undp.org/content/dam/sierraleone/docs/HDRs/Sierra%20Leone%20Explanatory%20Note.pdf.

– 2015a. "Human Development Report 2015: Work for Human Development." New York: UNDP. http://hdr.undp.org/en/content/human-development-report-2015.

REFERENCES

— 2015b. *Restoring Livelihoods and Fostering Social & Economic Recovery: UNDP Response to the Ebola Crisis in Sierra Leone*. New York: UNDP. http://www.sl. undp.org/content/dam/sierraleone/docs/Ebola Docs./SL UNDP Ebola Recovery Plan FINAL.pdf?download.

— 2017. *Growing Manufacturing Industry in Ethiopia: Case Study*. New York: UNDP. http://www.et.undp.org/content/dam/ethiopia/docs/Understanding %20African%20experiences%20in%20formulating%20and%20implement ing%20plans%20for%20emergence%20Growing%20Manufacturing%20 Industry.pdf.

— 2019. "Human Development Report 2019: Briefing Note for Countries on the 2019 Human Development Report. Ghana." New York: UNDP. http:// hdr.undp.org/sites/all/themes/hdr_theme/country-notes/GHA.pdf.

UNECA (United Nations Economic Commission for Africa). 2014. "A Country Mining Vision Guidebook: Domesticating the African Mining Vision." Addis Ababa: UNECA. https://www.uneca.org/sites/default/files/PublicationFiles/ country_mining_vision_guidebook.pdf.

— 2016. "Africa Mining Vision – a Compact between Business and Governments." Addis Ababa: UNECA. https://www.uneca.org/stories/africa-mining-vision-compact-between-business-and-governments.

UNICEF (United Nations Children's Fund). 2013a. "At a Glance: Ghana: Statistics." New York: UNICEF. Accessed 30 November 2020. https://www.unicef. org/ghana_statistics.html.

— 2013b. "UNICEF Annual Report 2013." New York: UNICEF. https://www.uni cef.org/about/annualreport/files/Sierra_Leone_COAR_2013.pdf.

UNIPSIL (United Nations Integrated Peacebuilding Office in Sierra Leone). 2003. *Sierra Leone Vision 2025: "Sweet-Salone" – United People, Progressive Nation, Attractive Country. Strategies for National Transformation*. National Long-Term Perspectives Studies (NLRPS). Freetown: UNIPSIL. https:// unipsil.unmissions.org/sites/default/files/vision_2025.pdf.

US Embassy, Freetown. 2011. *Sierra Leone 2011 Investment Climate Statement*. Economic Section, US Embassy, Freetown. http://photos.state.gov/libraries/ sierraleone/232497/Other/Sierra%20Leone%202011_ICS.pdf.

USAID (United States Agency for International Development). 2006. *Issues in Poverty Reduction and Natural Resource Management*. Washington, DC: USAID. https://www.usaid.gov/sites/default/files/documents/1862/issues-in-poverty-reduction-and-natural-resource-management.pdf.

– 2016. "USAID Country Profile: Property Rights and Resource Governance, Ethiopia." Washington, DC: USAID. https://www.land-links.org/wp-content/uploads/2016/09/USAID_Land_Tenure_Ethiopia_Profile.pdf.

van den Brink, R.J.E. 2006. *Consensus, Confusion, and Controversy: Selected Land Reform Issues in Sub-Saharan Africa*. Washington, DC: World Bank Group.

Van Der Ploeg, F., and S. Poelhekke. 2017. "The Impact of Natural Resources: Survey of Recent Quantitative Evidence." *Journal of Development Studies* 53 (2): 205–16. https://doi.org/10.1080/00220388.2016.1160069.

Van Gyampo, R.E. 2016. "Transparency and Accountability in the Management of Oil Revenues in Ghana." *Africa Spectrum* 51 (2): 79–91.

van Veen, E. 2016. *Perpetuating Power: Ethiopia's Political Settlement and the Organization of Security*. CRU Report. The Hague: Clingendael, Netherlands Institute of International Relations. https://www.clingendael.org/sites/default/files/pdfs/power_politics_and_security_in_ethiopia_2.pdf.

Veltmeyer, H. 2013. "The Political Economy of Natural Resource Extraction: A New Model or Extractive Imperialism?" *Canadian Journal of Development Studies/Revue canadienne d'études du développement* 34 (1): 79–95.

Vermeulen, S., and L. Cotula. 2010. "Over the Heads of Local People: Consultation, Consent, and Recompense in Large-Scale Land Deals for Biofuels Projects in Africa." *Journal of Peasant Studies* 37 (4): 899–916.

VibeGhana. 2012. "Government Reacts to Imani Statement on Master Facility Agreement." *VibeGhana*, 2 January. https://www.modernghana.com/news/369868/government-reacts-to-imani-statement-on-master.html.

Vidal, J. 2011. "Ethiopia at Centre of Global Farmland Rush." *Guardian* (UK), 21 March. http://www.theguardian.com/world/2011/mar/21/ethiopia-centre-global-farmland-rush.

Vidal, J., and P. Guest. 2015. "How Developing Countries Are Paying a High Price for the Global Mineral Boom." *Observer* (UK), 15 August. http://www.theguardian.com/global-development/2015/aug/15/developing-countries-high-price-global-mineral-boom.

Viveros, H. 2014. "Examining Stakeholders' Perceptions of Mining Impacts and Corporate Social Responsibility." *Corporate Social Responsibility and Environmental Management* 23 (1): 50–64. https://doi.org/10.1002/csr.1363.

von Braun, J., and R. Meinzen-Dick. 2009. *"Land Grabbing" By Foreign Investors in Developing Countries: Risks and Opportunities*. IFPRI Policy Brief 13.

REFERENCES

Washington, DC: International Food Policy Research Institute. http://ebrary. ifpri.org/utils/getfile/collection/p15738coll2/id/14853/filename/14854.pdf.

Wanyeki, L.M. 2003. *Women and Land in Africa: Culture, Religion and Realizing Women's Rights*. London: Zed Books.

Weis, T. 2010. "The Accelerating Biophysical Contradictions of Industrial Capitalist Agriculture." *Journal of Agrarian Change* 10 (3): 315–41.

Wendimu, M.A. 2016. "Jatropha Potential on Marginal Land in Ethiopia: Reality or Myth?" *Energy for Sustainable Development* 30: 14–20.

Wendt, A.E. 1987. "The Agent-Structure Problem in International Relations Theory." *International Organization* 41 (3): 335–70.

Wengraf, L. 2018. *Extracting Profit: Imperialism, Neoliberalism and the New Scramble for Africa*. Chicago: Haymarket Books.

WFP (World Food Programme). 2016. "Drought in Ethiopia: 10 Million People in Need." Rome: WFP. https://www.un.org/africarenewal/news/drought-ethiopia-10-million-people-need.

Wilson, S. 2011. "Sierra Leone's Illicit Diamonds: The Challenges and the Way Forward." *GeoJournal* 76 (3): 191–212.

Wilson, J. 2015. "Understanding Resource Nationalism: Economic Dynamics and Political Institutions." *Contemporary Politics* 21 (4): 399–416.

Wisborg, P. 2013. "Human Rights Against Land Grabbing? A Reflection on Norms, Policies, and Power." *Journal of Agricultural and Environmental Ethics* 26 (6): 1199–222.

Wohlmuth, K., A. Jerome, T. Knedlik, A. Gutowski, and M. Meyn. 2007. *Africa: Commodity Dependence, Resource Curse and Export Diversification*. Münster: LIT Verlag.

Wolff, S. 2011. "Post-Conflict State Building: The Debate on Institutional Choice." *Third World Quarterly* 32 (10): 1777–802.

Wolford, W., S.M. Borras Jr, R. Hall, I. Scoones, and B. White. 2013. *Governing Global Land Deals: The Role of the State in the Rush for Land*. Chichester: Wiley.

Woodward, S.L. 2010. "Soft Intervention and the Puzzling Neglect of Economic Actors." In *Strengthening Peace in Post–Civil War States: Transforming Spoilers into Stakeholders*, ed. M. Hoodie and C.A. Hartzell, 189–218. Chicago: University of Chicago Press.

World Bank. 2008. "Sierra Leone – Mining Sector Reform: A Strategic Environmental and Social Assessment." Washington, DC: World Bank Open Knowledge Repository. https://openknowledge.worldbank.org/handle/10986/8087.

– 2009. "A Simplified Handbook on the Government of Sierra Leone's New Operational Procedures and Guidelines for the Diamond Area Community Development Fund (DACDF)." Washington, DC: World Bank Justice for the Poor (J4P) and Network Movement for Justice and Development (NMJD). http://documents1.worldbank.org/curated/en/699581468167370138/pdf/52399 0BRI0P113100r0Simplified0DACDF.pdf.

– n.d.(a). "Doing Business Index: Ease of Doing Business in Ghana." Washington, DC: World Bank. Accessed 2 August 2018. http://www.doingbusiness. org/data/exploreeconomies/ghana.

– n.d.(b). "Doing Business Index: Ease of Doing Business in Sierra Leone." Washington, DC: World Bank. Accessed 8 January 2020. https://www.doing business.org/en/data/exploreeconomies/sierra-leone.

– n.d.(c). "Doing Business: Measuring Business Regulation." Accessed 29 November 2020. Washington DC: World Bank Group. https://www.doingbusi ness.org/en/rankings?region=sub-saharan-africa.

– n.d.(d). "Ghana – Extractive Industries Technical Assistance." Washington, DC: World Bank. Accessed 2 August 2018. http://projects.worldbank.org/ P163756/?lang=en&tab=details.

– n.d.(e). "GNI per capita, PPP (current international $)." World Bank Group Data. Washington, DC: World Bank Group. Accessed 6 February 2018. https://data.worldbank.org/indicator/NY.GNP.PCAP.PP.CD.

– n.d.(f). "The World Bank in Sierra Leone." Washington, DC: World Bank. Accessed 29 November 2020. https://www.worldbank.org/en/country/ sierraleone.

– n.d.(g). "2.4: World Development Indicators: Decent Work and Productive Employment." Washington, DC: World Bank. Accessed 6 February 2018. http://wdi.worldbank.org/table/2.4.

– n.d.(h). "2.18: World Development Indicators: Mortality." Washington, DC: World Bank Group. Accessed 6 February 2018. http://wdi.worldbank.org/ table/2.18.

– n.d.(i). "Africa Development Indicators." Retrieved 15 May 2016. https://data bank.worldbank.org/reports.aspx?source=world-development-indicators.

World Finance. 2015 "A New Age of Sustainability for South Africa's Mining Industry." *World Finance*, 23 March. https://www.worldfinance.com/markets/ a-new-age-of-sustainability-for-south-africas-mining-industry.

REFERENCES

World Gold Council. 2013. *Responsible Gold Mining and Value Distribution: A Global Assessment of the Economic Value Created and Distributed by Members of the World Gold Council.* London: World Gold Council.

Wright, G., and J. Czelusta. 2004. "Why Economies Slow: The Myth of the Resource Curse." *Challenge* 47 (2): 6–38. https://doi.org/10.1080/05775132.2004.11034243.

Yakovleva, N. 2017. *Corporate Social Responsibility in the Mining Industries.* London: Routledge.

Yelpaala, K., and S.H. Ali. 2005. "Multiple Scales of Diamond Mining in Akwatia, Ghana: Addressing Environmental and Human Development Impact." *Resources Policy* 30 (3): 145–55.

York, G. 2012. "In West Africa, a Canadian Mining Company Pioneers 'the New Humanitarianism.'" *Globe and Mail*, 20 March. https://www.theglobeandmail.com/news/world/in-west-africa-a-canadian-mining-company-pioneers-the-new-humanitarianism/article535009/.

Young, O.R. 1997. *Global Governance: Drawing Insights from the Environmental Experience.* Cambridge, MA: MIT Press.

Zhou, T.M. 2017. "Poverty, Natural Resources 'Curse' and Underdevelopment in Africa." In *Underdevelopment, Development and the Future of Africa*, ed. M. Munyaradzi, 279–346. Bamenda, Cameroon: Langaa RPCIG.

Zigomo, M. 2009. "China Asks to Plant 2 Million ha of Jatropha in Zambia." *Reuters*, 31 March. http://af.reuters.com/article/investingNews/idAFJOE52U0JN20090331.

Index

adding value, 108, 199–200

Africa Mining Vision (AMV), 21, 36, 42, 164

African mineral wealth/resources, 21, 42

Agenda for Prosperity (Sierra Leone), 126–7

Agricultural Development Led Industrialization (ADLI) strategy, 75, 175–6, 186, 188

Ahmed, Abiy, 169

AngloGold Ashanti (Sierra Leone), 83, 88, 102–3

artisanal and small-scale mining (ASM), 83, 89–90, 134–5, 139, 146, 153, 155, 162

artisanal communities, 79

artisanal extractive systems, 79

beneficiation, 13, 41, 60, 71, 92, 110–11, 118, 158–9, 165–7, 189–90; and value addition 63, 71, 91–2, 110–11, 117, 130, 157–60, 164–5, 167, 189–90, 197, 215, 217–18

Bio, Julius Maada, 136

biodiesel production, 196–7, 263

biofuel crop production, 196, 199

Biofuel Development and Utilization Strategy (BDUS), 195

booming resource enclaves, 80

case studies: introduction, 70–7

– Ethiopia: introduction, 168–71; contract farming, 198; lack of positive change in agricultural sector, 179–85; land administration and tenure, 171–6; threat of ethnic-based conflict and state fragility, 177–9

– Ghana: introduction, 78–81; emergence of hydrocarbon sector, 92–7; mineral resources, 82–6; mining fiscal regime, 86–92; natural resource governance, 81–2; role of foreign-owned private sector, 86

– Sierra Leone: introduction, 123–4; civil war, 123–5, 127–9, 133, 135, 154, 156, 205; conflict and security in mining sector, 132–6; illicit mining, 124–5; legal and regulatory framework, 137–42; London Mining Company, 149–50; and potential of iron ore companies to eradicate extreme poverty, 142–3; quest for inclusive economic transformation from mining extraction, 126–8; role of private sector in peacebuilding and reconstruction, 129–31; socioeconomic and environmental impacts of mining, 139–40, 156–7

certification bodies: role of, 51–2

civil war (Sierra Leone), 123–5, 127–9, 133, 135, 154, 156, 205

climate-induced conflict, 170

community development agreements (CDAS), 13, 41, 73, 137, 143–9, 160, 205–6

conflict-threatened states, 9, 55

Constitution of Ethiopia (1995), 74, 185

contract farming (Ethiopia), 198

corporate social responsibility (CSR), 21, 114–22, 130, 181, 203, 211

Council of Ministers Regulations of 2008 (Ethiopia), 187, 190, 199

Cox, Robert W.: critical approach to international political economy, 40–3

Derg regime (People's Democratic Republic of Ethiopia), 172

diamond area community development funds (DACDFS), 135, 163, 211; in Sierra Leone, 135–6, 146, 163, 211

diverse case method, 60–1

Dutch disease, 31–2, 40, 45, 49, 97; framework, 47

Ebola, 143–4, 149

Economic Community of West African States (ECOWAS), 159

Ethiopian People's Revolutionary Democratic Front (EPRDF), 169, 173, 176–8, 197, 199

ethnic-based conflict and state fragility, 177–9

ethno-federalist framework/model, 174–5, 186

ethnographic method, 63–4

Extractive Industries Transparency Initiative (EITI), 52–3, 84–5

Federal Democratic Republic of Ethiopia, 74, 173. *See also* Ethiopian People's Revolutionary Democratic Front (EPRDF); Transitional Government of Ethiopia (TGE)

federalist model of government (Ethiopia), 173–4

foreign direct investment (FDI), 4, 34–5, 38–44

foreign investors: role in Africa, 49–52

free, prior, and informed consent (FPIC), 41, 59, 184, 189, 213

governance: definition, 14, 29; global governance of natural resources, 14–16; structures of, 34–8

human rights violations (Ethiopia), 184

hydrocarbon resources, 16–19, 32; Ghana case study, 25–6; transformative potential of, 70–2, 78–97

illicit financial flows (IFFS) 23, 84, 165

illicit mining (Sierra Leone), 124–6, 205

imperial rule (Ethiopia), 171–3

Indigenous knowledge, 79

instability and conflict, 40, 45–6

international governance frameworks: for natural resource extraction, 52–3

international political economy (IPE), 40, 44; framework, 13; and natural resources, 38

INDEX

jatropha crop, 196

Kabbah, Ahmad Tejan, 125
Koroma, Ernest Bai, 125, 136, 138

land certification program (Ethiopia),
74–5, 174–5
Land Policy Initiative (LPI), 208
land resources, 21–4; of Ethiopia, 27–8
local content, 13, 50–1, 71, 80, 83, 92, 104–8,
114–19, 141–2, 157–8, 217
London Mining Company (Sierra Leone),
149–50

Mengistu Haile Mariam, 173
Mining Cadastre Office (MCO) (Sierra
Leone), 151–2
mining communities, 20, 38, 42, 66–8, 97,
103, 119, 135, 139–40, 142–9, 151, 156, 161–
2, 204–6
Momoh, Joseph Saidu, 124

natural resource governance framework,
202
non-state actors, 36

Organisation for Economic Co-operation
and Development (OECD): *States of
Fragility 2015* report, 76, 170
Oromia region (Ethiopia), 169–70

peace: definition, 11
peasant associations (Ethiopia), 172
People's Democratic Republic of Ethiopia
(Derg regime), 172
Political Economy of Natural Resource

Governance (PENRG) framework, 4, 13,
54–7, 121, 128, 157, 166, 184, 198, 201, 218
post-conflict management framework
(Sierra Leone), 135
Poverty Reduction Strategy Papers (Sierra
Leone), 126–7
private sector: role in Africa, 49–52
process tracing, 61–2
Productive Safety Net Programme (PSNP)
(Ethiopia), 193–4
Public Ownership of Rural Lands Procla-
mation (Ethiopia), 172

quasi-feudal land ownership structure
(Ethiopia), 171–2

research methodology, 58–70; case study
methodology, 61–3; case study selection,
60–1; ethnographic method, 63–4; institutional interviews, 66–70; literature review, 44–9; qualitative methodology,
64–6
research objectives, 6–7
research questions, 7, 15, 23–4, 203
research results
– Ethiopia: beneficiation and value addition, 189–90; considerations for developing effective governance framework,
193–7; possible approaches to effective
governance framework, 198–200; regulation and governance, 185–8; Saudi
Star, 191–2; violence in Oromia, 190–1
– Ghana: beneficiation and value addition, 110; community development,
102–8; CSR and local content, 114–19; hydrocarbon sector, 111–14; local content

policies, 104–8; regulation and governance, 98–101; technical training and education, 108–10
– Sierra Leone: beneficiation and value addition, 157–60; impact of governance and regulation 150–4; impact of private sector and local community development, 154–7; possible approaches for effective governance framework, 160–7
resource curse, 21, 31, 44–9, 78, 114–15, 128, 132, 202, 214
resource governance and management, 29–34
resource nationalism, 19–20, 50
Revolutionary United Front (RUF) (Sierra Leone), 124, 134

Sankoh, Foday, 124
Saudi Star, 191–2
Seawright and Gerring discussion, 60–1
Selassie, Haile, 171, 174
Sierra Leone People's Party (SLPP), 125
Sierra Leone Vision 2025, 126
smallholder farmers, 95, 172, 192, 194
Solagrow PLC, 190
States of Fragility 2015 (OECD report), 76, 170

Stevens, Siaka, 123
structural adjustment programs, 44
Sustainable Development Goals (SDGs), 3, 9

Taylor, Charles, 124, 132
theoretical framework: country case studies, 38–44
Tigray People's Liberation Front (TPLF), 173, 186. *See also* Federal Democratic Republic of Ethiopia
Transitional Government of Ethiopia (TGE), 173. *See also* Ethiopian People's Revolutionary Democratic Front (EPRDF); Federal Democratic Republic of Ethiopia
typological theorizing, 61–2

value addition, 13, 62, 71, 91–2, 98, 106, 110–14, 157–60, 164, 189–91, 202, 215, 217–18
villagization program, 183–4
Voluntary Guidelines on the Responsible Governance of Tenure of Land, Fisheries and Forests (VGGT), 53, 176

youth unemployment, 90–1, 156–7